HEART OF OUR HISTORY

COWSLIP.
In recent years the species has made a welcome return
to our local hedgebanks and roadside verges.
Along the Suffolk-Essex border they are often referred to
as peggles, with a common expression being,
'as yellow as a peggle'.

Cover photograph: The cottages on our front cover were originally barracks in Colchester. Dismantled at the end of the Napoleonic Wars, they were brought to Gestingthorpe and erected as parish workhouses. Following the New Poor Law of 1834, they were sold and again moved, this time to the bottom of Sudbury Road, Gestingthorpe.

HEART

OF OUR

HISTORY

Volume One

BY

Ashley Cooper

Best Wishes

Ashley Cooper

BULMER HISTORICAL SOCIETY

By the same author:

The Long Furrow
The Khyber Connection
Tales of Woodland and Harvest (fiction)

Published by Bulmer Historical Society 1994
Reprinted 1995
Reprinted 1996

©Ashley Cooper
Hill Farm, Gestingthorpe, Halstead, Essex, CO9 3BL

ISBN 0-9524778-0-7

Illustrations by Benjamin Perkins

Design by Colin Freeman
Printed in Great Britain by The Five Castles Press Limited, Ipswich

FOREWORD

This book has four objectives. Initially, to pay tribute to the 'great pioneers' of our local history – Basil Slaughter, Arthur Brown, Richard Deeks, and Edith Freeman – for so enriching my understanding of the Suffolk-Essex border.

Secondly, to 'push the frontiers forward', by writing of a locality – the Sudbury-Halstead-Hadleigh area – rather than a single specific parish or town. Thirdly, to provide a base of 'record office' research, upon which the later human reminiscences could be founded.

Finally – and most passionately – to incorporate the rich rural memories of all my contributors – who have allowed me into their homes and so frankly, warmly and humorously recalled a different – bygone – horse-drawn, 'pre-electricity' era. Their recollections are surely the most valuable part of this work.

In bringing this volume to fruition however, I must also thank everyone who has so generously supported my previous publications, and without which this present trilogy could not remotely have been conceived.
Thank you,

Ashley Cooper

In grateful memory
of

BASIL SLAUGHTER

of Bulmer
who introduced me to Local History

and
with special thanks to farmworkers:

Eddie Tuffin of Alphamstone
Alf Finch of Borley
and
Frank Billimore of Bulmer

– not only fascinating contributors, but very much more
–'guiding examples in life'

ACKNOWLEDGEMENTS

In addition to those already mentioned, many others must also be thanked. Most notably, Adrian Corder-Birch, the Chairman of *Halstead and District Local History Society*, who has been a veritable pillar of support, and whose own publications, together with those of his fellow members, Doreen Potts, Mary Downey and Dave Osborne have been especially useful. I must again record my thanks to Doreen Desmond, John Dixey, Peter and Alison Minter and Peter Rowe of *Bulmer History Group* for their constant encouragement, whilst to all the contributors who have invited me into their homes and entrusted me with their memories, I owe an utterly humble and heartfelt word of gratitude.

In particular to, Claude and Mary Alleston; Dolly Argent; Olive Bettinson; Frank and Phyllis Billimore; Tom and Bertha Bird; Ida Bird; the late Joe Blomfield; Jim Bryant; Edna Chapman; Fred Chatters; George 'Jute' and the late Rose Chatters; the late Hazell Chinnery; Cecil and Sylvia Cook; Janet Cooper; the late Gertie Coe; Dorothy and the late Jack Cornell; May and the late George Cresswell; Albert and Rene Cross; the late Percy Darlington; Ken Day; Horace Elsey; Chris Felton; Maurice and Ann Finbow; Alf and Maggie Finch; the late Dick and Ruby Finch; the late George 'Rover' Finch; Gladys Finch; John Frost; the late Harry Gilbert; Tom Gilbert; Dick Halls, the late George Harding-Payne; Lily Harrington; John Hart; the late Douglas Hasler; Tom Hastie; Michael Hills; Dennis and Mary Holland; Rev. Trevor Howard; Hilda Huggett; Fred Hunt; Jack Hunt; Edith Hurry; Jake Letham; Heiti Lawson; the late Ernie and Maud Lott; the late George Jackson; Charlie Martin; Dorothy Mills; Arthur Nears; the late Daisy Nice; Frank Nice; Tom Nott; Cecil Pannell; Doris Pannell; Popsy Parker; Edwin Partridge; Ken Partridge; Naomi Partridge; the late Cyril Philp; Oliver Prentice; Gordon Pritchett; Toby Rash; Evelyn and the late Horace Reeve; Elizabeth and the late Reg Rippingale; the late Mary Rowe; Tom Rowe; Jim Ruffle; Freddie Ruse; Stanley Sharp; Tony Self; Richard Slaughter; Lesley 'Luke' and Lettie Smith; the late Hilda Smith; Beryl Spillings; David Taylor-Balls; Jimmy Theobald; David Tuffin, Eddie Tuffin; Dorothy and the late Frank Turner; Rowena and the late Wally Twinn; the late Jack Wallace; John Waspe; Eric Warburton; the late Major Revd. Philip Wright M.B.E.; Bill Yeldham.

Finally I must record the constant support of my Mother and Father and offer them my sincere and grateful thanks.

CONTENTS

Publication Acknowledgements

I would like to thank Richard Deeks for material drawn from *Cavendish Contrasts* (published locally); Dave Osborne for allowing an excerpt from *Halstead and Colne Valley at War 1939-1945*; Adrian Corder-Birch for two quotations from *A History of Little Yeldham* and Mary Downey and Doreen Potts for references from *Schools and Scholars in Halstead and District*, all of which were published by Halstead and District Local History Society.

I must express my sincere gratitude to Essex County Newspapers for allowing me publish the photograph of Gosfield Hall, The East Anglian Daily Times for the photograph of Basil Slaughter and The Suffolk Free Press for the photograph of cricketing veterans.

Finally, I would like to acknowledge the courtesy of the National Gallery in London in permitting the reproduction of Thomas Gainsborough's painting *Cornard Wood*.

Record Office References

With the exception of certain details from Gestingthorpe – or unless otherwise stated – all other historic references in the text were extracted from the County Record Offices at Chelmsford or Bury St. Edmunds. All were initially located by using the parish indexes which provided the document reference for the School Logs, Manorial Courts, Perambulations, 'Settlements', Overseers and Constables accounts etc. At Chelmsford, particular use was also made of the bound Quarter Sessions volumes.

My sincere thanks to the staff of the two Record Offices for their immeasurable patience and continuous kindly assistance.

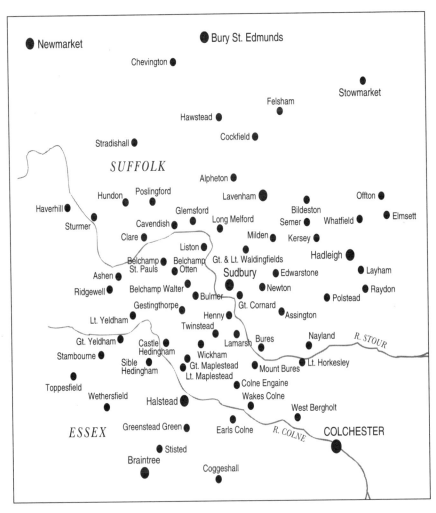

'Heart of Our History'

A note on names: In conversation I have sometimes repeated the colloquial 'Gestup' for Gestingthorpe and 'Gogum' for Goldingham Hall, Bulmer.

PART ONE

RECORD OFFICE RESEARCH

PARISH LIFE
1500-1930

– BACKBONE OF HISTORY –

*"There is no end of peoples coming on him,
on some pretence or other. The Magistrates and Overseers
and Churchwardens are always wanting his opinion.
They seem not to be able to do anything without him...
I do believe," continued Mrs Elton, "that this is the most
troublesome parish there ever was."*

from 'EMMA' by Jane Austen

Chapter One

ORIGINS: THE MANOR AND THE PARISH
Gestingthorpe, Great Henny and Little Yeldham

Late October
It was the year of the hurricane. Beside the Belchamp Brook hundreds of our 'cricket-bat' willows lay flattened and worthless. Around the farm scores of other trees were uprooted or dismembered – with great boughs cruelly rent off. At *Hill Farm* an ancient barn – lovingly preserved – had been heartlessly battered...worse it had been an awful harvest. Now it was interminably wet. Autumn drilling was weeks behind schedule.

"Try and come to the W.E.A. course – it will do you good," suggested builder Peter Rowe.

But in sodden conditions we were trying to 'muddle in' winter wheat...I arrived hopelessly late.

Clattering into the evening lecture at Gestingthorpe Village Hall the door banged loudly behind...everyone turned round to stare. And Arthur Brown – historian and speaker – had to momentarily pause...

"To re-cap," he eventually resumed, "there was a time, when the 'parish' looked after its own poor; its own roads; its own law enforcement; its own welfare."

Beside him sat Bulmer school teacher Basil Slaughter. Together they sowed the seeds of this book. For after Arthur's formal history, Basil continued with reminiscences of the old countryside. Of its unmetalled roads and isolated parochialism; of its bygone cottages and outside privies; of its 'straw plaiting', 'stoon picking' and 'after harvest boots', before finally showing old, black and white photographs of the erstwhile Suffolk-Essex border – with its narrow lanes, hedge rimmed views and shy children – posing many seconds for the camera's shutter.

This work was born out of the lecture they gave; upon the foundation of local knowledge they provided; and from their constant, kindly encouragement. It follows – unashamedly – along the route which they blazed.

Thus we begin our own journey. We take our first hesitant steps with an old horseman. He is Bert Surridge (b.1907) who a few nights after the W.E.A. lecture declared in the Gestingthorpe *Pheasant*:

"When I was young all the old men ever talked about was the parish. The parish 'this' and the parish 'that'. The 'parish field' and the 'parish charity'; a 'parish funeral' and the 'parish rate'."

Then I went home. To learn more about these parishes I opened *'Bulmer; Then and Now'*. And fell at the first hurdle.

"For Bulmer," wrote Basil Slaughter, "had four manors at Domesday."

"FOUR manors," I gawped, "but surely the manor was – the parish?"

Yet if there were FOUR manors in this one parish of Bulmer – what on earth was *the parish*? And what was *the manor* – of which there were dozens throughout our locality?*

'The manor' (to paraphrase *The Encyclopaedia Brittanica*), 'may have been born at the end of the Roman Empire but continued to evolve through Saxon times. Originally it grew its own food, tended its own livestock, provided roughshod protection for its weak and enforced 'common law' justice within its confines'.

Periodically the Lord's steward summoned manor courts. At these, grievances were aired and property transactions witnessed.

Some manorial records still exist. Those from Goldingham Hall,

*Bulmer's four manors were Binsley, Butlers, Goldingham and Smeetham. *See map on page 19*

13

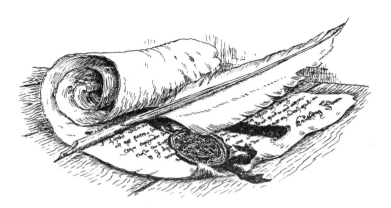

Goldingham's Manor Records were written on a parchment made from sheepskin – possibly a Bulmer sheep – in ink produced from either oak 'galls' or the bark of blackthorn (of which there is an abundance in the Belchamp valley), and with a pen that was fashioned from the feathers of a local swan or duck. Intriguingly one of the folios has a hole in it where the sheep's skin was imperfect.

Bulmer, reveal one fourteenth century rent of:

"XVI shillings; one capon and one garland of roses a year."

In 1533, a Sible Hedingham manorial court recorded that:

"John Mot, a butcher sells meat excessively dear – and is fined 2d."

If the latter sounds like a good reason for resurrecting manor courts today, the following also has a contemporary ring. For in 1536 one John Bynde of Gestingthorpe:

"unjustly encroached on an old church-path called a 'beerewaye' with his plough."

Sixteenth century ramblers would be delighted to know that he was:

"ORDERED to make the way into its former state."

Meanwhile, amongst numerous other complaints of, 'unscoured ditches', uncut hedges, and admissions of tenants, 'by the rod according to the custom of this manor', a real controversy was noted. For on Monday, 1st May 1559, Margaret Coo of 'Whights' (between *Delvyns Farm* and today's *Pheasant* Public House), was fined twenty shillings:

"for erecting a chimney on part of a certain way. Ordered to make good the encroachment under a like penalty of twenty shillings."

Twelve months later she had failed to restore the access. Again she forfeited twenty shillings. Again she was instructed to remove the obstruction – this time under penalty of 25 shillings.

The case was to continue. Margaret died. Her son Thomas agreed to provide the necessary track. One might have thought that the matter was closed. Was it indeed!

"Thomas Coo has not kept his bargain!' declares the court book of 1566, 'but blocked the way with a strong hedge. Ordered to restore the way to its former condition under penalty of SIX POUNDS, EIGHT SHILLINGS, AND FOUR PENCE."

Frantically one reads forward to see what will happen next. As if to heighten the suspense other items obtrude:

"A bay horse, very small, old and weak had come into the manor as a stray..."
"Thomas Milksop of Wickham St. Pauls has unjustly fed his sheep and cattle on the 'common pasture' called Westborrow Hill..." [near today's Bulmer Brickworks].

But what had happened to the controversial chimney near the Whight House. On Ascension Day, 9th May 1567 the court again met. And dramatically pronounced:

"Thomas Coo has forfeited his penalty of £6 8s. 4d. and is ordered to make the way good under penalty of forfeiting ALL HIS LANDS AND TENEMENTS HELD OF THIS MANOR."

✛ ✛ ✛ ✛ ✛

By the seventeenth century the power of the Manor Court was in decline. However, they still had one function. It was to formalise property transactions. Yet I was still surprised by their longevity. For

15

the Manor Court of 'Ballingdon within the Bridges' continued until NINETEEN HUNDRED AND FOURTEEN!
Other similar instances include:

Toppesfield (Camoys) ....Manor Court to 1919

Little Maplestead
Gosfield (Shardlowes) } ....Manor Court to 1925
Groton

Wethersfield..Manor Court to 1926
Chelsworth...Manor Court to 1930

Hedingham *(Borough & Upland)*
Lamarsh
Rectory of Lavenham } Manor Court to 1935
Kentwell Hall
Ashen (Claret Hall)

whilst on 30th June 1938* – barely fifteen months before the outbreak of World War Two – occurred the final 'tidying up entry' for the manor of Sampsons (Kersey) and Lillesley (Lindsey) in mid-Suffolk.†

Yet although the final courts were usually held in solicitors' offices there were still exceptions. Little Yeldham was one.

For on 28th September 1892 a manor court was actually held in the 'Court Room' at Little Yeldham Hall. (Hence also the expression 'court-yard'). Here Mr J. S. Gardiner presided, and tenancies involving the Mitsons and Cranfields are recorded.

Similarly on 14th July 1899 a manor court for Great Henny was held at the *Swan Inn* – overlooking the River Stour. Amongst the new tenants nine years later were a William Nott and an Oliver Stebbing.

How reassuring it is – in these fluid times – to report that there are still Notts and Stebbings in the area today. That at Little Yeldham there are Mitsons and Cranfields; that The Hall is still farmed by John Gardiner, (great grandson of J. S. Gardiner), whilst John's son Robert is the demon

* The dates of the last manor courts were obtained from the Essex or West Suffolk Record Offices, whilst the Gestingthorpe manorial records were translated at the expense of the late Miss V. Oates.

† Following the Manorial Incidents (Extinguishment) Act of 1925. These last meetings simply confirmed modern tenancies or arranged compensation of any remaining copyhold properties. Curiously at Sampsons and Lillesley it had been 'the custom of this manor, to be given to the youngest son'.

fast bowler who plays cricket for Gestingthorpe every Sunday afternoon of the summer – harvest excepted!.

We return to our initial query – into the number of manors in one parish – prompted by the cataclysmic discovery of Bulmer's *four at Domesday*. Fortunately a recent translation of Domesday,* enables us to deduce that many parishes had only one manor in 1086: e.g.

Assington	Brundon
Colne Engaine	Kersey
Edwardstone	Pentlow
Wickham St. Pauls	Foxearth†

Several larger parishes however had more: Belchamp Otten, Gestingthorpe, Lavenham and Long Melford all had two manors whilst both Cavendish and Hadleigh appear to have had three each.

Thus as we have asked before – if the parish was not a single manor – then what on earth was it? To my embarrassment the answer was surprisingly obvious.

"Quite simply," explains *The Encyclopaedia Brittanica*, "the area assigned to a single priest and to whom its tithes were paid."

However there are other tantalising idiosyncrasies about these parishes. For why is it that Little Henny should be a mere 419 acres; Ovington 716 acres; Chelsworth 877; Chilton 979; or Twinstead 1054 acres? Others in this intriguing scale include:

Alpheton	1222 acres	Assington	2986 acres
Milden	1343 acres	Toppesfield	3332 acres
Bildeston	1420 acres	Cavendish	3354 acres
Groton	1571 acres	Cockfield	3626 acres
Lt. Waldingfield	1574 acres	Wethersfield	4226 acres
Foxearth	1683 acres	Hadleigh	4288 acres

* Published by Phillimore, 1983

† Although the only manor recorded in Foxearth was Weston Hall, it did have like many other local parishes much other land belonging to Freemen. During the following centuries additional manors were created in many parishes. (According to *White's Directory* – and other sources – the original Weston Hall was later renamed Brook Hall).

Newton............................2197 acres	Long Melford...........5181 acres
Glemsford.......................2295 acres	Stoke by Nayland...5277 acres
Belchamp St.Pauls.....2623 acres	Sible Hedingham...5407 acres
Bulmer............................2801 acres	Finchingfield............8461 acres

...and Writtle (near Chelmsford), a staggering THIRTEEN THOUSAND, FIVE HUNDRED AND SIXTY EIGHT ACRES!

Doubtless the explanations might include 'workability' of the soil; accessibility to early man; previous habitation; proximity to rivers or degree of afforestation.

Either way, by 1600 these parishes were the central unit of our living countryside.

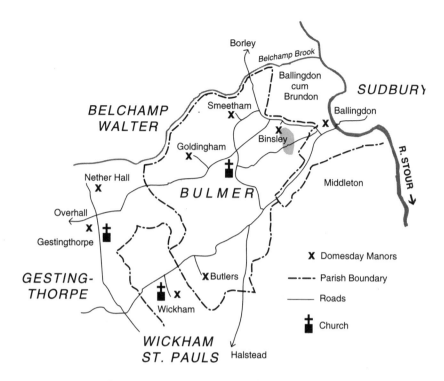

Bulmer's four manors at Domesday.

The Domesday Book compiled in 1086 provides an intriguing glimpse of local history. Why – for example – are there so many manors in Bulmer? (Binsley, Butlers, Goldingham and Smeetham). Basil Slaughter believes that the 'lost' manor of Binsley was near Kitchens Farm. However, Domesday records a second Binsley landowner – hence the shaded area.

Also shown are Gestingthorpe's two manors in 1086 and the single manor at Wickham St. Pauls.

Contemplating the reasons for the differing size of parishes – and their number of manors – has provided many hours of enjoyable speculation about the misty, dim years of the Anglo-Saxon era in conjunction with early Christianity.

One conundrum relates to Sudbury. Despite adjoining Babergh Hundred in Suffolk the town was actually attached to Thingoe Hundred near Bury St. Edmunds!

For more on Bulmer, see Simon Harris's superb new edition of 'Bulmer, Then and Now', available in local bookshops.

Chapter Two

THE SOVEREIGN PARISH
'Wethersfield, Little Cornard and Kersey'

"Frankly, the Parish Council of today has very little 'real' power at all. In Bulmer for example, we aren't even allowed to impose a speed limit in 'The Street'! Our principal role is to act as a sort of 'pressure group' on the District and County Councils. But our own authority is very limited indeed."

JOHN DIXEY
Chairman Bulmer Parish Council, 1967-1993

The journey into the area I love, with its sweeping views and undulating countryside was to continue...and so too were the surprises. The biggest was about these parishes.

"Historically," declares Arthur Brown, "they were like semi-autonomous kingdoms."

There was a pause, for 'how on earth,' I wondered, 'could these quiet, sleepy communities ever have been like 'semi-kingdoms'?' After a moment he continued:

"From 1601 *every single parish* be it Cavendish, Kersey or Pebmarsh became a rudimentary 'welfare state' – with Overseers who distributed aid where necessary."

"But where did the money come from?"

"From the rates of the parish's occupied properties."

"Who set and collected the rate?"

20

"The Overseers – who lived in – and were chosen by the Parish."

"And how was it kept accountable?"

"By the ratepayers – of which there weren't usually many – who could attend meetings of the parish government – which were originally held in the Church 'Vestry'. At these 'Vestries' constables and surveyors were also nominated…and the ratepayers could scrutinize *exactly* how their money was being spent."

"And did this 'experiment' last long?"

"For TWO HUNDRED AND THIRTY THREE YEARS! [1601-1834]. For over two centuries the 'parish' was a totally self responsible entity – answerable only to the magistrates at the Quarter Sessions."

"So there were only three layers of government?" I asked – thinking of the numerous tiers of administration that now exist from the 'European Parliament' downwards.

"Yes: authority devolved from the King to the Magistrates and then *straight* to the Parish. As such the magistrates – who were usually the landed gentry, 'officially' appointed the parish's Constables, Surveyors and Overseers and scrutinised the latter's accounts. But although power *ultimately* resided with the magistrates they tended not to interfere unless strictly necessary. For ninety per cent of the time the parish was genuinely independent – and responsible."

It was a responsibility as well. The overseers in particular were faced with weekly decisions of humanitarian welfare. If they were over generous their extravagance would be questioned… And if they were too mean the dissatisfied applicants could appeal to the J.P.'s – 'the higher authority' – who might over-rule the Overseer's astringency:

"Joanne Taylor of Stisted," declares an example from the Essex Quarter Sessions, "sets forth that she was born a cripple in that parish and is unable in any way to relieve herself, but that the parishioners have detained what she was formerly receiving." (July 1656)

21

The court instructed the Overseers to pay her "two shillings a week and provide her with some necessary clothes."*

It was not just the impoverished who appealed to the Quarter Sessions. In 1698, Sam Tiffin and Mr. Brewer of Belchamp Otten complained that the Overseers had 'illegally overcharged' them, whilst in 1768, a Bulmer farmer Thomas Eaton, queried his poor rate assessment, controversially adding, "that Robert Andrews (the Squire) and several other persons are underrated and assessed"!

How we can imagine the lowly labourers in bygone years, sceptical and quick to spot injustice comparing, 'the victuals supplied to old Widow ——' with those provided in an adjoining village. And how too we can picture the well-fleshed curate and leading farmers bemoaning that their rate was a shilling in the pound higher than that in neighbouring Edwardstone or Cornard.

Yet every eighteenth century parish was similarly structured. Most had their own parish building to house the infirm and destitute. (Called workhouses – but so dissimilar to their cruel Victorian successors as to demand a different name). Most also had a 'pest' house – where the sick could be isolated during outbreaks of

---

* From the Essex Quarter Sessions Book 1652-61. Essex Record Office Publications No. 65. (Stisted is between Braintree and Earls Colne).

There were also occasions when a single parish was unable to meet the needs of compassion. In these instances, the applicant or– village –could appeal for help at the Quarter Sessions. In 1635, for example, Lavenham applied to the Justices of the Babergh Hundred because they, 'could not support all of their poor following a smallpox outbreak'.

In 1698 a similar 'smallpox appeal' was received from Coggeshall to which Wakes Colne, Markshall, Copford, Aldham, Earls Colne and Colne Engaine were ordered to contribute. In Sudbury, All Saints Parish petitioned for assistance during a smallpox epidemic of 1711, whilst Nayland made appeals in 1772 and 1799.

Records show there were female overseers: Elizabeth Nice of Bulmer held the position during the controversy of 1768, whilst a Margaret Tiffin served at Acton in 1718.

contagion such as smallpox,† all paid for the apprenticeship of orphans, settled doctors charges for the impoverished, donated fuel to the elderly and obtained remuneration from the fathers of illegitimate children. As Arthur Brown concludes:

> "From 1601 – 1834 the parish ran its own 'D.H.S.S.' That is not an exaggeration – the Social Security benefits were uncannily like today... But don't take my word for it – go to the Record Office and investigate it yourself!"

Needless to say, I was hopelessly inept at Record Office etiquette. Slowly I learnt. Pencils not Biros; do not whistle outside; expect to wait for material; and don't always – always – be the last person scrambling out and dropping your papers when its way past time to close!

Yet it was a journey. A glorious memorable adventure through manuscripts and vellum into the great historical outback from whence all our villages came.

At Chelmsford I became fascinated by Wethersfield whose Vestry records read like a 'Hansard' of village history. Researching the year of 1764 was like visiting an erstwhile 'Ambridge', for there is:

"an overseer's account for each month (and presented at *The Dog* or *The Lyon*);
an inventory of the parish poor house;
a dispute about the cost of renovating the 'pest house';
and the appointment, 'at a public vestry in the church' of John Meadows to be the new governor of the workhouse – with the revealing instructions that:

> "the parish shall always find surgery, apothecary or midwife for the poor who in anyway become chargeable to the parish... The said churchwardens and overseers may inspect

---

† According to Richard Deeks, whose *Cavendish Contrasts* has recently been published, the isolation house in Cavendish was the erstwhile Overhall Manor House. To many, however, it is still known as 'Pocky Hall' from its previous association with smallpox. Other locatable 'Pest Houses' include Bulmer's, which stood in a remote position close to the Gestingthorpe boundary and Sible Hedingham's, "which," says Adrian Corder Birch, "was situated at the far end of Lamb Lane near the junction of Watery and Sandy Lanes." (From *A Pictorial History of Sible Hedingham*).

Wethersfield Church stands by the small green not far from the 'Dog Inn'. Commemorated inside is a Captain James Clerke who circumnavigated the globe three times with Captain Cook – during the very years of our study – before dying on Cook's last great voyage in 1779. Thirty years later the parish had a new curate (from 1808-1810). His name was Bronte. Later he was father to Charlotte, Emily and Anne – the famous Victorian writers.

the workhouse at all convenient times, and see that the (inhabitants) are 'WELL DONE BY, AND THAT THEY HAVE NO JUST CAUSE FOR COMPLAINT'."

How very different these sentiments appear from the horrible attitudes – and institutions – which were to replace them in the nine-teenth century. For the record, Gestingthorpe's 'workers house' stood in front of the Church, Bulmer had one in the Street and The Tye (but probably not simultaneously), Belchamp Walter's was near the 'cross roads', in Cavendish it stood in Stour Street, whilst at both Colne Engaine, Wickham St. Pauls – and doubtless many other villages – they overlooked the Green.*

* From *Cavendish Contrasts* by Richard Deeks and *Colne Engaine: Village and Parish* by Vernon Clarke.
For residents of the Waldingfield area, two most comprehensive local histories which cover 'parish administration' are: *Beyond Living Memory – The History of Little Waldingfield* by Harry Clive and *Great Waldingfield – The Babergh Village* by Louise Kenyon.
In 1801 Wethersfield's population was 1,296.

We return to Wethersfield. Today the village is on the commuter route from Sudbury to the M11. Yet in earlier centuries this parish *alone* was responsible for the:

"– erection of a bridge to Shalford in 1735;
– appointment of a schoolmaster in 1750;
– granting of extra allowances in 1804 – 'because of the high cost of provisions';
– distribution of coal to the 'necessitous poor' in 1808 and
– discussion on buying a fire engine in 1812."

How much the Record Office reveals! Later, as I drove home in the evening, I would detour from Braintree to the present day village – with its immutably solid church and 'Dog Inn' – and momentarily imagine those earnest Vestries where the squire, the farmers, blacksmith and Rector had discussed these very issues – of their 'semi-autonomous kingdom' – in bygone years.

Yet nearly every parish – with extant records – provides similar material. On Easter Monday, 1738 for example, the Gestingthorpe Vestry agreed:

"ye parish will pay to Mr. Tyrrol forty shillings a year for giving medicines to ye poor belonging to ye town."*

Likewise at Belchamp Walter. Here the Overseers' accounts for March 1826 reveal a payment of:

"7s 6d, to John Felton – for shaving and cutting hair at the workhouse for the old persons." (There were usually some 20-25 residents).

Amongst the mass of documents at Bury St. Edmunds is the agreement for the building of Great Waldingfield's Pest House in 1750, the bill for constructing Assington's workhouse in 1783 (which cost £229 15s 1d), and the engagement of William Causton, as, 'the keeper of Little Cornard's workhouse in March 1806. Here the inventory included twelve beds together with a homely description of a brew-

* From *Notes on the Parish of Gestingthorpe* by Alfred Patchett; 1905.

house, two coppers, and 'wearing apparel' consisting of:

"46 pairs stockings   4 coats
23 pairs shoes   4 waistcoats
15 gowns   4 pairs breeches
15 mantles   4 new handkerchiefs."

Causton additionally had to provide, "sufficient meat, drink, washing, clothing and the mending thereof," and to present his bills to the vestry meeting on the first Tuesday of every month.

There are, within our countryside a number of most enchanting walks. One of the loveliest is to follow the ancient trackway from Bulmer Brickyard to Jenkins Farm; then descend into the Stour Valley along the lanes of Little Henny, cross the river at Henny bridge and follow the path across the June-time meadows – with their beautiful array of purple-headed grasses...before gently ascending the by-ways to Little Cornard's 'Workhouse Green' – with its spectacular, panoramic views over Bures, Alphamstone, Henny...and that bewitchingly beautiful river plain.

The inmates of Causton's workhouse may well have been impoverished and infirm – but they had a stunning view of the Stour Valley – and the barges which passed on the river.

From Kersey's voluminous manuscripts we read of the special aid being given to the parish's poorer inhabitants – especially widows. During the winter of 1813 there was:

" 14 weeks flour allowance £22   2s 0d
13 weeks pensioners allowance £24 14s 0d
1½ chaldron of coals (for the poor) including
loading, unloading and carrying* ....£4   3s 6d"

There were also pauper or 'parish' funerals:

" 27th October 1824
William Cousens's coffin £1   4s 0d
Paid two nurses 8s 0d
Sexton ....6s 0d"

* These probably relate to the 'Speenhamland System'. In essence a form of Family Income Supplement to labourers' families. A 'chaldron' was approximately 36 bushels.

But whilst this dealt with the death of an impoverished parishioner – what happened if an injury occurred to a non-resident?

The answer was partly provided by Nayland's extensive deposits. For amongst them is a, 'Bond for Twenty Pounds', from Edward Kay yeoman of Clare. It is dated 5th July 1668 and was to:

"indemnify the parish of Nayland from any expenses incurred in the treatment of his servant Benjamin Turner, who had his limbs broken by a wagon and lodged in the house of Thomas Wright in Nayland..."

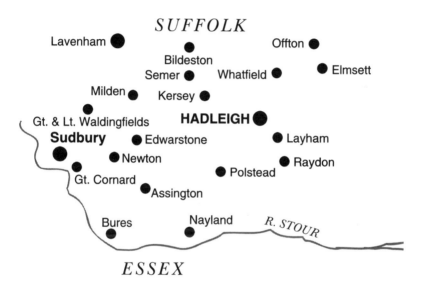

Then there were the 'Bastardy Orders' of which every village must have examples. The following was served upon a Bulmer man in 1703 and reveals that:

"He shall pay to the Churchwardens and overseers of White Colne [the mother's parish]...every week until the age of twelve, one shilling and sixpence, and at the end of twelve years shall pay £5 of lawful English money to bind the said child as an apprentice to some honest trade or calling..."

Whilst the figures in the Bulmer case appear reasonable, Stoke by Nayland's were significantly larger.

One June 22, 1714 a bond for no less than a *Hundred Pounds* was obtained from James Jacob of Westminster, 'to indemnify the parish from the upkeep and maintenance of a daughter born to Susan Hull singlewoman.' Yet even more extraordinary was that in 1737 and again in 1758 bonds for FIVE HUNDRED POUNDS were similarly secured.

By comparison, the villages' 'Apprenticeship Indentures' shed real light on population mobility. For between 1727-1780 we read of jobs being found for boys as:

" a glover in London;
a straw joiner in Little Bromley;
a cordwainer at Polstead;
a mariner at London;
a blacksmith at Thorrington;
and a chimney sweep at Colchester."

But most intriguingly of all was one Francis Tosspell who when aged just eleven, 'and being a poor child', was apprenticed in 1780, to Robert Dobby, a mariner of South Shields, County Durham.

Chapter Three

SETTLEMENTS AND PARISH PASSPORTS
Alphamstone and Bulmer

*"Tis five and forty years since I had my settlement
in this here town," said Coney...
(from The Mayor of Casterbridge by Thomas Hardy)*

There was more. Much more to learn of our 'sovereign parish'. One less palatable aspect was re-enacted at Bulmer's recent Eighteenth Century Festival. Here in full period costume:

"The gentry circulated with milkmaids and ratcatchers as a young Thomas Gainsborough, (Stephen Binks) painted Robert Andrews – the village squire.* Close to Church Meadow the ancient sport of 'camp' was played – passing off relatively peacefully – only one local farmer (Tony Minter) dying in the fracas and having his last rites performed by an upright and Godly clergyman (Trevor Howard).

Suddenly bedlam arose. A family of vagrants had been sighted (the Owens). Springing into action however the worthy constable, (acted by John Dixey) firmly escorted them to the parish boundary."

* Arguably Bulmer's most famous estate owner. Gainsborough's 'original' portrait hangs in the National Gallery and depicts Andrews standing beside his wife in the grounds of the 'Auberies' with Sudbury in the distant background. Like many of the landed gentry Andrews was also a J.P. administering local justice and auditing bridge building and road repairs etc. His observations on agriculture are included in both *Bulmer: Then and Now* and *The Long Furrow*.

Other J.P.'s at the time include Lewis Majendie of Hedingham Castle, Samuel Raymond of Belchamp Walter Hall and George Walker of Overhall, Gestingthorpe.

The parish was a kingdom in more ways than one. For the rate payers were determined that they should support ONLY the impoverished of *their* village.

For this reason was passed the 1662 'Act of Settlement' – which forbad residence in a new parish without a 'settlement' or 'pass'. (One might almost say a visa or work permit for the strictures applied were not dissimilar to immigration requirements today). As the overseers of Alphamstone declared:

"NO FOREIGNER SHALL BE ALLOWED TO COME INTO THIS TOWN WITHOUT PRODUCING A CERTIFICATE."
(Vestry book, 4th December, 1717)*

Whilst this might appear straightforward – if harsh – there were grey areas which must have caused intense distress.

In 1827 for example, Great Maplestead ordered William Younger and family to Gestingthorpe – claiming it to be his 'legal settlement'. But Gestingthorpe's overseers objected. The matter was taken to the 'higher authority' – where the J.P.'s reversed the decision. Younger again became Great Maplestead's liability.

Seven years later, Little Maplestead was more successful. For Robert and James Wendon, whom Gestingthorpe had recently expelled, were both 'ordered' back – the latter parish being adjudged responsible for them.

In the interim years however, five others had been compelled to leave Gestingthorpe.

1827 Isaac Warner from Gestingthorpe to Wickham St. Pauls.
1832 Elizabeth Coller from Gestingthorpe to St. Martins, London.
1832 George Cooper from Gestingthorpe to Wickham St. Pauls.
1834 Anna Wix from Gestingthorpe to Little Yeldham.
1835 Susan Evans from Gestingthorpe to Colne Engaine.†

How we can imagine these tragic cases. Sad bedraggled paupers. With

* (From *St. Barnabas Church, Alphamstone* by P. R. Tuffin). In 1795, the Act of Settlement was modified, so that nobody was to be removed from a parish until he or shebecame chargeable to it.

† Yet the ejections were not lightly undertaken. During these same years (1827-35) Gestingthorpe's overseers had also examined the credentials of four other men and one woman – who were subsequently allowed to *remain* – *AND* obtain parish relief.

downcast eyes and slumping shoulders slowly trudging the muddied tracks where today we blithely drive.

Yet the record offices have innumerable 'Settlement' and 'Removal' Orders. *Every single parish* in our area – from Hadleigh to Halstead and Cavendish to Colne Engaine is replete with its share. Little Waldingfield for example, 'admitted' fifteen people between 1705-1755, Belchamp Walter was ordered to receive fifteen between 1807-45, whilst Kersey was involved in thirty nine cases of 'receiving' or 'expelling' paupers between January 1805 and November 1834.

The following then provides an indication of how parochial authority over social services actually worked. We begin at Alphamstone – with its enchanting lanes, distant views and undulating countryside. On 24th June 1702, however, one of its residents, Thomas Horner:

> "received great damage by a horse accidentally going over him in the Queens Highway at Earls Colne and by so doing, did break his leg and bruise him in several other parts..."*

* From Essex Record Office Q/SBb 29/24.

Horner was looked after by an 'able chyrurgeon (surgeon) and good nurse'. However he could not be moved until July of the following year. Expenses of Fourteen Pounds and three shillings accrued – which Alphamstone's overseers were reluctant to pay.

Horner had to swear his life's history on oath. He had;

> "lived for the last 21 years in Alphamstone, his last employer was the minister, Rev. Fish, he had twice been married in the parish church – both times by Mr. Fish..."

Astonishingly – even with this case history it was not until two J.P.'s had examined the case, (upon the complaint of Earls Colne's overseers), that Horner's 'settlement' in Alphamstone was proved and the village compelled to reimburse Earls Colne for its care and attention.

Another local case was even less straightforward. For in July 1653 the overseers of Belchamp St. Pauls questioned the right of one Richard Fenner to be a legal charge on the village.

The matter again came before the magistrates who decreed Fenner's 'settlement' to be in Little Yeldham.

Life for some must have been depressingly unsettled. For two YEARS later, "upon a full hearing and debating of the case of Richard Fenner", his Settlement was subsequently ruled to be in Belchamp St. Pauls...

> "to where," declared the J.P.'s, "the constables of Little Yeldham are to convey him with his wife and child...and where on arrival he is to be received and provided for."

Another extraordinary incident involves Nayland. For in 1815 the overseers were instructed that Daniel Britton – a rogue and vagabond, aged about 82 had been apprehended in Chelmsford. *Fifty two* years previously, Britton had worked for George Holton, a Nayland butcher for one year, and been paid three pounds. Since that time he had not done any act whereby to gain a subsequent settlement. Woe betide Nayland! They had to provide for him.

Other cases are indeed pathetic. On 8th January, 1702, the constables of Belchamp Otten were empowered to remove Samuel Finch – 'a single man, and a person very lame and likely to become chargeable', back to the parish of Belchamp St. Pauls. Equally one wonders at the feelings evoked in 1827 when a removal occurred from Bulmer to Twinstead. It was of John Horsley and his wife Susan.

With them went their children, James aged ten; John aged seven; Sarah aged four and a baby named Anna. The latter was just five months old.

Sometimes I try to imagine the route the pauper took. Was is along today's A131 – the main Sudbury-Halstead road which passes through the Tye? Or were they escorted along the smaller lanes – possibly from Bulmer Church to 'Upper Houses', through the wooded track to Bulmer Brickyard and then up along the rutted path by Butler's Hall and on to Twinstead cross roads?

Yet worse, the year of Horsley's removal – and those quoted for Gestingthorpe from 1827-1834, coincided with the desperate unemployment which followed the Napoleonic Wars.*

Yet even here – and doubtless prompted by the growing social discontent, particularly manifest in rick burning and machinery breaking – the Vestries attempted to alleviate the situation.

"Some parishes," says Arthur Brown, "made a wonderful effort to cope. As early as 1780 a centralised 'House of Industry' had been built at Semer, near Hadleigh where paupers could spin wool into yarn for the Norwich market.† Similarly in Dunmow they set

* One contributory cause was a population increase – in *some* parishes of up to 30% – between 1801-1831. For example:

Population	1801	1831
Gestingthorpe	544	801
Foxearth	361	466
Belchamp Walter	422	670
Lamarsh	285	323
Little Cornard	274	345
Lavenham	1766	2107
Chelsworth	234	346
Kersey	513	700
Milden	130	177
Cavendish	1042	1214

Possibly this rise in population – and unemployment – makes it easier to understand the spate of Settlement cases and Removal Orders which occurred in those years.

† The 'House of Industry' served the Cosford Hundred, (basically the area around Hadleigh, Bildeston and Chelsworth). Semer itself joins Kersey and is some two to three miles from Hadleigh. There is still a 'Union Hill'.
The Labour Rate operated from roughly the mid-1820's to 1834.

up a sack factory, whilst in Sible Hedingham they tried to teach weaving. But in Bulmer – for a time – they GUARANTEED FULL EMPLOYMENT to the labourers through the labour rate... What an amazing thing to do. To guarantee full employment! No state in the world has done this, but our cheeky little village did. In the Bulmer of 1823 there were 28 people who were permanently getting assistance."

Many parishes in our area operated 'spade labour' or outdoor relief' schemes. In most the men were remunerated for working on the roads. At Gestingthorpe, however, an entire *twelve acre* parish field was literally dug – by hand. Further the pay of nine shillings a week – for the Able Bodied – was roughly comparable to being in 'proper' work. Interestingly at Elmsett (in mid-Suffolk) no less than sixty of the parish's 437 parishioners were at one time unemployed during 1833.

And how was Elmsett's 'outdoor relief' or 'spade labour' paid for? Quite simply, by a tax on the occupants of property. For every £11 of rateable value, eighteen weeks work had to be paid for.

To summarise then, it was an era when assistance was given solely, to 'genuine residents' of the parish. Further, it was levied from the more prosperous parishioners, collected by a parishioner and distributed by a parishioner. Those who were 'rated' could see *exactly* where the money was going.

Yet in reviewing this phase of history, from 1600-1834, there is an increasing conviction. That although parishes were ultimately answersable to the Magistrates and Quarter Sessions they nevertheless played an outstanding, fundamental role.

Throughout these decades, British history records many events, hereos and social developments. It saw the 'Gunpowder Plot' and Civil War, it experienced the Restoration, the Glorious Revolution and the subsequent birth of Empire. Its pages reverberate with illustrious names – of politicians such as Bolingbroke, Walpole and Pitt, of commanders like Marlborough, Nelson and Wellington, and of the giants of literature, science and religion – Byron, Wren, Wesley, Gainsborough and Constable.

Simultaneously society metamorphosed from insular to mercantile, from agrarian to industrial and from rural to increasingly urban.

Yet throughout it all, the parish – the simple humble parishes of Twinstead and Borley, of Little Cornard and Kersey were the foundation of our national life – like the base of a mighty pyramid – upon which all else was structured.

They have truly, indubitably been, the very 'backbone' of our social history.*

The following is extracted from their fascinating volume and reminds us, that we should not always view the era of 'parish government' with rose-tinted spectacles – for periodically civil disturbances would occur. (For example, in 1772 food riots were recorded at Belchamp Walter, Birdbrook, Great Yeldham, Pentlow and Wickham St. Pauls).

Twenty three years later, report Grimwood and Kay, a further scarcity of flour led to another dramatic escalation in price. Eventually – and in desperation – a miller's van was hi-jacked in North Street, Sudbury by the town's hungry and outraged inhabitants, who then proceeded to weigh out – and sell – the contents AT MORE REASONABLE RATES.

But what happened to the accrued money? In true British style, 'it was returned – with the empty sacks, horses and van – to the owners of Brundon Mill!

Chapter Four

PERAMBULATIONS

Belchamp Otten, Sudbury and Cockfield

"Parks Farm is in Maplestead – isn't it?" I murmur vaguely in the Gestingthorpe Pheasant.
"T'ain't so likely! That's Gestingthorpe – the ancient parish!" comes the instant reaction of Bert Surridge.
There is a pause. Then he asks me a question:
"What's special about the area near the 'Stone and Faggot' in North End?"
After a few unsuccessful guesses I admit defeat.
"Five parishes all nearly meet at one point there!"
"Five?"
"Gestup, Castle Hedingham, Belchamp Walter, North Wood and Little Yeldham."

Parish boundaries were crucial. Not only were the rector's tithes at stake, but so too was the 'rateable income from property'... together with the responsibility to care for the unemployed or distressed who dwelt, 'just within the boundary'.*

It was because precise knowledge was so vital that a procedure evolved for walking the parish's perimeter, known as 'beating the bounds'. The perambulators usually consisted of the rector, an assortment of village worthies and a number of children who were thus expected to learn the route and – according to some suggestions

---

* A good example comes from Earls Colne in 1654. Here, an illegitimate child had been born to one Joan Price. However, it could not be agreed whether the mothers's house was actually in Earls Colne or White Colne. Consequently the J. P.'s called inhabitants of both villages to determine in which parish the child was actually born and to whose overseers the father should provide recompense for its upbringing and apprenticeship. (E.R.O. Quarter Sessions).

– were themselves beaten beside particular landmarks. (A more likely explanation, however, is that whilst the lads were possibly encouraged to thrash trees and shrubs as evidence of their journey, the word 'beat' should be interpreted as 'walk' e.g. as in a 'bobby on his beat'). Either way, in 1680 the Churchwardens of Long Melford spent 3s 2d, 'when the boys went the bounds of the parish' whilst two years later they were more explicit:

"For bread and beer at ye perambulation ....3/-"*

So important was this knowledge of parish boundaries, (and the *Rubric* stipulates a yearly perambulation for Rogation week), that clergymen often recorded the route...

"To prevent the encroachings of our surrounding neighbours," declared the Rector of Belchamp Otten in 1705, "and also to prevent law suits in ensuing years, which may perpetually embroil the inhabitants in contentions, I have penned down the circuits of our parish..."

Irrespective of the *Rubric*, entire boundaries were seldom walked. Belchamp Otten's was done over two days – in separate years – (27th May 1700 and 16th May 1701 respectively). Bulmer's were beaten four times between 1762 and 1804. Gestingthorpe's do not appear to have been beaten between 1803 and 1823. Perhaps it isn't surprising. Those who did beat or 'gang' Gestup's 'bounds' effectively covered more than a half marathon, (14 miles 1 qr, 54 rods to be precise). But, undaunted, they were walked on May 9th 1823, by the vicar, the squire and nine others, (including John Carter, Edward Downs, George English and James Rayner).

Many readers will have seen perambulation records of their own villages, which so strongly evoke images of a more wooded and pastoral countryside. Gestingthorpe's was no exception and the walkers are typically told to, "cross a meadow from an oak tree in a ditch to a timber ash" – and elsewhere to a Field Maple, an Elm and even a Walnut tree.(† *page 38*)

However one part of the description was particularly interesting. For adjoining Great Maplestead the perambulators had to:

"get over the hedge into the garden of Little Chelmshoe

* From Sir William Hyde-Parker's *History of Long Melford* (published nineteenth century).

House...cross the garden in a line to Little Chelmshoe House door. Go through the house and MARK THE MANTELPIECE..."

A house built right over a 'parish boundary!' That was all I needed. Back to the record office once more!

To my surprise, Gestingthorpe was by no means alone. In 1701 the Belchamp Otten perambulators went:

"into Stettles Meadow...up to Eyston Smyths and then to Little Bevingdon' before 'going to the house in Snookes Hill and MARKING THERE THE BUTTERY END." Later they entered a field called Browns Bevingdon. Here the boundary was so precise that they had to, "count off 36 scootes or ridges on the south side belonging to Walter Belchamp," before "passing through a part of Henry Mayes' house and coming out at the highway."

Twelve miles to the south east is Mount Bures. Here the varied soil types gave rise to some pleasing descriptions. For the perambulators were instructed to:

"cross Daisy Broom, go through Peter Petit's wood, pass a pond near a boarded barn, throw a stone into Chapel Broad Meadow – 'for half an acre', take in Mr. Constable's 'hop ground', proceed to the top of Furze Croft...and then continue to the mantelpiece of the dwelling house of Samuel Wilkin and going through the same turn right..."[abbreviated]

Yet wherever the perambulation was held, a warm reassuring image of parish life emerges. When Cockfield beat its bounds in May 1832 the rector wrote:

"Old Nice the carpenter led the way, the Sexton Cocksedge followed with the flag, J. Payne carried the wheat and Martin the map of the parish as surveyed in 1803..."

† It may be of interest that whilst there were no less than NINETEEN references to Oak trees (in 1803) there were just two to Ash and only one each to the Elm, Maple, Hornbeam, Sallow and the Walnut tree. Interestingly, there were also two references to Hop Grounds, which at the time were an important crop in the immediate locality, with an annual 'Hop Fair' being held at Castle Hedingham. One of the most regularly walked parishes may have been Little Whelnetham. Here the bounds were beaten nine times between 1730 and 1800.

"At 12 o'clock we arrived at the *Greyhound* where cold beef and porter were in readiness..." (They would be needed – the total perambulation was over fourteen miles!), "and to which the officers of neighbouring parishes had been invited..."

Inevitably there were disputes. When neighbouring Bradfield Combust beat their bounds in 1838 and erroneously claimed, 'the whole of Outwood', the Cockfield rector – who was vigilantly present – not only produced a map, but perhaps as importantly, 'the best opinion of the oldest inhabitants'. It wasn't the only 'grey' area. For adjoining the road to Bury St. Edmunds, the Bradfield perambulators came to a house:

"but instead of passing through the centre of Stewards parlour – and out at the opposite window, (as WE did in 1832), the people of Bradfield entered a window to the north and passed through a kitchen – leaving the parlour AND the room above in Cockfield parish wholly"!!! *(For the full significance of 'just one room' see footnote)**

Inevitably there were also ponds and even moats on parish boundaries. "At Elmsett," retells Janet Cooper "a dog was made to swim the moat and thus complete the circuit."

However, our most endearing perambulation must surely be that of All Saints Parish, Sudbury. It was undertaken on 9th May 1877, when:

"The 'beaters' met at Ballingdon Bridge. They consisted of twelve adults and 24 boys – all of whom carried 'white rods'."

Initially:

"the party proceeded in boats – up stream – around Little Common, under Marsh Bridge, and round part of Great Common

* In *The Pattern under the Plough*, George Ewart Evans describes the extraordinary case of the *Dolphin* Public House – which was on the border of Burgate and Wortham parishes in North Suffolk. Here, the court had to decide whether the room in which the applicant for poor relief had slept as a servant, was in Burgate or Wortham; worse, how much of his body might have been in either parish as he slept. Locally we believe that the now defunct Belchamp Otten *Green Man* was also partly in Belchamp St. Pauls; whilst a portion of the Great Cornard *Maldon Grey* is in Chilton.

– to the precise distance of one chain 46 links from the corner of the Bathing Shed at Dobbs Hole."

Here they disembarked and continued through Mill Lane, Plough Lane and Straw Lane to Friars Corner and Quay Lane,

"before being rowed down the canal by the Great Granary (now the Quay Theatre) and under the first railway bridge...eventually reaching the foot of Ballingdon Bridge where we had originally started."

After partaking of refreshments at the *Bull Inn*, the beaters next proceeded to 'gang' an isolated portion of the parish known as 'The Island'.

It is at this point, dear reader, that the Pickwickian element in Sudbury's character, truly manifests itself. For having walked up Friars Street, and climbed over a wall to enter Mr. Andrews' garden, they then crossed the lawn:

"But in lieu of proceeding through the house of Mr. Andrews and passing through the window as had been done on former occasions", the perambulators decided to do something different – and easier.

So what did they do to avoid proceeding through the house – and climbing through the window? They completed the circuit by:

"THROWING A STONE OVER MR. ANDREWS' HOUSE INTO FRIARS STREET."

And what did the stone do as it descended into Friars Street?

"IT BROKE A PANE OF GLASS in the door of the house ON THE OPPOSITE SIDE OF THE ROAD – which belonged to Mr. Woolby, the stationmaster!"

Friars Street, Sudbury (the stone would have hit the house somewhere near the arrow).

But whilst this is delightfully Sudburian, let us pose another question. For although it is clear why houses were built over parish boundaries in towns, why were people so careless, where they sited their buildings in the open, depopulated countryside of Gestingthorpe, Belchamp Otten or Mount Bures?

Were the perambulations just too infrequent?

Finally, when travelling from Sudbury to Colchester, it is interesting to note that the parish of Leavenheath was not founded until 1863.* By comparison the neighbouring 'civil parish' of Wissington has 'officially' been absorbed by its neighbours.

When Wissington did officially exist, it covered nearly 1500 acres, but was always lowly populated with scattered housing. More to the point, the ancient parishes of Nayland and Wissington were both divided into two distinct parts – each of which was separated by a portion of the other parish!

Bet they had some fun beating the bounds there!†

Wissington and Nayland parish boundaries

* The 'heath' having been slowly 'enclosed' or converted to agriculture during the previous two centuries. Wissington still continues to be a separate Ecclesiastical Parish.

† Similarly, St. Peter's Church in Sudbury was, for many centuries, no more than a Chapel of Ease to St.Gregory's. The parish of St. Peter's is in fact an island surrounded by St. Gregory's parish.

Chapter Five

LEGACIES

Twinstead and Mount Bures

"In 1603, Thomas Appleton Esq., by his last will giveth to the Poor of Little Waldingfield 10 loads of wood to be continued yearly FOR EVER."

(From a plaque in St. Lawrence's Church, Little Waldingfield)

We have seen how the rates from village properties assisted the parish poor and how tithes from its fields supported its rectors, but there was an additional – and happier reason for knowing the boundaries. It was that charity was also of the parish born and was usually endowed to those living within its precincts. Often donations were disbursed at death.

In 1521, for example, John Coo of Gestingthorpe bequeathed;

"the sum of seven pence to be paid every Friday for one year after my decrease to thirteen poor folks – of whom four are to come from Belchamp Walter."

In a will dated 1611, clothier Robert Parke of Alphampstone left;

"to the poor of Bures St. Mary £3; to the poor of Alphampstone £4; to the poor of Henny Magna 10/- and to the poor of Pebmarsh 10/-"

However, our most endearing will comes from a small parish in Suffolk. To reach it we travel through the narrow lanes of Chelsworth, Bildeston and Nedging with their summer-time florescence of Cow-Parsley, Dog Rose and Elderflower until we arrive at the village of Elmsett – some four miles from Hadleigh. It was here, on

13th July 1635 that Elizabeth Haywood wrote her 'last will and testement', and charmingly included;

"to 20 families of the poorer sort of Elmsett, I give 12 pence apiece, a brown loaf of wheat bread as it comes from the mill, a piece of beef and a 'pitcher of beer' to be distributed on the day of my burial. I give 12d. apiece to the 4 honest poor men that shall carry me to burial, that is William Layt, John Largent, Samuel Lewes and Henry Ranson..."*

Many villages had almshouses. Possibly the best known is the Trinity Hospital in Long Melford (near the Church on the Green) which was established for twelve poor men, two poor women and a warden by Sir William Cordell in 1580. Meanwhile Brent Eleigh Church records the Colman bequest of Almshouses which are opposite the School.

Others – like Sir William Cordell (above) – left more permanent bequests. Every parish can provide examples. Many were of money, bread or clothes and were often distributed at Christmas time.

* Respectively from, *Notes on the Parish of Gestingthorpe*, by Alfred Patchett 1905; Parks Family documents and finally *Wills of the Archdeaconary of Sudbury 1630-1635*, edited by Nesta Evans, published by Suffolk Records Society.
John Coo was doubtless a relative of the Margaret Coo where problems with "a chimney built on the public way" were noted in Chapter One.

Local detail

Amongst several from Halstead there is a typical legacy to give, "a weekly allowance of bread to twenty-one poor parishioners attending church". At Toppesfield the rent of a let tenement was distributed in blankets to poor parishioners; at Pentlow, Susan Gooch left 16 acres and a house for the relief of "3 poor men and 3 poor widows above 55 years old".

Of Clare's many charities, 'clothing and Almshouses' were donated by William Cadge "for the benefit of eight poor widows", whilst at Ashen, a yearly rent charge of thirty-two shillings was paid to 32 of the oldest married couples.

At Acton there was an allocation of;

"two penny worth of bread every Sunday and one pair of shoes to six poor widows each Christmas Eve".

In 1722, John Brand – whose descendants today farm at Foxearth – bequeathed rents to buy bread for the poor of Edwardstone and Boxford. But perhaps the most colourful 'food' charity comes from Felstead where the poor were to receive, "a yearly distribution of red and white herrings during Lent"!

Many benefactors left land. Earls Colne parish was given a small farm of 14 acres called *Westons* in Wickham St. Pauls. At Cavendish, there is a *School Farm* of seventy nine acres. In Gestingthorpe a twelve acre 'Rents Field' provides grants for education. At Glemsford, a half acre meadow was left, 'to provide Bibles for the poor'; at Sible Hedingham seven acres were similarly bequeathed in 1732. At

Wethersfield – amongst numerous other bequests – was that of *Great Wisney Farm* to provide religious lectures, whilst at Foxearth, "a great part of the soil once supported Dr. Clopton's Asylum in Bury St. Edmunds".

Over the border in Lavenham, '1 rood and 34 perches' were entrusted to buy 'Bell Rope for the Church'.* At Kersey, 'two acres and three roods' were left for the relief of impoverished parishioners. In Chelsworth the rents from 'Smock Meadow' were given, 'to purchase linen for the poor widows of Bildeston', whilst at Hadleigh the 'Grand Feoffment' amounts to no less than SEVEN HUNDRED and TWENTY SIX acres.

Then there is Little Yeldham. Here in 1555 one Joseph Cook left the rent of a house, and 2 acres of land, to the poor of that parish and also Belchamp Otten. Despite many encroachments to one of the fields, Swingell Acre in the seventeenth century, the charity still continues.†

Little Yeldham's share of the revenue is used to provide coal to a deserving resident. The responsibility for delivering this falls onto the Clerk of the Parish Council – and Chairman of *Halstead Historical Society*, Adrian Corder-Birch.

Little Yeldham Church. Typical of many small parishes in the area, (e.g. Alphampstone, Ovington and Wissington), the church has a small 'bell turret', instead of a larger tower.

* Four square roods equal one acre (A rood itself consisted of 40 square rods, poles or perches. The latter were 5 yards in length).

† From *A History of Little Yeldham* by Adrian Corder-Birch. Published by Halstead and District Local History Society.

However not all of the gifts of property involved land or houses. In 1620 for example, 'the rents from CHEMFORD MILL' in Henny, together with two meadows in Lamarsh were given by Martin Cole to provide, 'linen clothes for the poor of Sudbury', whilst forty eight years later, Nathaniel King entrusted the rents from THE GEORGE INN to be disbursed in sixpenny loaves to those receiving Martin Cole's charity.

It is tempting to suggest that by the eighteenth century, Sudbury must have had some of the, 'best dressed poor in England', for in 1706 Thomas Carter left a house and lands to provide;

"coats for fifty poor men and cloaks for fifty poor women."

Thoughtfully he also donated twenty shillings, for a 'love feast' for the minister and trustees on the day of the allocation.

The sartorial donations continued. Twelve years later Roger Scarlin bequeathed rents to provide;

"stockings and shoes for those receiving Carter's charity."

Then in 1724 Susan Girling left, "tenements, and an acre in Friars Meadow", to supply shirts and shifts to those who were already receiving Carter's cloaks (or coats) and Scarlin's shoes and stockings!*

Yet two of our most evocative 'parish born' charities are those commemorated in the tiny parish churches of Mount Bures and Twinstead.

In the latter's enchantingly unusual, brick-decorated building is an ancient wooden board. It is hung on the Western wall. On it is written a will. It is that of landowner Isaac Wyncoll, who in 1681 bequeathed that henceforth;

"Such persons as enjoy the premises of Twinstead Hall shall cause to be killed at Christmas time one good Bull and give out all thereof except the Hide...to the poor of Twinstead, Great Henny, Pebmarsh, Lamarsh and Alphamstone" [Abbreviated].

* Some of Sudbury's charities still continue with vouchers being presented by the Mayor to Old Age Pensioners shortly before Christmas.
The legacies we have listed are only a small fraction of those which once existed. Thomas Carter and his bequests are commemorated on a magnificent memorial in St. Gregory's Church.

Thus from Twinstead to Mount Bures. But as we travel through the narrow winding lanes, let us muse on those who gave the legacies. The philanthropic squires; the earnest rectors; the sturdy yeomen – inwardly 'called' to leave 'three acres and two roods' – or the lowly smallholders, anxious to benefit the parish – or their souls – in perpetuity, with some few shillings or a humble tenement.

Yet none so completes this spectrum of donors as one commemorated in the porch of Mount Bures Church. The tablet dates from 1564. The benefactor's name was Love. And what is so remarkable about that?

Simply that Love – himself – was a beggar! A successful one. And the interest from his amassed capital?

It was left to be annually distributed. To the poor of the twelve parishes which had best supported him!*

✛ ✛ ✛ ✛ ✛

48

Chapter Six

GRIM TIMES

"They used to say – the old people did – that if anyone was near-
ing the end or being too much trouble in the workhouse in their
last days they'd 'slip the pillow' (i.e. take it away) – which would
hasten the end. I've got no proof of it ever happening, but Mother
and the other old people often used to talk about it"
George Harding Payne (1916-1993), Twinstead

As the decades passed problems had mounted for the 'sovereign
parish'. In 1805 Arthur Young noted the escalating costs of poor
relief.

Glemsford:				Hadleigh:			
1772	£678	5s	8d	1710	£604	9s	0d
1787	£783	8s	6d	1800	£4646	17s	0d
1795	£1594	4s	5d	1802	£1303	19s	6d*

Thus it was, that in 1834, the 'Old' Poor Law – which had tried so
valiantly to combat unemployment was finally abolished. In that year
was passed the 'Poor Law Amendment Act'.

It was a hated piece of legislation. It destroyed the rustic, parish
poorhouses. And replaced them with centralised – inhospitable –
workhouses. They were to serve a 'union' of parishes. And were

* 1800 and 1801 were years of scarcity and rates rose in all parishes.
Locally we know of the following increase in costs:

	Pebmarsh	Bulmer	Gestingthorpe
1776	£164	£115	£229
1803	£342	£285	£504
1813	£541	£884	£1066

(from *Notes on Gestingthorpe* by Slaughter and Brown).

administered by a 'Board of Guardians' – known locally as 'Guardeens'.

The consequences were awful. Gestingthorpe sold the homely workhouse which had stood before the parish church and with sixteen other North Essex parishes joined – or formed a 'union' – with neighbouring villages in south Suffolk. A workhouse was built in Sudbury. Today it is Walnut Tree Hospital.* Similarly the Yeldhams, Hedinghams, Maplesteads and others amalgamated with Halstead to build a workhouse (now demolished) for 400 people in the town's Hedingham Road.

To help defray costs, the redundant village poor houses were sold. Great Waldingfield's raised £95; Gestingthorpe's £200; at Bocking, "a substantial house with dining room, committee room, store house, three pantries, etc." realised £260; Pattiswick's made £50 whilst at Stisted, "all that which for many years was a workhouse and almshouse for the aged and necessitous poor" produced £360. Most were found a use. The north end of Lavenham's workhouse was converted into "a place of non conformist worship" whilst at Monks Eleigh, "a portion was made available to the mistress of the newly built school".

Yet the 1834 Act also did something else; it ended the 'outdoor' work schemes for the unemployed (page xx). For the working men of our villages, this was a bitter blow. For 'relief' (i.e. assistance or unemployment pay) would only be given to those in the stark new workhouses.†

Here conditions were draconian. Whistling was forbidden. Eating was conducted in silence. And married couples were separated. As a consequence, Semer's one time 'House of Industry' had to undergo:

"considerable alterations so as to separate the sexes – and also the young and aged – as required by the New Poor Law."

"It was," states George Cuttle, "a drastic measure of deterrence. The years of extreme hardship which followed were known as the

---

* St. Michael's Hospital, Braintree and St. Mary's in Colchester were also once workhouses.

† In Gestingthorpe's Vestry Book it was noted that the parish's charity field, "Which since 1828 had been farmed by the parish (who by this means employed their surplus poor labourers at spade husbandry) had to be let – the parish no longer being able to thus employ its paupers."

'hungry forties'."*

Elsewhere *The Times* vehemently attacked the Act as, "that appalling machine for refusing the crust to famished age and for imprisoning orphans in workhouse dungeons..." At Sudbury a J.P. and Alderman, G. W. Fulcher, wrote a scathing, evocative poem *The Village Paupers*. And a young writer, horrified by the new Law expressed his feelings in a famous work of literature. The novelist was Charles Dickens. The book – *Oliver Twist*.

Whilst 'Oliver Twist' is now part of our national culture few will know of 'Village Paupers'. Yet Fulcher's work is also deeply moving since it is partly reflective of the Sudbury area, (although not apparently the workhouse scenes). In essence, the poem tells the story of an 'idealised' rural labourer, John Ashford. The latter was a 'master of his craft', a 'Lord of the Harvest' (i.e. foreman), and a top ploughman, who is forced by ill health to enter a new 'union' workhouse. Here, abandoned and forgotten, he dies in squalor and degradation. The narrative is especially relevant since Fulcher was actually a Guardian of the recently built Sudbury workhouse, (which held 400-500 people), and is thus expressing the intense abhorrence of an affluent businessman for the inhumanities of the New Law.†

Reaction to the legislation was widespread.

"At Sible Hedingham 170 protesting labourers were restrained only by the reading of the Riot Act and the arrest of seven of their number. Later the workhouse was set on fire, and when firemen arrived they were pelted with fire brands. In villages around

* From *The Legacy of the Rural Guardians* published by W. Heffer and Sons, 1936.

† The poem – which is 1800 lines in length – appeared in segments between 1840-44, being published in its entirety in 1845. Fulcher (1795-1855), was educated at Sudbury Grammar School, becoming a prosperous tailor and stationer, with a printshop on the Market Hill – later to become 'Martens' printworks. He served in a range of public duties and was Mayor of the Borough four times between 1846 and 1854. (All from *The Village Paupers* by G. W. Fulcher, edited by E. A. Goodwyn, published 1981, available locally. Printed by Bidnalls, Beccles, Suffolk).

St. Gregory's Church, Sudbury. A monument to poet and mayor, George William Fulcher, stands near the porch. Carter (see charities) is commemorated inside, whilst Walnut Tree Hospital, once the union workhouse, adjoins the churchyard.

Wickham Market (in East Suffolk) over a thousand signed a petition for the restoration of the mild, humane, generous, benevolent and noble Old Poor Law."*

In 1836 the incomplete Sudbury workhouse was similarly damaged by fire:

"The poorer classes," reported *The Bury Post*, "made no secret of their satisfaction, clapping their hands, shouting, and some even going down on their knees 'to thank God for having heard their prayers'. In these feelings we are sorry to say they were not with-

* From *Chartism in Essex and Suffolk* by Arthur Brown, published by Essex Record Office and Suffolk Libraries and Archives 1982. The book provides a fascinating background to rural discontent in our area. The two newspaper reports were originally discovered by Arthur in the *Ipswich Journals* of 5th December 1835 and 30th May 1835.
    (Another interesting case of resistance to the closure of the village poorhouses occurred at Colne Engaine – where inmates refused to leave. See *Colne Engaine: The Story of an Essex Village*.)

out encouragement from persons of higher station." (The cause of the conflagration was not discovered).*

Some idea of the restrictive, prison like regulations of Sudbury's workhouse can be gleaned from *Gestingthorpe's Parish Magazine*. For in March 1899 the visiting hours were included:

"From 2-4pm on the first and third Tuesday in every month. Infirmary visiting every Tuesday from 2-4pm and on the FIRST Sunday in every month from 2-4pm.
In cases of urgency notice is sent to the relatives who may then visit the patient at any time."

(But what help was <u>Tuesday</u> visiting to farm labourers who worked six days a week with no holidays?)
Regardless of its unpopularity, a Board of Guardians continued to supervise the detested workhouses until 1930. In April 1931, responsibility was finally transferred to the county council.†

Although after 1834 the 'parish' did not directly look after its own workhouse it still had to contribute to the new institutions. Raising this money continued to be the responsibility of the village overseers, who often paid an assistant to collect the rates. In Gestingthorpe the 'assistant overseer' or 'tax collector' was one Alfred Digby Finch whose normal profession was that of a brickmaker. Today his granddaughter is the village's history recorder, Doris Pannell:

"Needless to say," she relates, "as a schoolgirl my poor Mother often got teased when they had Bible readings about dishonest tax collectors! Nevertheless Grandfather eventually covered twelve parishes and went round in a pony and trap. Later on, my own

---

* Again extracted from E. A. Goodwyn's reprint of *The Parish Paupers*. The booklet is an invaluable contribution to Sudbury's nineteenth century history, with a superbly researched introduction and accompanying notes.

† In later decades conditions mellowed. However several contributors like Sudbury's Oliver Prentice described:
"Tramps walking from one workhouse to another and then having to chop up firewood before they left in the morning. Some of the more permanent inmates of the 'spike' would then go round the town selling this kindling."

parents also 'took on' the job of collecting the rates.* Mother did Gestingthorpe and Dad did Belchamp Walter. They cycled around although I think they often had a job with farmers who would keep saying, 'can't you come back after harvest!'"

In earlier years many would have been glad to have paid rates. There were no old age pensions and the spectre of destitution haunted all but the most affluent. As the late Rev. Philip Wright explains:†

"The poor old dears were horrified of a parish funeral and poverty at the time was awful. Until at least the 1880's, if someone was in terrible distress – because for example, their house burnt down – the parson would call a 'brief' in local churches. At other times the churchwardens and rector might suggest a 'precept' or parish rate to help pay the expenses of the poor."♦

As a consequence of the austere times 'Friendly Societies' were formed to provide against the horrors of the workhouse, accident or injury. Again, these 'Mutual Insurance Societies' came from within the living body of the village itself. Bulmer had a 'Friendly Society' as early as 1803. Twenty years later Belchamp St. Pauls followed suit: "So that a fund may be raised for the relief of sick and afflicted

---

* For Belchamp and Bumpstead R.D.C. Rate collection was finally centralised in 1933-34

† Philip – who was well known for his interest in traction engines and heavy horses – was born on his father's farm at Hawstead, near Bury St. Edmunds in 1908. Before joining the ministry he was an early pupil at Chadacre Agricultural College and also a farm student at Byham Hall, Great Maplestead. In 1954 he was awarded a military M.B.E. for his services to the Army Cadet Force.

♦ As an example, in November 1897, the sum of £7 2s 6d was collected in Gestingthorpe for the Sandford family, to pay doctor's (and other) bills following an accident. The sum was equivalent to a farmworker's wage for fourteen weeks.
    Despite the strictures of the new law, parishes still attempted to alleviate certain cases of distress. (For example, the Gestingthorpe overseers account shows a deduction for the use of a room to pay the poor until 1871). Arthur Brown explains that, "a small dole was sometimes paid under the guise of Medical Assistance." The late Rose Chatters (b.1910), recalls, "when Father died, Mother got fourteen shillings a week, 'off the parish', to help bring up the family." Parish overseers continued until about 1927.

54

members...to which every member shall contribute one shilling monthly."*

In Gestingthorpe the 'Rayner Friendly Society' was similarly formed, whilst in 1827, the Stoke and Melford Union was founded, particularly for farmworkers. At its peak it had no less than 2000 members in 35 villages. Finally wound up in 1983, its last secretary, Henry Eady, explained to *The East Anglian Daily Times:*

"I think the association was conceived out of a real attempt to obviate poverty. In 1840 subscriptions were 1s 2d a month. It was not an easy sum for many families to find. People gave up their Sunday dinner if necessary to pay the few pence to the Union..."

The consequences of the New Poor Law and the impoverishment suffered by the rural labourer in the nineteenth century will again be referred to in, *Of the Furrow Born?*

This chapter has been a short one. It reflects a stark, bleak and unedifying episode in social history. Certainly the bitterness engendered was to be remembered not merely into the twentieth century but tenaciously up to its final years.

---

* From *Halstead and District Local History Society Newsletter, Summer 1989.*

Chapter Seven

SURVEYORS AND HIGHWAYS
Human Memories, Stone Picking and Ballingdon Hill

"We don't ever use these roads, bu!"
"Look at that 'ere waggon. Floundering about in weather such as this. Depend on it, he ain't a Gestup man!"
"All we do is work, work, work! All the bloomin' time. Just mending up roads for buggers from other villages to ride across and ruck up in the winter."

We continue with our exploration of how men lived, and worked, and how our parishes were governed. But what of the roads? The roads that linked these semi-states?

Each appointed 'Surveyors of the Highways'. Statute laid down that, "each male with a 'settlement' should do six days work on the roads each year." (In reality however, says Arthur Brown, "wealthy people would commute their service with payments of money, whilst employed men usually came at their employer's expense."). As Wethersfield Vestry meeting declared:

"Every farmer shall pick and lay one load of stones for every Five Pounds of his rates – on to such part of the highway as the surveyors shall direct." [24th January, 1765]

Not all parishes were so well organised. In 1597 no less than ELEVEN complaints were levelled against the inhabitants and parson of Toppesfield for the impassable state of their roads.* In 1656 fourteen men of Bulmer were similarly named for not doing their

---

* As early as 1535 a Highways Act required each parish to maintain the roads within their boundaries which led to market towns.

road duty, (although two years later the Bulmer – Ballingdon highway was again reported as being 'in a great state of decay'). Almost every single parish was likewise upbraided at the Quarter Sessions – be it Little Yeldham in 1597, Colne Engaine in 1767 or Mount Bures in 1823.

So unpredictable were the flounderous rural roads that discussing their condition became a standard 'ice breaker' in polite conversation.

"Am I only to talk of the weather and the state of the roads!" exclaims Marianne in *Sense and Sensibility*.

Yet concern for the highways extended beyond conversation. In 1518, one Thomas Paycocke of Clare actually left FORTY POUNDS, "for the 'fowle ways' between Clare and Belchamp and Clare and Ovington,"* whilst in 1584 Richard Goldinge of Henny bequeathed:

"Twenty shillings for the upkeep of the highways from Ballingdon to Great Henny...and another twenty for the repair of Ballingdon Bridge."†

Although Ballingdon Bridge is well known, the road to Great Henny – which Richard also supported – today provides some of our most enjoyable scenery. In places the road is an enchanting sunken lane with steep hedgebanks, eight to nine feet deep, which in summertime – when arched by the leaves of overhanging boughs – creates the exquisite impression of entering a tunnel. In these places it is not difficult to imagine those who passed this way in bygone years. Waggoners with their harvest sheaves, Rowe and

---

* Thomas Paycocke's family later lived at Coggeshall – hence Paycocke's House – renowned for its splendid pargetting. (Extracted from *The Discovery of Britain* by Jack Lindsay, Chapter Nine).

† From *Elizabethan Life: Wills of the Essex Gentry*, edited by F. G. Emmison – E.R.O. 1978.
    The Golding(e) family are one of the oldest in the area. The name repeatedly occurs in Bulmer and Belchamp St. Pauls (where five Goldings died in World War One), and a scholarly – and famous – namesake occupied the Hall in Shakespear's day. In the nineteenth century a Judith Garrod from Bures, whose mother was a Golding from Clare, married into the Constable family, and both the artist's father and brother were christened with the forename Golding. (From *John Constable's Correspondence*. Edited by R.B. Beckett, published 1962 by Suffolk Records Society).

Cornell's cumbersome threshing tackle, 'Wingy' Beaton droving sheep to Sudbury market or the horse-drawn 'baker's van' of Henny watermill. Parts of the road, moreover, have changed little since the sixteenth century – indeed landslides of the perpendicular banks still occasionally occur!

The recalcitrant parishes also – eventually – undertook their repairs. (And again it was crucial to know the *exact* position of the parish boundary!)

From Kersey comes some typical items from 1816:

	£	s	d
March 9th: Paid to James Wyatt for stones out of 'mony hole'	4	15s	0d
March 13th: Beer for 6 men for 6 days		12s	0d
April 1st: To sharpening pick axe			4d
April 15th: 2 new shovels		13s	0d
To laying and sharpening pick axe*		1s	6d
New facing to hammers			8d

whilst payments, 'for labour on the highway' were made to G. Cousins, T. Partridge, James Mann, E. Martin and J. Vince. (All being 'long standing' Kersey names).

Yet even in those days the volume of traffic was increasing. Eventually on the major roads neither the parish nor the Quarter Sessions could properly cope. From this situation began the era of turnpikes and toll-gates. On our most central toll-route (from Halstead to Sudbury), the Ballingdon Hills section was first turnpiked in 1695.

We have written 'Ballingdon Hills' in the plural, for in 1695 the road did, actually, consist of TWO punishing climbs. Then, in 1822, a new engineer was appointed. His name was James Macadam.

And he transformed those two, steep inclines into the single – and

---

* At times the sharpening of pick-axes became an almost daily occurrence. The blacksmith would have heated them up and then 'beaten out' a new point. In the last instance however he had 'layed' and fused on additional metal.

Ballingdon Hill – notice where the road has been raised beside the houses on the left

gentler – gradient that we know today.

Next time you drive up from Sudbury, notice the house opposite the *Kings Head* – now half submerged by Macadam's raised road. As you ascend, it is still possible to see where the highway is 'banked up' – across the previous valley – whilst in other places the road is like a giant sunken lane – where Macadam cut through the brow of the hills.

On lesser roads the parish surveyors struggled on assisted in the 1820's and early 30's by 'outdoor relief for the unemployed schemes'. Yet slowly the system was breaking down. From 1868-1880 existed a Hedingham Highway Board. The Lavenham area followed suit.

Thereafter Parliament placed 'main roads' under County Councils, whilst 'minor roads' became the responsibility of the newly formed Rural District Councils.*

* Local Government Acts of 1888 and 1894.

59

Yet there is still something special and significant about our winding, twisting, narrow country lanes.

For they were laboured on; kept drained and passable – through many manual centuries – by parish hands, and repaired with flints picked up by horsemen's wives and children.

Today, beneath the black veneer of tarmac is the backache of a woman. Beneath each road we drive on is a woman's torn and work-worn fingers; beneath each lane a windswept maiden; pale, forlorn, with infant child beside her, as with bended back and hail-lashed face she gathers up the stones. Yes! Beneath each highway in our area is the frail figure of a famished girl.

These then are our roads. They were wrought out of a Dark Age landscape; administered by surveyors of the parish born; repaired with flints from surrounding fields and laboured on – in every kind of weather, for many centuries – by those who lie now in our quiet parish churchyards.

We should sometimes drive slowly – and think of those who toiled thus...before our time.

Yet the memories of stone picking are not quite lost forever. Shortly after her *ninety seventh* birthday, Ida Bird – a farmworker's daughter from Wickham St. Pauls – vividly explained:

"We'd go in the springtime and do the wheat fields first and then the barley – while it was still low. Mother put her stones in the hollow of a big apron made of sacking that hung around her waist; but the younger ones like me used a bucket."

In an isolated cottage between Colne Engaine and Pebmarsh, gamekeeper Harry Gilbert revealed:

"We'd have to measure the stones in a special bushel – and then put them in 'yard' heaps (18 bushels), or half yard heaps (9 bushels). But the tumbril which took the stones away was also marked on the inside – so the roadmen knew whether they were getting good measure or not!"

At Twinstead, Dorothy Turner tells of the job which paid:

"about three ha'pence a bushel. But the problem was carrying

60

those buckets! When they were full of stones they were hard work for a little girl."

Not only is stone picking remembered. So too – and much more vividly – are the parish 'lengthsmen' who were responsible for defined stretches of highway.

"Old Barney," recalls Eddie Tuffin of Alphamstone, "did the beat from here down to Lamarsh. Just a keeping the drains clean, brushing the rubbish back and mending up the pot holes. You'd often see him breaking up stones – with his wire goggles on, and a long-handled hammer – and then putting them in the pot holes with red 'hoggin' from the pits."*

*SOME CONTRIBUTORS

Retired farmworker and shepherd, EDDIE TUFFIN (b.1903) – who is an Alphamstone Church warden in his *ninety first year* – is one of many new, warm-hearted and informative contributors to our research. (The Tiffen name recurs continually in our local history. A William Tyffyn is mentioned in Richard Goldinge's will of 1584 (p57), and as a constable at Gestingthorpe, whilst a Margaret Tiffin served as an overseer at Acton in 1718.

Others new contributors include IDA BIRD (b.1895) – who was not only an inspiration to meet – but an authority on all aspects of 'the cottage economy', whilst smallholder, station master and gamekeeper, the late HARRY GILBERT (1897-1986) of Colne Engaine had an almost encyclopaedic knowledge of bygone rural life.

Farmworker FRED CHATTERS (b.1906) today lives at Borley but spent nearly all his working life on the fields of Belchamp Walter, whilst the late DAVID TUFFIN (1903-93), was a village baker's son and smallholder from Henny Street. DOROTHY and the late FRANK TURNER (1903-92) were farmworkers' children from Twinstead and Pebmarsh, who lived for over 60 years in the former village – where Frank worked on the land, whilst Gestingthorpe horseman BERT SURRIDGE (b.1907), and Castle Hedingham farmer and 'steam enthusiast', the late CYRIL PHILP (b.1899) were two of our most knowledgeable and helpful contributors from *The Long Furrow*.

61

Many 'lengthsmen' are recalled as being real perfectionists who put, "lines down to meticulously edge back the grass," whilst regarding their 'stretches' with a fierce, competitive pride.

"My God!" declares David Tuffin of Great Henny, "if you dared go over our lengthsmen's verge because you'd met another cart or tumbril and he found out – cuh! You'd catch it!. That ol' man would 'go ahead at you' because you'd squeezed his bit of side down!"

But there were also friendly, warm-hearted, moments – particularly for the young. Fred Chatters (b. 1906) continues:

"Just occasionally the 'steam roller' would come round Belchamp Walter – to press down the granite and stones that the roadmen had put in – and do you know, for us village children it was the HIGHLIGHT of the year!"

Yet it was still an age – despite the steam roller, "when grass grew in the roads themselves," report Jute Chatters of Belchamp St. Paul, Harry Gilbert of the tiny lanes round Colne Engaine and Claude Alleston of the ancient routes from Boxford up to Groton and then Kersey.

"And in the middle of this grassy strip," retells the latter, "there would be a beaten down area – right in the centre – where the tumbril horses and cart-ponies had walked and trampled it down."

However, as farmer Cyril Philp points out:

"Being as the roads were only made of flint, gravel and hoggin, they weren't firm like today's surfaces. It made a waggon load of wheat much heavier for the horses to pull."

(As Tom Rowe points out, "it was twice as hard to ride a bicycle on a wet 'stone-hoggin' road than on a tarred surface").
There were however important exceptions.

"When you went up hills – like Ballingdon or Bardfield Hill," explains farmworker Fred Chatters, "the horses couldn't 'dig their toes in' once the roads were tarred. On the hills it was more difficult for them. In fact once the roads were tarred we needed an extra horse to pull a waggon load of wheat up Bardfield Hill."

In the towns there were other problems. As farmer Edwin Partridge of Raydon (b.1892) – whom I was privileged to interview shortly before his *hundredth* birthday – explains:

"Before they tarred the roads there were times when the dust would blow off them something terrible. Course what they'd do in towns like Hadleigh during the summer, was to go round the streets with a water cart – just to keep the dust down."

In the winter, when the horses might have frost nails added to their shoes, there was the additional hazard of snow. Many recall the old horse-drawn snow ploughs:

"You'd see them standing up on the village green – or on an old bit of waste ground somewhere" recalls Bert Surridge, "At Gestingthorpe it stood on the verge near Crouch Farm."

(Similarly, at both Groton and Elmsett they stood near the Blacksmith's, at Twinstead on the Green, at Pentlow 'at the top of the hill' and at Long Melford 'near Ward and Silvers').

But what of the snow ploughs themselves? At Alphamstone retired shepherd Eddie Tuffin enthusiastically continues:

"Ours was just like a great big pointed wooden divider with two horses on the front and two men who rode on the back of it...I believe it belonged to the council but the farmer I worked for has sent men and horses out with it all day long if there'd been a heavy fall."
"That was good of him," I murmured naively.
"Course the council had to pay!"
"Oh, did they!"
"Oh yes! You can trust an ol' farmer. He wouldn't have went out with two horses and a man for free – not that time of day! He wouldn't do it for goodwill. No fear!"
(The author shuffles uncomfortably in his chair..!)

Yet slowly the tentacles of progress percolated out to backward mid-Anglia. At Elmsett near Hadleigh, the author's father Harold Cooper (b.1918) was:

"walking home from school with my brother John when we suddenly realised that every hundred yards or so there were a couple of barrels laid beside the road."

The barrels contained tar. (But not the complete tar-macadam surface).

"But even so," says one source, "on the corners the charabancs pushed all the tar onto the side in hot weather – fat lot of use that was!!"

Moreover as Fred Chatters points out:

"When you went downhill with a horse and loaded waggon you'd drag an iron 'shoe' (or 'slod') in front of the waggon wheel to act as a sort of brake... Trouble was, after they tarred the roads, the tar would start smoking – because the shoe had got so blessed hot!"

Chapter Eight

CONSTABLES
Ridgewell and Little Maplestead

"On 14th October 1747, a vagabond family were apprehended wandering and begging in Ridgewell. Upon examination it emerged that their last legal settlement was in Newbury, Berkshire. The Ridgewell constables were instructed by the magistrates to convey them to the town of Bow, 'that being the first parish or town in the next precinct to which they ought to pass'."

(Essex Records Office)

We again return in time. To the last component of our 'semi-autonomous parish'. The village constables:

"who as likely as not," explains Arthur Brown, "would be the blacksmith, the publican or maybe a farmer. Able, sturdy individuals who knew how to look after themselves."

How one imagines these men – firm of character and strong of arm – as they dealt with brawling youths, rowdy drunkenness and most importantly the eviction of vagrants or those without 'settlements'.

Yet the constable's duties extended well beyond these confines. When Birdbrook was fined by the Quarter Sessions for not repairing their highways in 1655, it was the parish constable who was ordered, "to make a rate for the sum involved". When a water pump, "which supplied the alms people", fell into decay at Castle Hedingham in 1657, it was again the constables who became responsible for the repairs.

Now to Little Waldingfield. In 1681, Constable John Martin, not only "mended ye stocks", but was additionally – and more excitingly – involved in 'Hue and Cry', 'apprehending felons' and 'moving on vagrants'*, whilst in 1798 – when invasion threatened – it fell to Wethersfield's constable, one William Bentley, "to summon the 'supplementary militia' for the parish." (One wonders however, if he also proclaimed the news of Nelson's Victory on the Nile, as he strode to the outlying hamlets and farmsteads?).

Unlike other parish officers however, constables could at least charge for loss of time.

"constables bill for apprehending Robert Wendon for assaulting Mr. Ramsacre...19s 4d",† reads an entry in the Gestingthorpe accounts for 27th May 1836, whilst in 1776 one of Wethersfield's constables, Thomas Tanner, claimed the following expenses:

Oath of office..1s   0d
Three journeys to Gosfield and charges ..2s   6d
Return to justices 2s   6d

The above is deliberately selected since constables – like overseers – had to be officially 'sworn in' before a J.P. As early as 1543 however, one Gestingthorpe constable, William Tyffyn, was reprimanded for not having his appointment correctly legitimised and was consequently ordered, "to appear within fourteen days before a Justice of the Peace to take the oath".

Needless to say, not all constables had been angels. In 1694, Rob Prentice, a yeoman of Colne Engaine, was accused of, "diverse frauds under the pretence of certain monies expended by him in his office as constable", whilst in 1580, John Clerk the constable of Lamarsh:

"received a precept for the delivery of eight bushels of wheat, to the Queen Majesty's purveyors at Colchester, but did charge the said parish with the delivery of nine bushes and so...detained one of them for his own use."

* From *Beyond Living Memory* (the story of Little Waldingfield), by Harry Clive, published 1979. The earlier Birdbrook and Castle Hedingham references are both from the Essex Quarter Sessions Order Book 1662-1661, edited by D. H. Allen, published by Essex County Countil as E.R.O. No 65.

† We have met Robert Wendon before when he was the subject of a Settlement dispute (see page 30).
The constables were John Carter, James Rayner and George Nott.

A more endearing lapse occurred in 1720. For at Sturmer – just south of Haverhill, the petty constable arrested a man for cursing and beating his wife. Doubtless the constable performed his duty well. Doubtless he wished to relax, and to enjoy the accolades of fellow villages whilst celebrating his sterling deed…(need one really write more?). For yes, when finally drunk he allowed his prisoner to escape!*

Yet it is wrong to be flippant. For year after year, century after century, the parish constables played their role; upheld the law and kept the peace. They needed to be the formidable, upstanding characters Arthur described. Anyone with less than a 'strong personality' would have found the task onerous indeed.

Consequently it was not always a popular job, and there are several petitions to the Quarter Sessions for discharge. In January 1654 for example:

"William Borling and John Sach – lately elected petty constables of Halstead, set forth that they were poor men and unfit to serve in the said office". The parishioners were ordered to make a new election.

Yet despite the irregularities an overriding impression prevails. It is this. That within the interlocking structure of constables, Petty Sessions, Quarter Sessions and Assize Courts, 'Law and Order' was not only maintained – but justice was seen to be done.†

Sometimes however the constables' actions reveal surprising attitudes. In 1789 for example, John Alston of Pebmarsh apprehended thatcher Samuel Binks:

"for suffering persons to game and play with dice for Plum Cakes in his house…on the evening of 25th day of December."

* In 1758 a similar incident occurred at the Petty Sessions at Castle Hedingham Bell. On this occasion the prisoner was yeoman George Hanchett of Great Yeldham. Did his gaoler, one David Crufell, also become…'distracted'?

† For a more authoritative account (especially of the magistrates, and the Petty Sessions held at the Castle Hedingham Bell), the reader should refer to *Law and Order in North Hinckford* (i.e. North-East Essex), by retired Hedingham school teacher Frederick Pawsey D.F.C., J.P. (Published by Halstead and District Local History Society).

67

How tempting it is to picture that dark Christmas night – with Alston and his NINE witnesses peering through the window of Binks' cottage to observe the candle-lit scene! (But does the fact that nine witnesses came forward suggest that it might also have been a case of 'settling old scores' – or that Binks and his friends were repeatedly unruly? Amongst the witnesses with strong local names were an M. Coe, G. Rust, Henry Laver, Jerimiah Hunt and Edward Parker).*

Yet possibly we should not forget the differing standards of earlier times. In 1596 a Castle Hedingham alehouse keeper was indicted, "for keeping a disorderly house in which veal was eaten during Lent". In 1589 a Halstead woman was, "whipped for leading an immoral life". As late as 1782 a Sudbury woman was publicly whipped for "stealing ninepence worth of cloth..." In 1825 the Chelmsford Quarter Sessions frequently imposed punishments of hard labour:

"Six months to Samuel Ashford for stealing fowls the property of Timothy Kemp of Little Yeldham", and "Three months to John Laysell for stealing a leg of pork from Richard Spalding of Great Yeldham"... are but two examples.

Additionally there was transportation...or the death penalty. In 1824 four men were hanged at Chelmsford for a series of robberies from farms and houses in Bulmer, Gestingthorpe, Foxearth and the Belchamps. (They had stolen sheep, cloth, malt and fowls). Vast crowds, estimated between ten and fifteen thousand witnessed their executions.

From these darker, sobering reflections we return to the parish's own authority. In 1798 White Colne had its own 'cage', stocks and 'whipping post'. Castle Hedingham's 'cage', "was made of wood and stood in a small piece of garden near Tenty Meadow".† At Sible

* A century later, Pebmarsh suffered a genuinely horrific crime. For one morning a madman committed a murder. When the policeman, P.C. Cook arrived he is reported as finding:
"the murderer in a state of frenzy, walking about with his victim's head in a bowl under one arm with two dead chickens and a gun in his other hand". (From *An Essex Pie* by T. M. Hope)

† Extracted from, *Castle Hedingham in the Olden Times*, by Edward Bingham (from a lecture he delivered in 1894). This copy reprinted by Maurice and Anne Stockhill.

Hedingham the stocks stood outside the *Three Sugar Loaves* until the early twentieth century, whilst Gestingthorpe's, (which were in front of the church), were last used around 1850, "on the occasion of some young people quarrelling and disturbing a funeral one Sunday afternoon".

Some parishes also had overnight 'lock-ups' (about the size of a privy) for drunks or vagrants. Bert Surridge believes that Gestingthorpe's may have been near the 'Barracks', (but possibly when the latter stood near the Church?). Local towns similarly had jails. In the eighteenth century Sudbury's was in genteel Friars Street. As a possible deterrent the chains and manacles were left hanging outside.

In earlier times there were localised gallows. Usually they were erected on the edge of manor or parish boundaries. Those we know of, and where we can still imagine the stark wooden frame and awesome figure – dangling against a darkening sky – include:

Gallows Green .... on the Gestingthorpe-Bulmer boundary
Gallows Hill .... near Waldingfield Road, Sudbury
Gallows Hill .... near the Hadleigh by-pass
Galleys Corner   on the outskirts of Braintree, beside road to
                      Witham, just in Cressing Parish.
Gallows Green   on boundary between Great Easton and
                      Lindsell.
Galewfeld .... recorded at Castle Hedingham
                      (circa 14th century.)*
Gallow Green .... Aldham near Colchester
Gallows Lane .... leading off the road between Lavenham
                      and Cockfield.

We have deviated slightly from the era of the sovereign parish. Let us return then to a village constable's duties. We first go to Ridgewell – beside today's A604 – where on 10th May 1824, John Chaplain, "being a 'respectable farmer', and one of the constables, was summoned to *The Kings Head*". Here, two men, John Woods and Charles Mickley, "were behaving in so riotous and disorderly a manner as to cause a breach of the peace".

What does our gallant 'parish constable' do? Was he a strong silent

* From *Place Names of Essex*, by P. Reaney

man of the Gary Cooper mould? Or was he rather, 'a spit in the fire and grab the culprit John Wayne type'? Either way he eventually got John Woods into the stocks. Mickley however, resisted with great violence. But hurrah! the 'respectable farmer' stood tall; was not overawed and with his assistants eventually overpowered Mickley – whose hands were secured in the stocks... The 'parish constable' had restored law and order...The streets of High Ridgewell were at peace once more.*

The Case of the Maplestead 'Cock'.

Now to today's A131 – the main road between Sudbury and Halstead. Just over two miles from the latter, near a leafy junction to Pebmarsh and Maplestead, stands *The Cock* public house.

Here, on 10th August 1822, a more intriguing incident occured. The misdemeanour was conterfeit currency.

Although there were several similar cases at the time, the testimony of John Davis, the ostler at *The Cock*, was particularly entertaining, being delivered – one suspects – with rustic if theatrical conviction. He had seen the two defendants – Peter and Mary Young – enter the inn with two bundles. About the same time a butcher came in, "warning that the couple had been passing off bad money all over Halstead".

"Determined to watch them", the ostler sat down in the same room. "He kept his eyes upon the parcels the whole time".

About half an hour later, the female prisoner;

"in a very quick and artful manner, put her hand into one of the bundles and took out a bulky parcel – which was tied up with, 'an old dirty handkerchief'. She then left the room. A few moments later her husband followed."

Realising that one of the shillings exchanged in the pub was false, ostler Davis was instructed to follow the couple and change it. Surprisingly they obliged. The ostler then 'pretended' to return to

* To complete the story, the farmer "who had some business of great moment" was replaced by Ridgewell's other constable, William Fitch. The latter decided it was unwise to leave the couple in the stocks in the 'open air all night' and with assistance took them to an upper room in *The Kings Head.* Later the Constables and Landlord formally swore their evidence before Lewis Majendie of Castle Hedingham – the nearest J.P. (All from Essex Records Office).

70

The Cock – but actually;

"continued to observe the couple's motions on the road". The parcel was concealed in a ditch. Davis "hid himself behind the hedge nearby."

Thinking they were no longer observed, Young and his wife returned to the ditch – but could not find the parcel. At this point, a violent altercation took place between husband and wife. The ostler heard, "a great deal of very bad language!"

Being spotted, Davis informed a little girl to get a constable. Young and his wife ridiculed the ostler, since neither they – nor he – actually had the parcel, when, "on pulling the grass aside it was found..." As for the constable, he arrived in the nick of time. For the counterfeiters were accusing Davis and his master of having no right to stop them...as they were not 'official' constables!*

How we can now imagine Davis – garrulous and well-meaning, telling and RE-TELLING the story in later years!

But where did 'the action' take place? Was it on the Sudbury to Halstead road – or along the smaller lanes to Pebmarsh or Little Maplestead?

Adjoining the latter (Cock Road), and almost opposite the pub, is Gestingthorpe's parish field (see pages 31 and 45). In those days a Gestingthorpe 'town house' stood nearby – where paupers lived. Indeed it was this field which was dug  by hand during times of high unemployment. Was it their ditch – we wonder – in which the 'money' was concealed and ostler Davis hid?

A hundred and seventy years later, the contemporay 'parish land' trustees – who include Frank Nice, Rev. Ken Belben and the author, together with Clerk Cecil Pannell, still conduct a perambulation of the field each September. (The rents today provide grants for education). Inevitably, however, as we amble beside the beautiful autumn hedgerows of Hawthorn bushes, Field Maple and Oak trees, at least one trustee's mind begins to wander as he imagins those moments of heady – if faintly bizarre petty crime in 1822!

✤ ✤ ✤ ✤ ✤

* In the *Chelmsford Chronicle* of 25th October, 1822, we learn that the pair were sentenced to two years imprisonment in the County Goal. Their parcel of fake coins was found to contain 71 half crowns, 554 shillings and 190 sixpences. (Extracted from Essex Record Office, Quarter Sessions bundles).

Although the necessity for appointing parish constables was reduced after the Police Act of 1839, (introduced by Sir Robert Peel – hence the soubriquet of 'Bobbies'), the official policemen who followed were often 'of the furrow born' and truly reflected rural life.*

"If you were a youngster and you played truant," recalled farmer Bill Yeldham, (b.1908) as we sat in his house overlooking the fields of North End and Gestingthorpe, "the policeman gave you a good cuff on the side of the face. They had long leather gloves in those days – and they really stung. What's more you didn't go and tell your parents – because if you did, you'd get another one from them as well. But it didn't do us any harm and that way a kind of local law and order was maintained".

Not surprisingly the smallest misdemeanour by the early policemen was soon recounted with dry, soul-preserving East Anglian humour. With a wry chuckle, threshing contractor and smallholder Jack Cornell continues:

"Before bikes were very common the Bulmer Constable was meant to walk right down to the bottom of Finch Hill, every afternoon, and meet the Belchamp policeman on Bardfield Bridge.† Well one day he was 'all over and behind', so naturally he jumped on his 'brand new' bike and pedalled off. But as he came in sight of the bridge he saw the Inspector trotting up in his pony and trap! So he jumped off – and threw his bike behind the hedge. But then, after he'd met this 'ere copper from Belchamp the Inspector gave him a lift home in his pony and trap! Huh! The first thing he had to do when he got back to Bulmer – was walk all the blessed way back to the bottom of Finch Hill to get his bloomin' ol' bike!!"

Across Bardfield Bridge is the parish of Borley. Bearing left – and then right – one travels up a long, elm banked, 'sunken' lane to arrive

---

* The Police Acts of 1839 and 1840 enabled counties to form their own forces. Essex was one of the first eight counties to do so and by 1841 there were already constables at Belchamp Walter, Foxearth and Bulmer. Thereafter the force slowly expanded although parochial constables were still appointed for some years. We think that Gestingthorpe continued to appoint a constable until 1872. (Again, see *Law and Order in North Hinckford* by Fred Pawsey.

† The bridge crosses the Belchamp Brook and is near the T-junction to Borley and the Belchamps.

The idyllic tranquillity of Cavendish Green masks other aspects of local history. The parish's smallpox 'isolation house' stood not far behind the Church, whilst the War Memorial records that in World War One, thirty three young men paid the supreme sacrifice. (The village's population was then about 900). Contributor Frank Billimore remembers that his father – a shepherd – sometimes camped on the Green at night when droving sheep from Bury St. Edmunds to Colchester.

A typical carter or carrier, C. Bragg of Halstead, near Pebmarsh Church.

In earlier years the 'parish' was entirely responsible for the upkeep of its own roads. For brief details of Kersey's road repairs and 'poor relief' see pages 26 and 58.

"Very few people had bikes!" John Dixey's grandparents proudly display theirs about 1910. Behind them is the Sudbury to Halstead road at Bulmer Tye. To the left is the lane to Jenkins Farm; in the foreground is the road to Castle Hedingham. The present road is somewhat busier!

Gainsborough's Statue on Sudbury Market Hill was officially unveiled in 1913 by Princess Louise, Duchess of Argyle. One of those to witness the occasion was schoolgirl Dorothy Mills (page 109).

Lavenham Church was one of several to be left the rents of a small field to pay for the 'bell-rope' in the tower.

GAINSBOROUGH
1727   1788

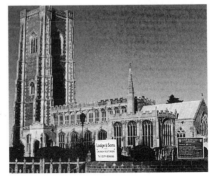

A Diamond Couple! Dorothy and Frank Turner
reminiscing about the Twinstead and Pebmarsh of their youth.

Retired horseman Fred Chatters of Borley recalls
the Belchamp Walter of his youth.

Wally and Rowena Twinn providing their
memories of Alphamstone and Pentlow.

The late Basil Slaughter. Headmaster of Bulmer School and stalwart of the W.E.A., Basil was also an early pioneer of oral history in the area, resulting in numerous lectures accompanied by old photos of the locality. In the above photograph he stands with his own version of Thomas Gainsborough's 'Mr

and Mrs. Andrews', ready for the recent Bulmer Festival and Eighteenth Century re-enactment. (Squire Andrews's portrait was actually painted not far from the 'Auberies' with Sudbury in the distant background. Gainsborough's original can be seen in the National Gallery, London). (Photograph by kind permission of the 'East Anglian Daily Times')

Cecil Pannell of Gestingthorpe with the hand bier in Gestingthorpe Church. Cecil's father and grandfather were both village wheelwrights and undertakers and the bier – a beautiful example of craftsmanship – is believed to have been made by the family business – in 1897.

at 'The Green'. It was here, in a small farmworker's cottage that another of our contributors – with whom I spent so many happy afternoons – humorously recalls the village policeman of his boyhood:

"...and he was always after me!" laughs life long farmworker, Alf Finch (b.1900). "I did get in some scrapes when I was at school. One time, I climbed up Mr. Abel's walnut tree – to shake the branches whilst my mates picked up the walnuts. Then they scampered off shouting 'Copper's coming! Copper's coming!' 'Course I tried to hide in the branches. But he just took one look up and groaned – 'Oh no! Not you again!'"

But it wasn't only youngsters who had brushes with the law. Tom Gilbert (b.1922) tells of his father's fruit and vegetable business at Little Yeldham.

"Father was meant to have candles on the pony cart, especially on dark nights in the winter. Well, times were hard in the thirties with the depression on and so forth, and of course everyone tried to avoid that sort of thing. But just occasionally he'd meet the policeman."

"Where are your lights?" he'd demand.

"Sorry constable, I – er – haven't got any matches" would come the reply.

"You never have!" the policeman would snap as he lit the candles"Go on, Gilbert!" he'd growl.

PART TWO

RURAL LIFE

"There were 'higglers', dealers and carriers. And they could basically do people's shopping for them. They usually had a donkey cart and would collect or deliver items that had been ordered – often 'wheeling and dealing' rabbit skins, or the like on their round. In Bulmer we had a chap called Bill Humm. He didn't just have a donkey cart, but a great, big flowing white beard – well, he became quite a celebrity!"

The late Jack Cornell, 1918-1988.

"Whenever my father (Harry Rowe)had to walk a long distance – like to Colchester and back, he'd always put Silverweed or 'Footsease' in the sole of his shoes. The leaves are lovely and springy and it also kept his feet cool."

The late Hilda Smith
of Twinstead and Wickham St. Pauls.

"At school we always had to celebrate 'Empire Day'. At Belchamp Walter we'd go into the playground and stand around the Union Jack – and then we'd have some sort of ceremony – and finally we'd have to salute this flag. As luck had it, it was actually Charlie Martin's birthday – so we used to say they'd put the flag up a purpose for him!"

Fred Chatters (b. 1906), now of Borley.

[At some schools, such as Pebmarsh and Wickham St. Pauls, the children attended a Church service before having part of the afternoon off].

75

Chapter Nine

DELIVERIES, HATCHES, MATCHES, DISPATCHES

*"Gestingthorpe's first Post Office was established around 1848
– about the same time as those in Pebmarsh and Gosfield"*

DORIS PANNELL

They strode along muddied tracks and meadow paths, beside bram-
bled hedges and narrow lanes. They passed fields of turnips, clover,
mangolds, beans and wheat. They crossed pastures grazed by sheep
and cattle, and came eventually, to isolated farmsteads – with grunt-
ing pigs and straying chickens. And as they walked, they met horsemen plodding with their teams to work; 'stallion leaders', drovers,
stockmen with their cows, and maybe also, a kitchen maid – scurry-
ing to the 'big house' – with a blush upon her face for the strapping
wheelwright's lad she had just met beside the stile.

They were the early village postmen who trudged, and later biked,
for miles around our countryside – in all weathers and every season.
Many stopped about midday in 'little tin huts', (painted 'official' red),
with a bench and fire inside, where they often did some cobbling
whilst waiting for the second collection. One such was Teddy Heard,

"Who," recalls Alf Finch, "walked from Sudbury up to Borley
and then went round the village – right up to Eyston Hall and such
places as that – twice every day. Of course, when the Inspector
came with him he deliberately did it the longest way round!"

"Even more remarkable," relates John Dixey, "was a postman
named Harry Wilson who walked from Sudbury Post Office, all
round Middleton to Henny Ryes and then right up to Twinstead...
Then he'd walk back to Sudbury to get the letters for the afternoon

76

delivery. But once he'd got them he'd march right back to Twinstead, have his dinner in the Postman's hut on the Green and then do a bit of cobbling until it was time to do the second delivery – which finally brought him back to Sudbury!"

In an age before the telephone, the work was truly essential.

"To warn people he was coming," explains Fred Chatters of Belchamp Walter, "the postman would blow a whistle before he got to any of the 'big houses' like *Mary Hall*. But on a still day we could often hear Otten's postman blowing his as well."*

In time the mail was delivered by bicycle:

"But villages were still 'real villages' in those days," declares retired postman Albert Cross† of the Twinstead, Wickham and Great Maplestead round, "and for some of these 'old dears' it was quite an event to get a letter. I mean they hadn't got any electric lights or running water and on winter evenings you'd knock on the door and they'd call out."
"Who is it?"
"Posty!"
"Then they'd draw the bolts back and nervously peer out."

"But what about Christmas?" I wondered.

---

* Although it was doubtless unpleasant in wet weather (when he wore a big oil-skin cape), the Belchamp postman had a most scenic route: "He came" relates Fred, "from Sudbury Post Office up to the 'Auberies', along Bulmer Street, down to Gogum Hall and then across Belchamp Meadows on the footpath, (which the council actually maintained as a cinder track) to Belchamp Walter Church. He then went up to Clarkes Farm and did 'the village', before going right down to Mary Hall, Hopkins and Northeys before finally coming back to the Postman's Hut (which was opposite today's council houses). Well he'd stay there until mid-afternoon and then strike off back to Sudbury doing the afternoon collection and blowing his whistle as he went!"

† After being out in the heat of India in World War II, Albert returned to England becoming a postman – and biking some thirty miles a day. "But in that first winter – after India – it was perishing cold. I used to put brown paper under my leggings to help keep warm!" More recently, Albert has been a founding member of Halstead Local History Society and contributor to *The Khyber Connection*.

"Well that's another thing. Years ago country people didn't actually post their Christmas cards until Christmas Eve. And we delivered them *on Christmas Day!* We used to start especially early – at 4 a.m. and get finished about two o'clock in the afternoon. Christmas was a game though! Sometimes there were so many parcels stacked up in front of the bike that I could hardly see where I was going!"*

Things had certainly changed from the early days of the mid-nineteenth century;

"When," records Adrian Corder-Birch, "one of Sible Hedingham's postmasters was heard to speak of a particularly heavy mail one day ... It consisted of just thirteen letters!"†

Yet other – more elemental – deliveries also took place. I was first reminded of this when visiting retired horseman Frank Billimore at his home near the *Cock and Blackbirds* in Bulmer Street. As we talked however, the conversation turned from memories of bygone farming to childhood reminiscences, and wife Phyllis happily – and proudly – remarked:

"My Mother was the midwife for Monks Eleigh, Milden and Lindsey. But when we were young, we children often used to wonder, 'where on earth is Mother going in the middle of the night with her apron on?' Of course she wasn't properly trained or anything – but then they weren't in those days. But even so she still brought several sets of twins into the world!"

It was the same at Alphamstone where the village midwife was Popsy Parker's grandmother. However, recalls Popsy with a smile, there was one particularly memorable birth.

"She used to go to her maternity cases in a donkey trap but I've often heard my father talk of one bitterly cold, snowy night when someone had trudged across the fields to get her. So she woke up

* "When the mail was delivered on Christmas Day," commented a different source, "the postman was often invited in for a quick drink. But there were occasions when by the end of the morning – well you can work out what had happened! In fact at ——— we once had to send out a search-party and finish old 'George's' round for him!"

† From *A Pictorial History of Sible Hedingham*. Published by Halstead and District Local History Society, 1988.

78

my father and he got up and harnessed the donkey to the cart. But being as it was so rough and the snow was beginning to drift he actually took her out – nearly all the way to Bures – and then had to wait there until she had actually delivered the baby!"

Ironically, Popsy's father, George Amos, was also the village wheelwright – and undertaker. "Oh yes! we often used to say that we saw both ends of life!"

In fact village undertakers usually were wheelwrights or carpenters. As George 'Rover' Finch of Gestingthorpe wryly explains:

"You'd see wheelwright Geoffrey Pannell walking down the road with his measuring rod and you'd think '–Oh dear, someone else have got some bad news'."

Traditionally the bad news travelled quickly. Blinds were drawn; straw – to cushion the noise of passing waggons – was put on the road outside. And church bells were tolled.

"At Glemsford," states historian Richard Deeks, "it was rung once for a man; twice for a woman; three times for a child."

The age of the deceased was often added. As a boy, the author's father wondered why a horseman would sometimes leave off work at strange times. "Ah. He's going to ring the bell, someone's died you see," came the explanation. Also when a child, Mary Alleston once asked if the tolling of the funeral bell meant that old ———— had finally died.

"Well they ain't practising for it!" came the quick retort.

The Rev. Trevor Howard, latterly of Bulmer, Belchamp Walter and Belchamp Otten, more seriously explains:

"It was from this practice that John Donne wrote his famous lines:

Any man's death diminishes me,
Because I am involved in Mankind;
And therefore never send to know
For whom the bell tolls;
It tolls for thee."

As with everything in that era the grave digging and the coffin making were usually undertaken by parishioners themselves. In making a coffin for someone he had known all his life, Gestingthorpe's Geoffrey Pannell would be assisted by his brother – who took time off from farm work to help. By the nineteen twenties the finished article would be transported to the deceased's house in Harry Rippingale's coal lorry (which also doubled up as the village bus). Before motorisation however, the coffin was usually carried on the finely crafted hand bier, which now stands in Gestimgthorpe Church. But despite its elegance it also had to be functional in the worst of weathers.

"Oh yes," recalls son Cecil, "I've heard both Father and Grandfather talk of pulling and pushing coffins in all conditions – downpours and snowdrifts included!"

Not all villages had their own hearses. At Elmsett, in mid-Suffolk, a fund to buy a 'wheelum bier' was opened as late as 1922. Meanwhile at Alphamstone:

"A big heavy hand-hearse was hired from Twinstead Church for five shillings." explains Popsy Parker, "But for very long journeys, Father might rent a 'horse hearse' from Sudbury. Pulling a hand-hearse up some of Alphamstone's hills was quite a business!"*

She is not the only contributor to recall that the hand hearses seemed unnecessarily heavy.

"At Belchamp St. Pauls," reminisces farmworker 'Jute' Chatters, "it was like a big four poster bed. Two people would pull it on a pole and there might be two more to push. Think of that in the pouring rain on those rough, muddy roads!"

---

* The Twinstead hand hearse has produced a range of memories: "It was a noisy ol' thing!" recalls Dorothy Turner. "I'll never forget my grandfather being buried. I mean the wheels used to squeal enough as it was – but when they turned a corner, oh dear, they 'grated' something awful!"
    Alphamstone shepherd, Eddie Tuffin, was one of those sometimes 'borrowed off the farm' for undertakers duties.
    "Me and another chap would be sent to Twinstead to borrow their hearse. One to push and one to pull – but according to where we were going we'd perhaps come the long way round – to avoid the worst hills. 'Course once the coffin was on, it needed four of us to work it."

But not everyone was similarly conveyed. Farmers might travel on a 'harvest waggon' whilst for others the final journey was made on the shoulders of old friends and contemporaries. Indeed the impression prevails that the hand hearses – or 'wheelum biers' were quite recent introductions. As Fred Chatters recalls of Belchamp Walter:

"I can remember eight men carrying a coffin from Mill House [between North End and *Hopkins Farm*] all the way to Walter Belchamp Church and that must be well over two miles. They'd have to come past *Mary Hall*, along to Puttock End, then to *The Eight Bells* and finally down by *Springates Farm*... 'Course, they changed over and took it in turns."

Where possible footpaths were utilised. As Gestingthorpe's Bert Surridge (b.1907) explains:

"People were carried to church on 'bier ways'. They were funeral paths and had to be wide enough for two men to walk side by side whilst shouldering a coffin. But if they had a tidy step to walk, they reckoned on being 'found' some beer before they set out. They used to reckon that if you didn't leave enough beer, then you wouldn't get yourself buried!"*

The concept of carrying a coffin to church on a sleet-grey day against a backdrop of inky woodlands and leafless trees, along a squelching and slippery track, is one which underpins this work; for it illustrates how totally involved the villagers were – both in each other's lives and the parish itself. And because the East Anglian attitude to death is so completely uncomplicated, one can imagine also the grunted remarks, as the coffin on the bearers' shoulders, got heavier and heavier.

"Never thought old George weighed so much..." says one.

"...well, it weren't his brains bu!" comes a reply.

Similarly there were the cryptic comments of many a village undertaker:

* We remember the manorial controversy of 1536 when a 'bierway' was ploughed up (See Chapter One). Meanwhile at Ridgewell Church a fifteenth century oak 'hand' bier is believed to be the oldest in Essex, whilst a more recent 'wheeled' bier stands in Brent Eleigh Church.

"Hate to say it," mutters one, "but I shan't be a mite sorry to see that 'ok-urd owd darvil' screwed down."

But even here the quaintest things could happen. In a white brick cottage not far from the Henny *Swan*, smallholder David Tuffin (1903-93), recalled one, unforgettable morning's work:

"An old man died in Henny Street and the undertaker asked me to get the coffin with my horse and cart. Anyway I got the coffin to the cottage and then gave him a hand to get it up the narrow stairs. Well he put the body in and screwed the lid down – but then – we couldn't get the bloomin' coffin downstairs! ... It-just-would-NOT-come! 'What are you going to do now?' I wondered. Come the finish, do you know what he did? Took the bloomin' window out! ...And then leant a couple of planks up against the window sill – and slid the coffin down on them!"*

There was still a grave to be dug. For many it was in the soil of the parish on which they had performed their life's great work; of ploughing and seeding, harvesting and shepherding: and where too they had been christened and confirmed as their forefathers had for generations before them. Almost all would be known to the Church Sexton – who had the sombre task of digging the grave, and was himself an integral part of parish life. Indeed at Belchamp Walter one previous sexton is still fondly commemorated:

Here by this wall lies old Sam Cook
Who with his Spade, his Bell, his Book
Serv'd Sexton Three Score Years and Three
Until his Master grim Death cry'd
Enough – your Tools now lay aside
And let a brother bury Thee.
Died 6 May 1800: Aged 89 years

(from plaque on North Wall)

* Bee keepers had an additional duty as Gestingthorpe's Lesley 'Luke' Smith explains: "My grandfather had twelve hives of bees – but if ever anyone died in the family he'd go and knock on top of the hives three times – to let the bees know – otherwise he reckoned they'd swarm".

Yet footpaths and grass lanes were used for more than carrying coffins and the repetitive journeys of workaday life. There was also the happier business of courtship and weddings:

"It wasn't at all unusual," says the Rev. Philip Wright, "for both the bride and groom to walk to Church for the ceremony."

It is undoubtedly a more pleasing thought; of summer afternoons and flower garlands, and of meadow scents and wild flowers beside the tracks on which they walked. However we should not be too romantic – for there were also thunderstorms and showers.

"My mother lived at Bures Croft," retells Dorothy Turner, "and when she got married in 1903, she walked from there to her wedding at Bures Church. Well apparently that was raining TORRENTS! But do you know – *that old vicar ticked her off for being late!!!* Miserable old so and so! But they didn't have any honeymoon or anything. When the ceremony was over they just walked back to her mother's house and then after about a week there they found a house at Alphamstone."

For longer distances however a wagonette might be hired for the bride. (A wagonette held about six people – but was still open-topped).

"The man at the pub hired them out," reminisces Gestingthorpe's 'Rover' Finch. "But when I married we both went in wagonettes."

Smallholder George 'Rover' Finch (1895-1990), is the oldest Gestingthorpe contributor to this book. He spent his entire working life on just seven acres of land, not far from *The Pheasant*. And sitting in his cottage nearby, he suddenly revealed the last vestiges of an ancient custom. It is 'The Rough Band' – which the great East Anglian historian, George Ewart Evans, investigates so fully in *The Pattern Under the Plough*. To have 'caught' a final memory of this archaic practice in the heart of our area was particularly exciting. With bright twinkling eyes George spontaneously exclaimed:

"After the wedding was over we'd give them the 'Rough Band'; Oh yes, we'd go outside their house and bang on any old thing that we could to make some music or noise with, and then we'd stay there until they gave us some beer! We even gave the 'rough band' to Mr. Ruffel – a farmer! But when I got married, I left some jugs of beer out a' purpose for them."*

Despite the optimistic hopes and earnest supplications for good health and happiness, there was sometimes the need for a doctor.

"When I was a boy," recalls Bert Surridge, "the doctor came and took out the tonsils of the girl next door. The charge was seven shillings and sixpence, and I believe they did it on the kitchen table."

"If anybody was badly ill in Little Yeldham," relates Bill Yeldham, "someone would have to walk to Castle Hedingham and knock up the doctor. Well, first off this 'ere doctor would have to tell his horseman to get his pony and trap out, and then take him to wherever he had to go. But if it was a quiet night, you could hear him coming for miles as the wheels rattled round on the old flint roads."

It wasn't only doctors who seemed to be a long while arriving in emergencies.

"When they had the fire at *Clickets Farm*," laughs Gestingthorpe's Dick Finch, "they had to get the fire engine from Castle Hedingham. But it was pulled by two horses and of course they had to be caught and harnessed up first! What a palaver! Anyway, when they did finally arrive the men jumped off and started pumping. It took some pumping as well! We gave them almost as much blessed beer as they put water on the fire!"

* The origins of the 'Rough Band' lie in expressing disapproval – often of wife beating or adultery. In mediaeval times, the Rough Band was approximately synonymous with the 'drumming out' of people from villages. By making the biggest din that they could, the Rough Band intimated the hostility and frustration that society felt with miscreants.

By the twentieth century, the original purpose of the Rough Band had been forgotten and when resurrected at weddings, was no more than the boisterous 'joining in of village lads'. (At the conclusion of *Far From the Madding Crowd*, Thomas Hardy describes a similar practice in Wessex).

It is interesting to speculate whether the contemporary practice of tying old cans and fireworks onto the cars of newly married couples can be traced back to the Rough Band of 'Rover' Finch's day.

Then there was the village baker.

"Gestingthorpe's," says Doris Pannell, "was Dick Felton – and everyone knew him. Every two or three days he came round the village in a cart drawn by a faithful old horse delivering bread and flour. And the aroma of that freshly baked bread! But best of all he always had a smile and a friendly word."

Despite the nostalgic memories we must never forget the hardness of those times. Farmworker Fred Chatters elaborates:

"You got paid for Christmas Day on a farm years ago. But you still had to come in and attend to your horses or whatever – and of course you didn't get nothing extra for doing that, and then on Boxing Day – well that was just an ordinary day. If you wanted it for a holiday then you 'lost it' [i.e. weren't paid for it]. And it was much the same with Easter Monday. There wasn't nothing years ago. They might perhaps give you Good Friday afternoon – but only on condition that you went to Church. And that was it. There was just no such thing as holidays. It was six full days work a week except that on Saturday afternoons you could leave off one hour earlier. And that was your lot."

At Twinstead Frank Turner is not alone in recalling a small milestone in social history:

"When farmworkers' wages went up from twelve to thirteen shillings a week – my God! There was a HELL OF A TO-DO!. One ol' horseman – who lived on the farm said, 'I'm due an extra shilling now.' 'So you may be,' his boss replied, 'but your rent is going up a shilling as well!' Oh yes, some of them – not all of them mind – but some of them were really rotten years ago."

Wet weather presented other problems. Charlie Martin of Belchamp Walter continues:

"If you were ditching or hedging and that come on wet – so you couldn't stand it no more – and went off home to get dry, your ol' governor would come to you at the end of the week and say, 'How many hours have you 'lost' this week?' …and you'd tell him and then he'd reckon up what he owed you. And I've been in a ditch plenty of times when the wind's been up and the rain's been driving down and you've put old corn sacks round your shoulders and legs to try and keep dry but you dursn't leave off. As for being ill! I mean there weren't no sick pay that time of day. Oh no. You'd have to be very, very poorly before you stopped away from work."

Even when the long hours of farm work were over, there was still the crucial vegetable garden to be dug and weeded. And yet they were *never* worked on Sundays.

"It's extraordinary really," says Eddie Tuffin, "because for years and years my father worked a full 'six day week' at *Middleton Hall*. And yet apart from just 'taking up' a few vegetables for our dinner he wouldn't *dream* of working in his garden on a Sunday."

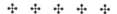

Silverweed or 'Footsease'

Chapter Ten

TRANSPORT
Early Bicycles and Buses: 'Bluffy's Bus Remembered!'

A meeting has been held in The George Hotel with a view to forming 'The Halstead Cycling Club'. There were said to be more than 30 riders in Halstead and the vicinity.
Halstead Gazette, 28th February 1891

We have told of the postman's lengthy perambulations. Yet it was the same for rural women when visiting the market town. Indeed the memories of 'fast walking mothers' striding into Sudbury or Halstead from outlying villages like Gestingthorpe or Pebmarsh are legion.

"From Wickham St. Pauls," says Ida Bird, "Mother walked to Sudbury and back for her weekly shopping."

"At Pebmarsh," states Tom Nott, "parish washerwoman Nancy Bishop walked to Halstead and back each Saturday."

"From Bulmer," recalls Gertie Coe:

"Mother would stride down to Sudbury during harvest, buy some meat, and then bring it back and cook it, before taking it out to Father – wherever he was in the fields."

Yet once a year the shopping expedition involved the whole family. Twinstead farmworker's daughter, Dorothy Turner, provides a stirring – if poignant – memory:

"When Father took the harvest money Mother would take all us children – including the youngest in a pram – and we'd walk all the

87

way to Sudbury and buy some new 'once a year' shoes and maybe – just maybe, some clothes. Then, on the way back we'd load this pram up with parcels – and the baby – and take it in turns to push it up the Ballingdon Hill. But when we got to the top, Mother would stop and get out a lovely Swiss Roll and we'd sit down and eat it – and that was a real treat...and then we'd walk the rest of the way home, and that's what we did every year."*

By comparison there were also vendors who regularly tramped the villages selling their wares.

"Old Golden," recalls Alf Finch, "used to come up to Borley from Sudbury with a big basket of fruit and another of 'bloaters' on his arms – and he'd come across the meadows and walk all round Borley – and he'd still be able to sell the bloaters at three half-pence each!"

It was the same at Kersey. Here, recalls Claude Alleston:

"Old man Martin would walk round the villages with a basket of kippers and bloaters."†

* Dorothy's mother also kept the wax from her husband's bees. "She'd get a little bit about the size of your thumb nail and then she'd walk to Sudbury with it and go to Brown and Jays the chemists – and because it was so special, she'd get quite a nice bit of money for it.And then she was allowed to spend this money on clothes for us."

† Many shops provided a weekly delivery service around the villages.
    "In Gestingthorpe," says Beryl Spillings, "you didn't need to go to Sudbury more than about twice a year. It isn't that we had a couple of shops in the village, but so many more other stores, bakers and butchers also came round. From Castle Hedingham we had Bains and Mortimer, from Sudbury we had the International, 'Holland and Barrett', Kings and the Co-op, whilst from Melford a Mr. Wash came round with paraffin, drapery, candles and cloth. What's more, there was never any charge for delivery. People would run around all over the place to sell a pound of sugar!"
    There was also the business of haircuts. At Belchamp Walter, "roadman Walter Deal would do it on a Sunday morning" whilst at Alphamstone, wheelwright George Amos charged, "1d for a haircut and 3d for a shave." (More than one contributor however, recalled that during sheep shearing youthful high jinks might result in an unwary village lad receiving an 'unexpected haircut'!) But what about women, I wondered. "They just cut their own – or got their friends to do it for them," remarked one source.

Yet not only have the distances which were walked changed with the generations:

"So too," declares Peter Minter of Bulmer Brickyard, "has the actual manner of walking – particularly amongst men. Years ago country people – especially horsemen – walked with a rolling, lumbering gait – with the legs wide apart – and for a good reason. You see on dirty, wet roads or on muddy fields, it stopped the insides of their knees getting dirty... It's a shame because nowadays you hardly ever see a genuine 'horseman's walk' in Sudbury."

But still we might ask – other than by walking – how *did* rural people reach market towns? One June evening as we sat in his house overlooking St. Barnabas' Church, Eddie Tuffin (b.1903) cheerfully explained:

"Well at Alphamstone, John Stuck – who I worked for – was also a Jobmaster. He had a Victoria, two wagonettes, a dog cart, a pony trap, a 'Brougham' and a 'brake'."

"What was a brake?"

"A 'brake' carried about 14 people and in the winter it could be covered in. It was pulled by two horses and he'd do regular runs with it to Sudbury – just like a modern bus. He'd pick up as he went along – almost until they fell out!"

"What about if there were just too many people?"

"Well quite often I'd follow behind with a wagonette. That used to seat five – but we often got seven in at a push! However, they were open to the elements. Whatever the weather."

"How long did it take?" I wondered, thinking of the narrow lanes and steep hills.

"What to Sudbury? Oh, thirty to forty minutes. We used to come away from Alphamstone about quarter past one, stable at *The Christopher* in Gainsborough Street and then come back at 4.30. 'Course on the return we'd be all be stacked up with parcels! And in the winter time it was dark and we only had those little lamps to

A Brake

see by. There again we never met anything much – except for perhaps another cart, and we didn't used to blunder past each other – not that time of day. But if we had a full load coming up some of these hills – especially Ballingdon Hill – it used to make the horses what you call 'dig their toes in'."

For a few moments I frantically scribbled down Eddie's comments: (Of the charge to Sudbury being 'a shilling round trip'; of wagonettes being hired to take people to – or from – Bures Railway Station; of the horses being 'half bred hunters' – that could also be used for lighter farm work; and of the nearest other 'Jobmasters' being Cousins and Chambers – both of Bures).

When however, I at last looked up – a broad grin had appeared on his face.

"You had to work though!" he exclaimed. "I remember one Christmas time I took Oliver Stebbings, from *Street Farm*, Henny to a 'do' near the *Saracen's Head* at Newton. We didn't come away 'til after midnight! I was fast asleep in the kitchen of the 'big house' when they came for me! Anyway it was suffen' severe that night and Sudbury Market Hill was white with ice. There was a full moon and it regular shone on it! 'Course I couldn't travel very fast on account of the ice, so you can see what time it was when I finally got back. 'You're suffen late,' hollered Mr. Stuck from out his bedroom window'. 'I know that!' But next morning I still had to be at work by six o'clock! Oh no. You didn't get many hours sleep."

Nor did one of Sudbury's jobmasters who took party-goers home from Christmas Balls in the Town Hall. His name was Decimus William Harvey and he operated out of the yard of *The Angel* public house with five horses. From here he not only met every train to arrive at Sudbury station, but was also available for weddings and funerals and additionally offered an ostling service.

Today, his daughter – Dorothy Mills (b.1902) – lives in the town's newly built 'William Wood Home for the Aged' – on the site of the old Grammar School. It was here, in late June, that we enjoyed an afternoon of delightful reminiscences.

"Father was always busy on Market days," she explains. "You see farmers would leave their ponies and traps at our stables – and we would look after them while they went to the Corn Exchange or livestock market and their wives went shopping."

"What about the funerals?" I wondered.

"Well the coffin usually went on a trailer. You see only very rich people could afford a glass hearse. The minister always walked in front and then another trailer came behind with the wreaths on. But Father also did weddings – and then he'd put bows of ribbons on the harness and so forth. Oh! Those horses did look a picture as they went up the Market Hill – all groomed down and with their brasses polished up!"

Trying to recreate the scene I asked if springtime had been the most popular season for weddings – and received an unexpected answer.

"It might have been, but the most popular day of all was actually Christmas Day! In fact it was so common that we usually had our Christmas Dinner on Boxing Day – so we could all be together."

The descriptions of jobmasters and ostlers remind us what a dramatic – and recent – breakthrough bicycles were to isolated rural people:

"Bikes!" exclaimed Maud Lott of Bulmer (b.1901); "I couldn't afford one till I was over thirty."

Numerous contributors concurred. "Father never had a bike!" declared Dick Finch (b.1910) – when I asked how his parents had mastered the new invention on the rough granite roads. Indeed as Bert Surridge recalls:

"The first person to ever have a bike in Gestingthorpe was ol' Revd. Bromwich – and he was the first by several years."

Similarly at Bulmer:

"There was only one person (Ted Emmerton) with a bike when I went to school," says hurdle-maker Tom Rowe (b.1903) "and his had solid tyres!"*

At Boxford, records Claude Alleston:

"Johnny Whymark actually used to make bicycles. He'd buy lengths of tube and braze them together and then put the spokes in the wheels – but there was a lot more skill to that than anyone would think. He was a clever ol' boy."

Slowly however the new-fangled 'traptions became more common. In time even Gestingthorpe had a bicycle shop – which was run by Percy Downs. Indeed it was here that Dick Finch bought his own first machine – but only after he'd started regular work. By comparison Eddie Tuffin tells of his first velocipede.

"The boss bought it for me. That was for something I'd done I suppose; but it'd only got one brake – and that was on the front – and of course if you put it on too hard, you know where you went that time of day...you went over the top into that ditch at the

---

* In the Hadleigh area Edwin Partridge (b.1892) was; "six or seven years old when I first saw a bike – and that belonged to my Father. What's more, you couldn't just bike around anywhere. Before the roads were tarred you had to steer carefully over the tufts of grass and through all the potholes and ruts!"
By comparison, Naomi Partridge tells of the 1930's. "At Whatfield, Jimmy Johnson would hire my Father's bike on Saturday evenings to deliver the Salvation Army's 'War Cry' newspaper...I think that Dad used to charge him about fourpence."

bottom of Burnt Hill!"

Eventually however, Eddie was able:

"to buy a proper one. A Humber. It cost £5 15s 0d. And I had it all those years. And then, a few years ago I gave it to the Church for a Gift Auction. And do you know! It fetched over £20!"

Perhaps because Little Maplestead's Cecil Cook (b.1918) is a little younger he was able to obtain his from Chaplin and Keeble's of Halstead, after working his first harvest. However, of the £3 19s 6d price tag, it was still paid for: "a pound down and the remainder at five shillings a month"

There was also the business of illumination. When Gertie Coe finally bought her first bike after a year's silk weaving, (at Kipling's Factory in Sudbury's Gregory Street), she had to get used to the carbide light.

"And it smelt awful! You had to turn on the water to make the gas and then if it got flooded, it wouldn't work. And being as we worked from 8am until 6pm we needed it both journeys in the winter. And I ought to know – I've been up and down Ballingdon Hill thousands of times in the dark!"

By comparison, housemaid Maggie Finch's first bicycle had an oil lamp. But when she was biking home from work at Borley Rectory the wind would sometimes blow it out:

"and then you daren't ride any further because the police were on the lookout!"

But if I was intrigued at the thought of roads on which a bicycle – let alone a motorised vehicle – was an unusual sight, we should not forget the advent of our first rural bus services.

"In Gestingthorpe," recalls horseman Bert Surridge, "'Bluffy' (Harry) Rippingale bought a Model 'T' Ford lorry for delivering coal after World War One. Then in the evenings he'd sweep it out and put a row of seats and special roof on the back and it became a bus! But I shall never forget that bus. Especially going up Ballingdon Hill. I mean, we young'uns could jump out and walk up quicker than he could drive!"

Scores of contributors spoke with real, glowing affection of the days of 'Bluffy's' bus. Farmworker – and now brickmaker – Tom Bird of Wickham St. Pauls is one of many:

"When he first started the roof and sides were made of green canvas with something like cellophane for the windows. Inside there was a little oil lamp which hung at the back of the cab. Then he bought an old Chevrolet and made a better top. It was clever really, because it had a hook on, where he winched it off to convert it back into a coal lorry."

In time – after he got established – Bluffy was able to afford a 'proper bus' and make regular runs to Sudbury, Halstead and Braintree. However, as Tom points out:

"them that really benefited most were the girls at Courtaulds Silk Mill in Halstead. You see, once he had enough to get a bus full he did a 'round' and took them every day. Before that they had to go each week in a wagonette. But it wasn't only a boon for them. It made it easier for all village girls to get jobs in the towns."

Amongst our contributors the nostalgic memories of Bluffy's bus – and especially the Saturday night cinema runs to Sudbury are legion. Two who particularly recall Bluffy, 'with his pipe and trilby hat on' are Dick Halls and Chris Felton – both Gestingthorpe lads in the late nineteen thirties:*

"He was ONE OF THE VERY BEST!!" they jointly exclaimed one memorable night in *The Pheasant*.

"But my word," continued Dick, "did he love a pipe! He even had a special wooden rack for them and if he went to Clacton (4/6d return) he'd have five pipes filled up and ready in this rack above him!"

"You can't help smiling," chuckled Chris, "for old Bluffy would never ever refuse a fare. 'Push up a little together,' he'd say. We were packed in like sardines! I believe the first bus was only meant for fourteen but I'm damn sure that he sometimes squeezed on thirty! There were people standing on the steps, and hanging on

* Dick Halls today lives at Lindsey near Hadleigh where he runs an agricultural haulage business, whilst Chris, who was also a lorry driver, now lives in Bulmer.

the rail, with another one or two in the cab, and then he'd smile and say, 'Hang on together now!' But no-one minded. We were all friends and neighbours in those days. Besides, it was still a bloomin' sight better than walking."*

And as Dick points out:

"The thing that really made it was ol' Bluffy himself. He always had a smile on. He wasn't greedy. And he never left anyone stranded. If there were just too many at Sudbury on a Saturday night he'd always come back and get them. 'Hang on together' he'd say. I'll come right back'. No , I can honestly say that no-one ever saw him put out."

"Did he ever take the cricket team about?" I queried slyly.

"DID HE! Cor, Cricket evenings out on the bus were FANTASTIC! We never left until they kicked us out of the village pub where we had played and in those days the whole team – everyone – went on the bus. For us country boys it was a really good night out. As for Bluffy – well so long as he had some dominoes – and his pipe – he'd have waited for us all night long!"†

Someone else to be involved with 'Bluffy's bus' was Gladys Finch – who for many years served as conductress. Today, she still lives in a small cottage almost opposite *The Pheasant*, and close to the sheds where Bluffy once kept his legendary 'bus'. For Gladys however there was one particularly unforgettable passenger:

* Gestingthorpe's 'Luke' Smith adds with a laugh, "when the bus really was 'over full' on his Saturday night run to Sudbury, he used to drop some of us off in Ballingdon – before anyone spotted him – and then go up to the Market Hill where the majority got off – before coming back to Ballingdon to pick up the rest of us!"

† The business was scrupulously obliging. On one occasion – just once – the bus accidentally became 'double booked' with a seaside party to Yarmouth – and a 'once a year' cricket outing to Southend. Within the steady speeds of the nineteen thirties, Harry Rippingale's reaction is justifiably legend:
"He took the seaside party to Yarmouth and then drove back to Gestup; collected the cricket team and took them to Southend. He then went back to Yarmouth and collected the seaside group and brought them back – and then immediately set off for Southend again to collect the cricketers!"

"His name," she recalls with a laugh, "was 'Marpy' – and he had a wooden leg. But sometimes he would have to have it repaired and so he'd put on a spare one. Then, just as the bus was about to leave Sudbury, he'd come stumping over and call, 'Wait a minute. I've got to go and get my other leg!' Oh, that did used to make me feel queer!"

Gladys is not the only one to have 'felt a little queer'. So too, it seems, did some of the horsemen who became lorry or bus drivers, but discovered that the traditional ruse of 'letting the horses have a blow' (as an excuse for a drink in a roadside pub) had to be amended. May Cresswell of Foxearth, tells of, "one old driver pulling up at the pub where he used to stop with the horses and muttering vaguely, '...just 'er...got to get some water for the radiator...' Oh well, we soon knew what that meant!"

Across East Anglia there must be countless other anecdotes of these early buses. Farmworker Fred Chatters provides one example:

"I'll never forget one time ol' Henry Cornell picked someone up on Bardfield Bridge [near the Belchamp-Borley-Bulmer 'T' junction]. But when he went up the hill to Bulmer, he happened to 'miss a gear' and that bloomin ol' Chevrolet ran back – downhill – until it chanced to hit a telegraph pole – well it pitched this bloke right out the back! Huh! He'd only just got in!"

Others spoke of having to 'give a little assistance' to the under-powered vehicles.

"Like at Whatfield," reminisces haulier Claude Alleston. "You see Jimmy Johnson had a Model T Ford – but when he went up 'Ipswich Hill' some of us would very likely have to get out and give it a shove! Even more commonplace," he continues, "was the sight of 'Model T' buses backing up hills [reverse gear being lower than first]. At Bulls Hill, Hitcham, and Thorpe's Hill, Hintlesham, it was a regular thing," he says. Similarly, "At Henny," says farmworker Horace Elsey, "they'd often have to 'back-up' Amos Hill."

Then there were the other 'passengers' which were sometimes transported. I first learnt of this at Raydon Nursing Home in mid-Suffolk. For as bright June sunshine flooded through the open window of his bedroom, Edwin Partridge, in his hundredth year, suddenly, and proudly exclaimed:

"My uncle – Charles Partridge of Layham – had the very first bus around Hadleigh way and it was driven by Harry Clarke. But I'll tell you this, on the days when he didn't go to Ipswich he took loads of pigs in it instead!"

"Didn't anyone mind?"

"No! Not in those days! I mean once they'd unloaded the pigs they just used to wash everything out and it would soon be ready for people to ride in again!"*

As we have seen the bicycle and then the bus, represented a fundamental liberation for rural people. Employment – and social life – was no longer governed by 'walkable' distances. Conversely however, motor transport has exacerbated the decline of the cohesive, organic community that the parish had previously been.

Similarly we have witnessed the steady emasculation of the one-time, all-powerful, parish 'Vestries'. In 1894 they were finally replaced by parish councils. Perhaps the greatest democratic step forward was that henceforth all adult male parishioners were enfranchised.†

Yet a century later the very concept of the 'village community' is

---

* The story is not unusual. Oliver Prentice retells of one of the first genuine 'double deckers' in Suffolk which was owned by Jim Wyartt (brother of the famous Barney Wyartt) and which did a run from Bildeston to Ipswich and other market towns. "Course on the very first journey, we spent the whole time cutting back the overhanging branches! But the other thing was this – we actually used to cart cattle and sheep around in it as well. We'd go to whichever market was on. I've ridden on top with lambs."
"How did you get them up there?"
"We just used to carry them up. Either under our arms or on our shoulders. 'Course we'd put the bullocks in the bottom. You see, the wooden seats would fold back onto the wall which made more space for them."

† In the same year parishes were also grouped together to form Rural District Councils. (In 1934 Halstead Rural District Council was formed which absorbed both Belchamp and Bumpstead Rural District Councils, whilst between 1972 – 1974 the Halstead District was amalgamated into the enlarged Braintree District Council.)

arguably under greater threat than at any time since the Black Death. Sadly many older inhabitants feel cut off – even stranded – without the shops or services of their youth and surrounded by new faces who know nothing of their past endeavours. Thankfully, in every parish, a few – usually 'the same few' – have struggled to keep community spirit alive. We owe them all, our gratitude.

PART THREE

YOUTH

"There was a HUNDRED and FOURTEEN children at Belchamp Walter School when I went and now I doubt you'd even get fourteen.

But I've picked acorns for farmers at 4d a bushel – and as for mushrooms! When I was a boy Belchamp meadows were renowned for them! I've often been down there at four o'clock in the morning – and so have others – and they've come from miles around! But do you know what our most common play was when I was a boy?...Our play was work."

Charlie 'Bommy' Martin (b.1902)

HENNY NATIONAL SCHOOL 1863
Monday, November 30th.

Children assemble for school *8.41*
Test and prayers at *9.00*
Reading, Arithmetic, Writing on Slates &copy books until *12.00*
Grace sung, children dine in the school room and
  recreation in the playground until *2.00*
Needlework for girls at *2.00*
Writing and reading for boys at *2.00*
Straw plating from ....*3 until 4 o'clock*
Writing for those not having straw until ....*4 o'clock*
School visited by Miss L. Barnardiston & Lady Parker at *3.00*
School dismissed with singing and prayers at *4.00*

Emma Darby; Teacher

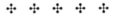

There are those – who even in these latter days,
  Against instruction, vain objections raise
On all attempts this hackneyed adage fling,
  "A little knowledge is a dangerous thing",
'Once educate the children of the poor
  And willing service they will yield no more'.
Such gravely argue, 'if they're never taught,
  Their duties – they'll perform them as they ought'

from *The Parish Pauper* by Sudbury's George Fulcher, (published 1845).
In the above, Fulcher challenges those who questioned the wisdom of
'educating the poor'.

Chapter Eleven

EDUCATION COMES TO THE PARISH
Log Books and the Harvest of 1879

"Look at those big isolated clumps of buildings," said Holmes.
"Schools!" exclaimed Watson.
"Lighthouses my boy! Beacons of the future! Capsules with
hundreds of bright little seeds in each, out of which will spring
the wiser, better England of the future."

The Case of the Naval Treaty
by Sir Arthur Conan Doyle

Whilst the public houses provided relaxation, the vestries government and the chapels guidance, it was the village schools which were
the 'hope', indeed 'salvation' of families who for centuries past had
been enmeshed in rural poverty.

A good picture of education in our area emerges from a question-
naire sent to all clergymen in 1839.

"At Great Maplestead," the vicar answered, "a benevolent lady
[Mrs. Mary Gee] has founded a school for a hundred children which
she runs from her own private funds."

In Little Maplestead, however, "half the children are wholly
without education."

The two Maplesteads well illustrate the piecemeal – but growing –
interest in education. At Gestingthorpe:

"Two schools in cottages cater for about two thirds of the children. Each pays twopence a week... the total expenditure is twelve
pounds per annum. If more is required, it is paid by the vicar."

101

At Belchamp Walter, 'a sort of school' was in existence. The scholars paid a penny a week. Additionally, 'a poor woman keeps a small school in connection with a 'meeting house' (possibly on Chapel Hill?). But if Belchamp Walter was 'behind' Gestingthorpe, it was certainly 'ahead' of Belchamp St. Pauls. Here there was only a Sunday School, although:

"an evening school for boys is attended by about twenty."

By comparison, Bulmer not only had a proper school but additionally:

"an evening lecture twice every fortnight – for scholars after they have left school!"

Education was indeed entirely of the sovereign parish born. Gosfield had a schoolroom for seventy five, whilst at Great Henny there was no schoolroom:

"but the children assemble in the chancel of the church...also there are two or three Dames Schools."

And finally to Ashen. (Between Stoke by Clare and Great Yeldham). Here, in a village of some 320 people, there was only a Sunday School which was supported by the Rector, who austerely observed:

"As the parish consists entirely of farmers and their labourers, it would be very difficult to raise adequate funds for a National School ... there are one or two daily schools to which the labourers send their children...but reading is very little attended to, the great object being to learn the straw plating for bonnets which is the universal employment for children of both sexes in this parish."

signed Edmund Squire. Rector of Ashen

Most early schoolrooms were built with donations from wealthy parishioners. At Bulmer it was Squire Alexander of *The Auberies* who financed the rebuilding of 1840, (considerably extended by J. St.

George Burke in 1874), whilst at Foxearth the philanthropic incumbent Father John Foster founded the National School in 1849.*

These 'model' villages were imitated and our remaining schoolrooms were erected between 1850-1876. Today they are still identifiable, frequently having slate rooves and red brick walls with white brick around the windows, doors and corners.

Year of building:

Monks Eleigh	1834	Kersey	1873
Belchamp St. Paul	1842	Birdbrook	1873
Colne Engaine	1845	Little Maplestead	1874
Foxearth	1849	Lamarsh	1875
Wickham St. Pauls	1852	Gt. Yeldham	1875
Gestingthorpe	1855	Middleton	1875
Little Yeldham	1856-57	Alphamstone	1876
Long Melford	1860†	Ashen	1876
Cavendish	1863	Borley	1876
Chelsworth	1870	Pentlow	1876
Belchamp Otten	1871	Brent Eleigh	1876
Belchamp Walter	1872	Raydon	1878

(For this, and other information I am indebted to 'Schools and Scholars in Halstead and District' by Mary Downey and Doreen Potts. This fascinating book includes numerous photographs of the schools and their pupils – including a number of contributors to this book. I am sincerely grateful to Mary and Doreen for the help their research has given this chapter. Published by Halstead and District Local History Society).

* Similarly at Colne Engaine, a National School was erected in 1845 due to the efforts of the Rev. John Grimwood, who raised most of the £360 required. (Unusually for the immediate area, both Colne Engaine and Foxearth Schools are built of flint).

In 1833 a Treasury grant of £20,000 was made available for building schools and distributed through the National Society. Some villages may have received a proportion of their costs from this source.

† As early as 1670 'The Lady Chapel' in Long Melford Church had been used as a schoolroom and continued as such until 1860. Part of a multiplication table still exists on the East wall. (See *Long Melford Through the Ages* by Barry L. Wall).

Clare School is typical of those built in the area. Note the pleasing attention to architectural detail – even the slate roof having two different patterns. Some schools (e.g.Belchamp Walter) also had ornamentation on the roof's ridge tiles.

In 1876 Elementary Education finally became compulsory. (Following the Education Act of 1870 – hence the flush of building between 1870-1876)

Taking control at Gestingthorpe on 4th January 1875, the new teacher, Frances French, wrote:

"The school is for the first time put under the Government... The children's attainments are very low indeed...few could do a simple multiplication sum of more than one figure..."

At Chelsworth the children – who had previously attended a dames school – were, "extremely backward in every subject," whilst at Glemsford, the teacher found them "wretchedly backward, not any child being able to do a simple addition sum."

How lucky we are to have so many of the school Log Books in the local Records Offices! They are a riveting source of human history and all too soon the author was seduced into reading page after page and requesting ever more villages!

Immediately apparent is the teachers' commitment. Many were pioneers. The occupants of newly built schools. In villages unused to formal schooling – but which were now to experience 'compulsory education' for the first time.

One wonders especially what Celia Nicholls, the new appointee of Borley School actually felt when she wrote in the Log for March 25th 1879:

"I commenced duties this morning at nine o'clock."

But who was Celia Nicholls or Frances French of Gestingthorpe? How old were they and what experience did they have of rural life? One suspects they were often young, for Frances French 'was a student from Whitelands'. Yet they were trailblazers. Pioneers of education in rural areas and also of careers for women. But whatever their backgrounds and aspirations they would soon have learnt of the dependence between farm and village.

"Many children at work hay-making" (Wickham St. Pauls, June 29th, 1878); "Several boys absent picking charlock from the wheat" (Gestingthorpe, June 4th, 1875); or "Many children away pea-picking" (Earls Colne June 20th 1884) are typical entries. Nevertheless Bulmer's teacher must still have felt sorely aggrieved when, no less than EIGHTY out of a HUNDRED children were: "away collecting acorns as pig feed" (October 1877).*

Conversely, on 10th April 1867, the teacher at Bures exclaimed – with almost triumphant glee:

"school better attended on account of weather hindering field work."

Compromises were usually achieved. At Pebmarsh, Earls Colne and Alphamstone, the schools annually closed, 'for a week, owing to pea-picking', (e.g. in 1900, Alphamstone's break began on June 25th), whilst in 1869 the headmaster of Sudbury Boys School phlegmatically remarked:

"gleaning…still requires a number of my country boys"

At Cavendish in 1906, the summer holidays were still described as the 'harvest vacation', whilst in 1920 Newton school, 'did not re-open until September 13th, an extra weeks holiday being given as the harvest was not finished'.

* From *Bulmer, Then and Now* published by Bulmer W.E.A.

Yet although 1920 might have been a fractionally late season, there was, during the nineteenth century, one harvest which was so backward, rain-drenched and disastrous, that its shadow has passed down into modern times. Indeed quite recently the author's father spontaneously declared:

"WET! THIS IS NOTHING TO COMPARE WITH 1879!"

As a child he was not alone in hearing of that catastrophic year from elderly people. At Bulmer, John Dixey was told that Cutters Field had not been harvested by Christmas Day, while several contributors repeated anecdotes of sheaves being carted on Boxing Day. Almost certainly they were referring to the same year.

With this in mind the Log Books are of absorbing *agricultural* interest. For Earls Colne did not even have its pea-picking 'absentees' until the second and third weeks of August. Elsewhere it was AUGUST TWENTY EIGHTH before Bures, Long Melford, Chelsworth and Wickham Schools eventually *closed* for the corn harvest (re-opening on September 29th) whilst Borley School did not re-start until October 6th. A week later on October 13th, Chelsworth's teacher admits: "attendance still very small, gleaning not yet done."

But perhaps the most serious testament to that bedraggled and sodden season was that at Poslingford, the lessons did not resume until OCTOBER 13th and even then, "some of the children had not finished gleaning". At Long Melford it was November 7th before "a number of boys attended who have not been present since the holidays", whilst at Poslingford it was Novem-ber 24th when the last boys finally returned.

Yet the distractions were not always agricultural. In 1877 the schoolmistress at Little Yeldham wrote:

"Kate Mitson sent home for insisting upon doing her straw plait... I find the straw work a great nuisance in the school."*

At Gestingthorpe, it was at the village's brickworks where John Turner, Henry Raymond and Arthur Finch were reported working one afternoon in the May of 1879, whilst on April 4th 1884, Alice Mann of Earls Colne was not untypical in being, 'kept away from school to go stone picking'. At Long Melford, there were regular references to 'boys being absent as beaters' on the Kentwell or Melford Hall shoots. Interestingly, as late as 1919, several boys at Newton School were, 'kept away doing partridge driving'. Seven years later, however, when '3 children went potato picking', the Attendance Officer was duly informed.

But it was not simply 'piece-work' that withheld the pupils. 'Several children absent on account of being forced to pay 2d a week' (Wickham St. Pauls School Log, June 9th, 1878), or, "Sent several children home for 'school money' that was owing", (Belchamp Walter, August 18th, 1879), reveal understandable – and not isolated instances – of parents resenting – and occasionally refusing to pay their contributions in the early years.

(The charges varied in different villages. Ashen's were two pence a week for the first child and a penny a week thereafter. In 1891 all contributions for elementary education were abolished).

In January 1903, Pebmarsh school was, 'closed for three weeks by the Medical Officer of Health', while later in the year a whooping cough epidemic swept the village and again reduced the register. At Borley, there were several instances when 'the Liston children could

* From *A History of Little Yeldham* by Adrian Corder-Birch, published by Halstead and District Local History Society.

not get through because of floods'. On November 19th 1879, real tragedy struck:

"One of the infant boys (Arthur Barber) drowned on his way to school. Was not able to begin lessons 'til 9.30 the scholars being so shocked at the loss of their schoolfellow."*

Scarlet fever lurked ominously. On December 12th 1879, two pupils of Long Melford Boys School:

"suddenly died, although present at school a few days ago."

At Chelsworth on 18th October 1879:

"numbers were low on account of a child's funeral taking place in the afternoon...four of the elder girls acting as bearers."

Similar entries were not unusual. Yet the classes continued. At Twinstead's tiny school with its attendance of barely twenty, the object lessons for Autumn 1905 included:

the whale	beaver	tea
cocoa nut	balloons	cotton
camel	rice	

Songs and hymns were also taught. In front of Alphamstone's School Board in December 1898 the children sang: 'Life is Full of Ups and Downs', 'Tom Jones' and appropriately 'The Farmer's Boy'.
Doubtless all teachers yearned for the remarks of Inspector H. W. Claughton who a year later observed:

"the school has become very small but the children get a very good elementary education."

---

* Yet again the year was 1879. Two days later on November 21st, Gestingthorpe's teacher records that a snow storm had resulted in low attendance. Fires at Borley School had been commenced on October 20th. At Sudbury in November 1879, the teacher wrote: 'we are not able to see across the room after 3.30 – for although we light the gas the old piping seems quite corroded'. At Glemsford in January 1893, the teacher described the rooms as 'intensely cold', whilst at Belchamp Walter similar – and persistent complaints were made until the 1950's.

Whilst of Twinstead:

"in spite of the difficulty for one teacher in having so many 'standards' the general tone of the school is excellent."

Yet the schools were visited by more than Inspectors and clergymen. Occasional farmers' wives ('the upper ones') – but more usually the lady of the 'Big House' or her daughters – are often recorded as visiting. (At Gestingthorpe, Bulmer and Alphamstone there were frequent afternoon calls from the Misses Oates, the Misses Burke and Misses Stebbings). As Basil Slaughter points out, "It was a popular way of doing good."

Inevitably, truancy occurred. On 23rd May 1879, Celia Nicholls caned eight Gestingthorpe boys in one go, whilst at Alphamstone, 26 years later, "Frank Harrington played truant after asking for half a day to have his boots mended". (11th October 1905).
Possibly Frank was thinking back to May 21st 1900, when his teacher Mrs. Amelia Wells, wrote of the school's twenty five pupils:

"Work as usual this morning, but gave holiday this afternoon to celebrate the RELIEF OF MAFEKING."

In fact, Frank is in good company, for on Tuesday June 10th 1913, the children of Borley school were given a half-day's holiday for the unveiling of Gainsborough's Statue in Sudbury. *
And what's that got to do with truancy, and pretending to have your boots mended?
Simply that according to legend, young Thomas Gainsborough reputedly forged his father's handwriting – to get out of school and go sketching instead!

---

* Someone who was actually there, was Dorothy Mills, then a pupil of the Council School in Friars Street.
"Oh yes," she explains, "A group of children went from every school. We were trooped up to the Market Hill and all had to stand around for quite a long time and then the Mayor came – with his robes on – with all these people in top hats, and then they must have unveiled him and we sang God Save the King. The other thing was that 'Sepulchre Street' was re-named 'Gainsborough Street' – so that was something else we all had to get used to!"

109

Chapter Twelve

THE VILLAGE COMES TO THE SCHOOL
Mice, Mathematics and Mischief!

"Ah there's too much of that sending them to school these days! It only does harm. Every gatepost and barn door you come to is sure to have some bad word or other chalked upon it by the young rascals...their fathers couldn't do it and the country was all the better for it".

Captain Vye in *The Return of the Native*
(Thomas Hardy)

Maybe the impoverished fathers – desperate for every penny of 'piece work' their children could earn – quietly agreed. Yet until 1900 children could still legally leave school at the age of eleven.

Significantly the grants which schools received were made 'in proportion to the numbers attending'. And Inspectors made surprise visits to check the accuracy of the register. So keen were Governors to induce maximum attendance, that at times, Gestingthorpe's Parish magazine reads like a propaganda sheet. In January 1898 it proclaims:

"the school is to receive 2/6d per head on the average attendance."

(i.e. the higher the average attendance – the higher the grant). Happily this had been 89 for the past year. In July the rector hosted the annual School Treat where prizes for attendance (one might almost call them bribes!) were formally presented:

110

"3 shillings to children who had never missed.
2/6d to those who had only missed once or twice.
2/- to those who had not missed more than ten times.
1/- to all who had made 400 attendances (i.e. a morning or
afternoon session)."

At a time when farmworkers were paid about ten to twelve shillings a week the total prize money amounted to over SEVEN POUNDS and was presented (and presumably provided) by the widow of the late squire, Mrs. Caroline Oates.

Despite the inducements, most children were still expected to do little jobs before going to school. Ida Bird (b.1895) of Wickham St. Pauls, "had to milk the goat before a breakfast of pea soup or boiled up bones". At Belchamp Walter, Charlie Martin (b. 1902) used to:

"run down the meadows and get Olly Pearson's cows up to Springate Farm ready for milking. In fact I'd even started to milk some of them myself – by hand of course – but that suffen' made my wrists ache to begin with!"

For many others the early morning chore also involved milk:

"Oh yes! There was a real team of people out getting the milk from the farms," exclaims Rose Chatters of Belchamp St. Pauls, "you'd see some old dears with up to six cans in their hands. But it was an effort – especially before school! I used to go right up to The Cherry Tree for ours – so it was nearly a mile and a half's walk."

Meanwhile the boy who was later to be her husband, George 'Jute' Chatters, earned a penny a week by collecting a neighbour's supply, but still had to make, "nearly half a mile round trip for a pail of water". Like others, Phyllis Billimore was typical in "getting people's milk to earn a few coppers for the Sunday School treat".*

* "It's a bloomin' wonder the milk kept at all really," says Jack Cornell. "I mean they never used to do any steaming or sterilising of buckets – they just used to wipe them round with a bit of cloth. In fact when I was young they used to milk the cows at *Brickwall Farm* in an old straw yard with pigs and chickens running about... I know they tightened up on it in time, but that's how it was when I started school!"

Others described the walk to school from their outlying homes. Ruby Finch who lived at Wesborough Hill, near Bulmer Brickyard, recalls:

"It was well over a mile to the school at Wickham St. Pauls but we went in all weathers. When it was raining, we just put on a couple of coats and if there were large drifts of snow – well it wasn't at all unusual for one of us to fall right through!"

Similarly, when just five years old, Bertha Bird (b.1913) had a mile and a half's journey from *Hodgson's Farm* to Great Maplestead school:

"unless it was too wet to cut across the meadows in which case we had to go 'the long way round' – and that was over two and a half miles!"

David Tuffin – who went to Middleton School – provides his own recollection of wet weather:

"Well," he observes, "you'd just set off running – like an old horse slopping and splashing through all the mud. You finally got there in the end!"

Yet there were also compensations. Farmworker's daughter Hilda Smith nostalgically described her own two mile route from *Hill Farm*, Twinstead, to Henny School. The area has some beautiful valleys and one can well imagine the enchantment of the walk in good weather.

"On nice days it was really lovely. We walked beside the stream, through lots of meadows full of flowers – oh, cowslips, buttercups, meadowsweet, ragged robin – and if it was hot, we would have a little drink from the sparkling water."

However we shouldn't paint too idyllic a picture:

"Of course, if it was raining, we still had to go – and there weren't any macs or wellingtons in those days, just lace-up boots!"*

* Hilda, who recently passed away, was also our most enthusiastic contributor to the Wild Flower Survey of *The Long Furrow*. Her late husband Cecil was a principal influence on *The Khyber Connection*.

For Bulmer children, there was an additional problem:

"The thing was," explained one, "although you didn't have to wear any uniforms in our time, they were suffen' fierce about your shoes being clean. Course we only had hob-nail boots in those days, but one family had to come through Brundon wood – so their poor mother always had to come to the end of the muddy lane with a clean pair for them!"*

But what facilities existed if it was bitterly cold or pouring with rain during the journey. At the Gestingthorpe *Crescent*, Dick Finch explained:

"Most schools had a big round Tortoise Stove which you could stand around to dry yourself out. But once the lessons began it was the teachers who sat next to that; we were put at the back!"

It was the same at Bulmer: "It was all right at the front – but perishing cold anywhere else," exclaimed Ernie Lott of the room which was heated by an, 'open fire with a big guard around it'. As retired threshing contractor Jack Cornell sardonically sums up:

"It wasn't what you'd call very wonderfully boiling at the back of the room. Oh no; you didn't lose a lot of sweat in there on a cold day!"

Perhaps the most telling comment is of the school being swept and scrubbed out every Friday :

"but you may depend on it – quite often in the winter the floors would still be wet on Monday morning!"†

Many of the schools which the caretakers cleaned were of similar layout. There was an infants' room, for children under seven or eight and then the 'big room' for those who had been 'moved up'. Each

---

*"At Gestingthorpe," says Bert Surridge, "the oldest boys at the school were paid a shilling a month for getting a pail of water from the pond opposite the school and washing out the toilets each Friday."

† 'Luke' Smith adds of the hobnail boots, "At night time we boys would go along the roads scraping the flints – to make the sparks fly – but woe betide if our parents caught us!"

morning there were prayers or the singing of a hymn and the Register was taken. Eventually the lessons began; there was the reciting of tables; the repeating of the alphabet; the reckoning of sums; the needlework and in some schools like Bulmer, relates Evelyn Reeve, 'the learning of the catechism'.

Invariably also, there were the slate boards and pencils which both 'Rover' Finch and Philip Wright recall, "squeaking awfully and putting your teeth on edge". At Bulmer School, says Jack Cornell, "the slates had squares on one side and three lines on the other." However, when he 'went up into the big room' Jack graduated to dip-in pens and ink wells. Writing had to be 'thin up and thick down'. But stop! Look! The poor lad next to Jack has suddenly got a dry inkwell. Surely some mischievous neighbour hasn't dried it out with blotting paper? Meanwhile at Gestingthorpe, recalls Dick Halls, "the ink was made from powder which was mixed up in the schoolroom and taken round by monitors."*

Yet some children still had real problems with writing, for as Dick explains:

"Quite simply, you were NOT allowed to write left-handed at 'Gestup' School."

Many must have sorely regretted their left-handedness.

"The teachers insisted I used my right hand and rapped my knuckles if I didn't," commented the late Daisy Nice of Gestingthorpe (b.1900).

But whether the lessons were of reading, writing or 'arithmetic, the time soon began to drag. Playtime seemed an eternity away and the old school clock was longingly looked at. Wethersfield's had a noteworthy peculiarity:

"It was actually," states retired farmer Jack Wallace, "proven to be the *slowest one there ever was...*"
"Really! Fascin–," I almost said.
But he caught me with a smile. "Although it was looked at so much that the glass nearly fell out!"

---

* By comparison Mary Holland and Frank Billimore had learnt to write on "sand in trays". (The trays were about twelve inches square).

For all the fidgeting children, distractions were difficult to avoid:

"It might sound funny," remarks Jack Cornell, "but in those days we children got an awful lot of pleasure from seeing very simple – but slightly unusual – things. About twice a year, there would be a real 'highlight' because 'Sooty' Hills, or ol' Golden from Sudbury, would bike up to Bulmer and sweep out the chimney in one of the houses near the school. I know it sounds silly, but when the brushes finally came out at the top – we just couldn't contain ourselves. We'd be thrilled to bits!"

Gestingthorpe children had a different distraction:

"Nearly every day," records the late Douglas Hasler, "the Reverend Greening came to the school. But the thing was this. The Church had tall elm trees on two sides and then a rookery. So sometimes when he arrived he had a white streak down his back where the rooks had 'christened' him – and oh yes – that used to make us boys smile!"*

For Little Maplestead's Cecil Cook, however, there was one unforgettable morning.

"In October 1924 two Handley Page bombers got lost in the fog – and landed in May Field. Next day we were all marched down to watch them take off…and that was the best morning's school that I can remember!"

With thoughts of military aircraft, we are drawn to World War One and more sober statistics:

"At Parkgate Farm, Gestup, where my father worked," relates Bert Surridge, "eight good men went off to the war: only one came back. School numbers fell as well. There was only 28 there when I left.† But our teacher, Miss Harrison was very, very good. She had taught a lot of those boys and she used to send them parcels. When

---

* Douglas's memories were typed out for us – one letter at a time – whilst he was suffering from Motor Neuron Disease. Earlier he had been a carpenter and D-Day veteran.
(In many schools it was the parson who administered justice – usually by caning the backside).

† In 1900 there had been around 100 pupils and in 1912 about 50.

the War was over, it was Miss Harrison who raised the subscription for the War Memorial. She got up a Hundred Pounds. A lot of money that time of day. And then she had them build it of special Devonshire stone".

Repeatedly one hears similar testaments to these village teachers. Initially they had endured the reserve of parents who wished that their children were out at work; usually they came from different backgrounds ('there was more class distinction then, and teachers were more in the 'parson' category'). Yet they managed – sometimes unassisted – to provide a thorough grounding for their children. They have gained, from the perspective of adulthood, an almost unparalleled degree of affection and respect.

In Gestingthorpe it is Miss Harrison who served for over thirty seven years and who was, says Dick Finch, "a wonderful woman. She was firm and strict and good." In Bulmer, older residents spoke with real gratitude of the two Miss Mayes. Without doubt one could hear similar testaments from other parishes of these steadfast women – so many of whom remained single, seeming to adopt generations of pupils rather than enjoy married life and parenthood.

But perhaps most importantly of all,they helped to establish the new, emerging 'middle ground' in parish life and having once arrived, remained to teach and rigorously instruct the children and even grandchildren of their earliest pupils.

But possibly that old school clock which moved with such excruci-ating slowness has finally reached lunch time:

"But there were no school dinners," exclaims Gertie Coe of Bulmer, "so we had to take dinner with us – and then go to the pump in the caretakers yard for a drink of cold water."

It was the same at Wickham St. Pauls: "Except," points out Ruby Finch, "that the pump was on the further side of the village green!" Dorothy Turner elaborates, "We used to have lunch in the infants' room, but if it was too wet to play on the green we'd have to sit in the porch instead – some playtime that was!" By comparison, one farmer's daughter recalls taking a can of milk to school for the dinner break; "I'd carry it as far as one telegraph pole – and then my sister would take it to the next."

But although facilities were Spartan, there was still the all important playtime. Among the 20 odd pupils of Pentlow School, the late Wally Twinn (b.1902) joined in the normal games of "tag, hoops and hopscotch – which we could play on the road because there weren't any cars." At Bulmer, Tom Rowe (b.1903) played "'breaking in the colt', 'fox and rabbits', leapfrog and football – using an old 'cover' stuffed full of leaves".

Yet perhaps the most revealing comment in this entire chapter is that when Tom and his contemporaries were at last able to get 'a proper football':

"It was bought by the whole school collecting acorns for pig feed."

Maybe it was also during the dinner break that the school 'know-all' would approach a fellow pupil and say:

"Choose a figure beneath Ten Pounds – but with the pence _less_ than the pounds.
After some thought the younger lad suggests Eight pounds, sixteen shillings and five pence.
"Chalk it on the ground," says the 'scholar' **£8   16s   5d**
"Now reverse it," comes the order.
The instruction is meekly obeyed. **£5   16s   8d**

"Now subtract it," comes the confident instruction.
Slowly the sum is worked out....................................**£2   19s   9d**

"O.K. Reverse it again."
The figures are duly inverted to give **£9   19s   2d**
                                    ————————

"Now add the last two figures together..."
                                    ————————

The calculation is hesitatingly begun, but before it is finished, the 'know-all' has produced from his pocket a grubby slip of paper, and on it would be written _£12 18s 11d!_

(For anyone who is attempting to follow the arithmetic, do not forget there were 12 pence to a shilling and 20 shillings in a pound! It must have been a superb trick to do at Christmas parties).

But if all this is a little overpowering we will now return to Borley – where it is still dinner time...

117

"I got into some wars when I was at school," exclaims Alf Finch. "One time in the dinner break the man from Brundon Watermill was passing with his donkey cart and by accident, I hit him with my catapult. Well I ran back to the school toilet to hide – but the mistress saw me. Out she came to cane me!"

As a further punishment, Alf was forbidden to remain in the school playground:

"So I went and set ag'en the wall – outside in the sun – but I wasn't many minutes eating my dinner, and then I went down to the railway hut – where the boy was that done the gates, with 'Hub' Gardner, the stockman from Borley Hall, whose dinner time it was, and they were playing at cards. But they kept me in there too long! When I went back they was a singing in the school and I thought 'Good God, I'm late'. And I got a caning for that as well! That night when my father heard, he looked at me and said: 'Huh! Your trouble is that you're a-tearing out too much boot leather boy!'"

With the toll of the school bell, the playground emptied. Lessons resumed for the afternoon. As did the well recorded moments of

Scene of many a mischievous moment...Borley School with Schoolhouse adjoining.

118

school-boy mischief.

Today, every single rural history contains its 'evergreen' stories of pranks in the schoolroom – usually involving mice. With this in mind, it was with some scepticism that I asked threshing contractor Jack Cornell if any of them had ever really happened.

"…OF COURSE THEY BLOOMIN' HAPPENED!!!" he exploded as a preamble to his own adventures with the young Tom Radley.

"We caught some mice and put them in a tin – and then trundled off to school with them. Trouble was that the bloomin' things died. Then Tom went and dropped the blessed tin and the damned things fell out dead, so he didn't make himself over-popular with the Miss Mayes on that occasion!"

"At Wickham St. Pauls," remembers Tom Bird (b.1912), "one of my mates, George Honeywood, passed the 'sheen' (threshing machine) and caught a whole sackful of mice. When he let them go there was pandemonium! The teacher was so frightened she stood on the desk! Oh dear. There was a price to pay as well! We didn't get much play for a month or two after that!"

Of his Gestingthorpe boyhood, Dick Halls jovially explained:

"If you couldn't catch a mouse you'd take bumble bees instead!" Whilst Jack Cornell 'claims' that he and Tom Radley, "let a sparrow go in the classroom (…well, we thought about it anyway!)." By comparison, Alf Finch and his Borley friends made some brick sparrow traps* in the playground, "and then kept asking to be excused to see if we'd caught anything." Eventually they did and the sparrow was 'toasted' over a hedgecutter's fire.

"At Gestingthorpe School," recalled two other male contributors one night in the *Pheasant*, "we used to get long stinging nettles, wait at the toilets and then push them under the doors into the girls cubicles…that used to make them squeal!"

At Bulmer, there was a window between the two classrooms:

"And I shall never forget Percy Lott," recalls our usual *enfant*

* See diagram on page 74 of *The Long Furrow*.

terrible, "being made to stand to attention in the corner – because when the headmistress wasn't looking, he would be pulling faces at the 'littl'uns' through this 'ere window and they would be curling themselves with laughter!"

Needless to say, it wasn't always profitable to misbehave. Uncannily realising that in eighty years time his experiences would become invaluable material for local historians, young schoolboy Alf Finch of Borley generously, heroically, and public spiritedly, exposed himself to all manner of discomforts – *purely of course* – to benefit the research for this book.

"Do you know – the mistress caned me on the hand five times in one day! FIVE TIMES!"

"However did you manage to get it five times?"

"I don't know! I did something wrong, didn't I!"

"Did your father find out?"

"Yes." He said, "'Well it weren't for your good behaviour boy!'. That's all he said to me. You know, he didn't hold with me."

But there were also other punishments.

"You'd have to stand in the corner holding slates above your head," continues our valiant Borley source, "but one time my arms got so tired that all these blessed slates came crashing down... Oh dear, I was in even more trouble... That meant even more canings!'

Meanwhile at Bulmer, a variation of the 'dunces cap' was 'being made to wear 'a long red tongue''. At one school a misbehaving infant stood on a chair while everyone pointed at them. Even worse, was that most tedious of punishments – of being made to 'stay in' – after lessons were over.

"The trouble with that," recalls 'a certain Bulmer threshing contractor', "was that your parents soon figured out why you were late – and then you would be in the hot water with them as well."

However the 'little scheme' which Jack and his friends devised (of 'nipping out through the back door and clambering over the wall into the Churchyard') was not very fruitful either.

"We thought of ourselves as being proper little heroes. But of course, the teachers never forgot and then we'd have to stay behind and say all our tables – right up to 'twelve times twelve' every bloomin' night for weeks on end!"

But despite the lessons and the punishments, the chanting of tables and the object lessons, it came about – eventually and imperceptibly – that the time for 'leaving school' finally arrived.

"At Alphamstone, during the labour shortage of World War One," retells Eddie Tuffin, "farmer John Stuck applied to the Board of 'Guardeens' to get me out when I was twelve – and that was it – I carried on with him for the next fifty eight years!"

A few years earlier, Ernie Lott of Bulmer also obtained his 'Labour Certificate'.* His first job was crow scaring: "and I was on my own, all by myself, in a big field – all day long!"

Possibly, like so many others, the sneaking suspicion may have crossed his mind that 'school wasn't such a bad place after all'.

Girls sometimes stayed on. Another Bulmer pupil, Emily Hearn (1890-1983):

"did about six months helping to teach the small children – as a 'monitor' – before I went into service."

Meanwhile the boys of Bulmer School who, 'always had to touch our hats if ever we saw the schoolmistress walking round the village – now adamantly refused to do so.' Maybe the offended teacher hissed in return: 'civility costs you nothing, Cornell!' "It was one of her favourite expressions," recalls Jack. "I've often thought about it since."

Happily from Colne Engaine, there is a more romantic story of schooldays; for it was here that Harry Gilbert (b.1897) met the girl who was to be his wife.

* Born in 1899, Ernie was another of the farmworker contributors who inspired *The Khyber Connection*. (Ernie was actually stationed near the famous Pass in 1920).

"We were sweethearts then," she exclaimed, some eight decades and sixty five years of married life later. "Nothing very serious of course, but we used to pass little messages to one another and he might help me do my arithmetic."

Let us leave it however to retired farmworker Frank Billimore, to sum up – for all of our contributors – his appreciation of those dedicated teachers.

"If someone misbehaved and didn't try hard enough, they'd be right strict with them – so that they'd miss their play and that was enough to make them cry. But the truth of the matter was this. We basically had a very good schooling. We did a lot of nature study and went for walks around the village and up to the farms and then we'd go back and write about what we'd seen"*

* There were also 'fee paying' dame schools. Usually run by the unmarried daughters of the local gentry in their own homes, they catered for children from slightly more affluent backgrounds. Those we know of include May Viall at Gestingthorpe and Violet Stebbings of Twinstead.

There was a shadow beneath which all of our contributors grew up. It was World War One. Gestingthorpe War Memorial *(above)* records the Twelve men and women who died in the services from a village of some 450 inhabitants. (1915 population). Inside the Church a wooden plaque commemorates all forty nine who served.

Other parishes record similar stark details. Bulmer War Memorial reveals that eighteen paid the supreme sacrifice from a population of just 600. Inside the Church and Village Hall a Roll of Honour records the names of no less than NINTY SIX parishioners who actually served.

For many years to come Armistice Day – Remembrance Day – was accorded very special status.

"It made a terrible impact. The memories of the First World War were very, very vivid.

"At eleven o'clock on Armistice Day, you'd see horsemen stop in the fields where they were ploughing and if the threshing tackle was on the farm, they'd call a halt and stand in silence. And in towns it was the same. The siren would go and then everyone – men in factories, clerks in banks, pedestrians, shoppers – and all the traffic on the road stopped for the two minutes remembrance".

Dennis Holland – recalling Remembrance Day always being held on November 11th – irrespective of it being a 'week' day.*

* At Newton School, the log for 1926 reads:
"This being Armistice Day, at 10.45am the children attended a short service held on the green near the memorial."

At other schools the two minutes silence was formally observed in the classrooms. At Cavendish the log for 11th November 1941 reads:
"The rector came to the school at 10.55 and stayed until 11.15. Silence was observed, prayers were said and a hymn sung."

Chapter Thirteen

RURAL CHILDHOOD
Christmas and Harvest, Brick Ovens and Coppers

"Just before Christmas – when I was a little girl – Father would send me up the Market Hill and I'd go to the shopkeepers and say: 'Please will you give the ostler at The Angel yard a Christmas box?' They might perhaps give me sixpence and I'd enter it in my book. When I got back Dad would divide it out amongst his three men – and if I was lucky I might get sixpence for doing it!"

Dorothy Mills, b.1902, Sudbury

So it was finally three thirty or four o'clock and lessons for the day were over.

"But despite the long walk home," says horseman's daughter Ida Bird – who lived at *Netherhouse Farm*, Wickham St. Pauls, "there was always something to be done. And it wasn't just collecting eggs, weeding the garden or getting in firewood! There was the seasonal piece-work! Every year we went stone-picking, pea-picking and potato-picking; then we'd help to 'single-out' mangolds and swedes, do 'docking' in the cornfields and always go gleaning after harvest."

Yet there was still time for 'children to be children'. It is this notion of 'play' that I most wish to explore – since it preceded either television, 'Sports Centres', or the family holidays, which today we so take for granted. In their absence, there were possibly two compensations. The roads were free of motorised traffic; and the villages were full of children.

"Even though Wesborough Hill was so isolated," says Ruby Finch of the lonely hillock near Bulmer Brickyard, "there were still ten of us children up there...we just made our own fun."

They also made their own toys. It was this subject that I first discussed with the late Harry Gilbert – gamekeeper, smallholder and World War One veteran – as we sat in his cottage between Colne Engaine and Pebmarsh, with the fields and the woods that he loved so dearly, stretching out, in a wide arc around us.

"Most years we'd have a craze on 'hoops'. First off, you'd look for an old piece of railing or thick wire. Then you'd take it to the blacksmith and ask him to make it up for you...I know it sounds daft but an ol' hoop would hully help get you to school you know! 'Course if it got cracked it would be straight back to the blacksmith again – and he'd charge about a farthing to mend it!"

Later in the year there were marbles, and then 'tops':

"Well the slow'uns didn't go far, but you could whip others for yards even though the roads were only made up with flints."

Eventually it was autumn:

"And once the Hunt started, we'd be off imitating them. About fifteen or twenty boys would meet up in the village and two of us would be the 'foxes' and head off into the woods somewhere. We used to run miles and be absolutely dead tired by the time the game was over!"

All of our contributors provide similar memories. At Bulmer, the boys had, "races with cotton reels propelled by a matchstick through a 'wound-up' rubber band", whilst at Hartest, relates Rev. Philip Wright: "the steel stays from ladies' corsets were utilised to make pop guns". At Belchamp St. Pauls, 'Jute' Chatters played cricket with "an old board for a bat and a ball made up of old socks all stuffed together", while with autumn came the sound of, "*Billy Billy Onker, My first Conker* – it's what we Belchamp boys said to get first go".

From the Horse Chestnut to the Sallow of pond and stream. From the latter Jute made 'bows' which fired 'arrows' of Elder complete with 'feathers' of reed. Yet despite the improvisation, "with a good bit of string, the arrow would still go out of sight...well a fair distance anyway!"

And if the arrows remind us of an earlier age, so too did some of the surviving superstitions. Jack Cornell paid the blacksmith at Bulmer Tye threepence, and then ninepence, to buy two of his warts – and they did actually go away! Yet while this practice still lingers on, our next is surely historic:

"If people got cut by something sharp," recalls Jack's sister Evelyn, "they would smear grease onto the object that had cut them...even BEFORE getting bandaged up. When we kept *The Blackbirds*, a man came in and asked Mother for some grease because he had cut himself on a nail – and he wanted to grease it!"

Several contributors recall the archaic reaction to thunder and lightning:

"Curtains were shut, mirrors were covered up and cutlery taken off the table."

But if the older generation were nervous of unusual noises, the youngsters, as always – revelled in creating them:

"Around Guy Fawkes night," explained Harry Gilbert, "the things that were really at a premium were old fashioned keys."

"Whatever for?"

"For making bangs with! You'd get a box of matches, rub all the brimstone off, stuff it into the 'hole' of a key and then drive in a nail to make a bang with!"

127

With the ever longer evenings after Guy Fawkes night, the children inevitably began to think of Christmas:

"You'd hang your stocking up on Christmas Eve," says farm-worker's daughter, Gertie Coe (b.1906) "and you might get –
a couple of oranges,
a sweet mouse,
a few nuts,
a packet of sweets and maybe a game."

Most contributors testified to something similar. Yet despite the frugal times, it was still the festive season:

"At Christmas," recalls the late Hilda Smith of Wickham St. Pauls, "Dad would get the little hessian bag from the passage way – which we'd filled in the autumn – and then say, 'Now – let's have a few nuts!'."

At Alphamstone, Popsy Parker's Christmas dinner was usually a chicken, "a big treat in those days, and on Boxing Day, a rabbit pie". But one of the most endearing memories is of Christmas Eve when,

"We went carol singing.* We had a big choir in those days and

* "At Sudbury," remembers Dorothy Mills, "the brass band came round the town playing carols. They'd come about ten or eleven o'clock and stop outside *The Angel* and call out, 'Merry Christmas and Happy New Year to Mr. Harvey and family'. Then they pushed a little box on a long pole up to the bedroom window, and we'd put a few coppers in."

Bulmer schoolboys of the early 1930s, (Back row left to right): Ken Raymond, George Harrington, Freddie Hunt, Leslie Downs, Bernard Pryke, Derek Felton. (Front row): Chris Rash, Ken Raymond, Billy Messant, Jack Cornell and Emrys Bird.

1894, Parish Council's were formed. Celebrating the centenary of Bulmer Parish Council are left to right): Barbara Rawlins (parish clerk) and councillors Richard Stewart, Ron Mansfield (Chairman), John Dixey, Dawn Allen and Richard Tomlinson. Unable to join the celebrations are Margaret Mills and Peter Rowe.

BLUFFY'S BUS!
Few local people can have been so enduringly popular as Harry 'Bluffy' Rippingale who pioneered the Gestingthorpe bus service in the 1920's. Above: Bluffy with his first Model-T Ford lorry-cum-bus.

The final journey, Harry pictured on his retirement in 1956. Conductress Gladys Finch stands behind with Stanley Baxter in the door. Bluffy's premises were almost opposite the 'Pheasant' public house.

ylvia Cook holds the 1884 enrollment certificate
of her grandfather, John Cracknell into the
'United Patriots National Beneficial Society'.
Before unemployment pay or sickness benefit
Friendly Societies played a crucial role in
alleviating distress for working families.

Retired farmworker – and keen historian –
Cecil Cook with his own account of the
Maplesteads before World War Two.

Mary Downey and Doreen Potts whose book
'Schools and Scholars in Halstead and District'
rovided much valuable background information.

Continuing the tradition of local publicans who
have fostered community spirit are Adrian and
Tricia McGrillen of the Gestingthorpe 'Pheasant'
with daughter Laura.

Dorothy Mills of Sudbury recalling the unveiling of Gainsborough's statue.

Leslie and Lettie Smith of Gestingthorpe in their immaculate garden.

The late Jack Cornell – threshing contractor and smallholder. Brought up at the Bulmer 'Cock and Blackbirds' Jack's vivid, enthusiastic memories of his boyhood, village cricket and rural life did much to inspire the book.

"Years ago children went to Sunday School and Church – and then Church again in the afternoon." During one service however a certain lad's mind began to wander as he doodled with his penknife... Surely the initials – which can still be seen on the second pew in Bulmer Church bear no association with any contributor to this book – or page!

Scene of many a happy evening – the Castle Hedingham 'Bell'. Like other traditional inns, stagecoaches called here on their way to the capital, whilst Petty Sessions were held – and local justice administered – in the 'Disraeli Rooms' upstairs.

Harvest scene, circa 1910

"The countryside was so much more interesting years ago – there was much more for children to do," recalls Gestingthorpe's Beryl Spillings. Many remember taking tea to their fathers in the harvest fields.
 The above photograph is probably of haymakers although the crop could possibly be barley as this was also mown and 'carted loose'.

Gosfield Hall from the air. The second largest house in Essex and temporary residence of Kings and Queens, it was here that Edith Hurry, Horace and Evelyn Reeve worked as domestic servants. (Photography by kind permission of 'Essex County Newspapers'). The servant's hall was near 1; Butler's pantry 2; housemaids' bedrooms 3; kitchen 4 and laundry 5.

The late Horace and Evelyn Reeve. Interviewing Horace, the erstwhile Butler – and Evelyn, a one-time house-maid – was especially good fun. After Gosfield the couple moved to Gestingthorpe.

When Iris Harrington of Alphamstone was 'in service' she was photographed in both her 'morning uniform' (left) and 'afternoon clothes' (right).

An early introduction to work – riding the trace horse.

A centurion remembers! Edwin Partridge of Ponds Farm, Raydon recalling rural life in his youth. It was especially exciting to record Edwin's first-hand memories of the "Church bell being tolled every morning and evening during gleaning". Although the practice was widespread in East Anglia, The author had previously had to rely on written reminiscences rather than direct evidence for lectures and slide shows. (The explanation was that it gave all women an 'equal chance' at the gleaning – irrespective of whether they had young children or not). Photograph by kind permission of the 'East Anglian Daily Times'.

Eddie Tuffin

Emily 'Popsy' Parker

Ruby and Dick Finch

Claude Alleston

Eddie Tuffin

*I sometimes felt that leaving the open country-
side of Gestingthorpe and Bulmer for
Alphamstone's narrow lanes and hilly fields was
almost like going to a different part of England
– a bit like Wales or Cornwall.*

*On many occasions when I visited Eddie, it
was after a hectic day's crop spraying and I
would arrive late and full of tension. Yet in only
minutes, Eddie's kindly, warm-hearted
personality would transport me back to a
different, earlier age, when life was governed by
the pace of a horse and the rotations of
traditional agriculture.*

*In his own years as a shepherd, Eddie –
who is now an Alphamstone Church Warden –
would make a lambing pen beside the churchyard on hurdles that had been made by Tom
Rowe of Bulmer.*

Emily 'Popsy' Parker

*A life long resident of Alphamstone where her
grandmother was the midwife and her father the
undertaker. Popsy was not only a fund of local
knowledge but also a wonderful source of kindly
encouragement and support.*

Ruby and Dick Finch

*Gestingthorpe born and bred, both provided
some vivid insights into the village life of their
youth. Dick's wry, kindly sense of humour could
not long be suppressed and he often spoke to me
when I was tractoring near his home at the
'Crescent'.*

*On one occasion he and Ruby were returning
from one of their long countryside walks when
they paused to watch me drilling. When I finally
stopped the tractor, he chuckled slightly and
then, teasingly asked:*

*"We wondered," he said, "what is the particu-
lar advantage of drilling it crooked?!"*

*But before I could even answer, Ruby had cut
in:*

*"Now do you have it with 'milk and sugar' –
or just milk?"*

*And hospitable as always there would soon
appear not just a cup of tea but a slice of creamy
rich chocolate cake of enormous proportions and
second helpings all but compulsory...*

Claude Alleston

*"Do I remember Claude Alleston? I should think
I do!' declares Freddie Ruse of Long Melford.*

*He – was – a – terror – when he was at
school. "I don't know how he did it, but somehow
he'd get back into the classroom during the
dinner break and put a drawing-pin on your
seat – then when you sat down you'd scream out
and the master would give you such a look! The
other thing he'd do is catch a sparrow and put
that in your desk – so when you opened the lid –
in the middle of the afternoon – it would suddenly fly out and create havoc!"*

*Claude was actually born at Kersey and later
lived at Boxford and then Sudbury where he
ran a haulage business. He was a fund of local
knowledge and was one of our most helpful –
and humorous – contributors!*

'Extra-parochial' areas of land are also of interest. Presumably ceded by
landowners in early times, to provide tithes for a specific parish priest, they must
have surely complicated the Poor Law administration of later centuries. One of
the most intriguing is at Little Yeldham. Here an eighteen acre block of land –
almost adjacent to Little Yeldham Hall – was actually a part of Great Yeldham!

Parish Boundaries

Parish boundaries never fail to fascinate. By what process of ancient acquisition did they become so irregularly shaped? Note especially Gestingthorpe – which begins to 'lap round' Wickham St. Pauls; observe also the contorted boundaries at Little Horkesley, Tilbury-juxta-Clare and Little Waldingfield.

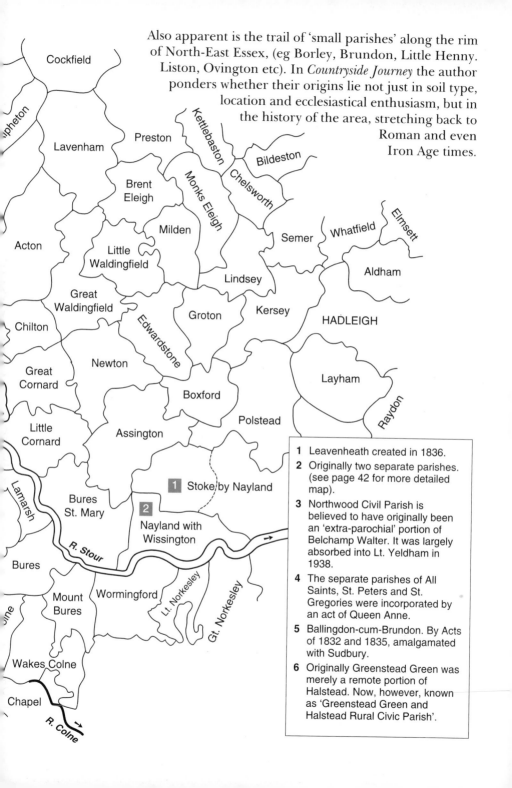

Also apparent is the trail of 'small parishes' along the rim of North-East Essex, (eg Borley, Brundon, Little Henny. Liston, Ovington etc). In *Countryside Journey* the author ponders whether their origins lie not just in soil type, location and ecclesiastical enthusiasm, but in the history of the area, stretching back to Roman and even Iron Age times.

Cockfield

upheton

Lavenham

Preston

Kettlebaston

Bildeston

Brent Eleigh

Monks Eleigh

Chelsworth

Acton

Milden

Little Waldingfield

Semer

Whatfield

Elmsett

Lindsey

Aldham

Great Waldingfield

Edwardstone

Groton

Kersey

HADLEIGH

Chilton

Newton

Great Cornard

Boxford

Layham

Raydon

Little Cornard

Assington

Polstead

1 Stoke by Nayland

2

Bures St. Mary

Nayland with Wissington

Lamarsh

R. Stour

Bures

Mount Bures

Wormingford

Lt. Norkesley

Gt. Norkesley

une

Wakes Colne

Chapel

R. Colne

1 Leavenheath created in 1836.
2 Originally two separate parishes. (see page 42 for more detailed map).
3 Northwood Civil Parish is believed to have originally been an 'extra-parochial' portion of Belchamp Walter. It was largely absorbed into Lt. Yeldham in 1938.
4 The separate parishes of All Saints, St. Peters and St. Gregories were incorporated by an act of Queen Anne.
5 Ballingdon-cum-Brundon. By Acts of 1832 and 1835, amalgamated with Sudbury.
6 Originally Greenstead Green was merely a remote portion of Halstead. Now, however, known as 'Greenstead Green and Halstead Rural Civic Parish'.

Exploring our local villages with their breathtaking views and repeated visual surprises was a recurring joy. On many of the lanes between the Maplesteads and the 'Colnes', Henny and Little Cornard there are beguilingly steep inclines, whilst in summertime the verges are festooned with the white blossom of Hawthorn and 'cowmumble' – until the banks open out –to reveal panoramic vistas of rolling East Anglia that stretch many miles.

On some occasions I returned home from my contributors as an enormous harvest moon hung low in the skyline and illuminated the surrounding fields with a silent, almost mysterious peacefulness. It was on these same fields that some had performed their lives' great work of seed time and harvest, threshing, shepherding and stockmanship.

Alf and Maggie Finch

At Borley one cold February afternoon, I met two of our most endearing contributors, Alf and Maggie Finch whose cottage overlooks the fields where Alf was a horseman for all of his working life. With rich North-Essex vernacular, bright twinkling eyes and most of all a warmth of willing humour, we had some wonderful afternoons recording the Borley of bygone years.

Yet like so many contributors, the couple provided far more than enjoyable memories. As one of their grandson's wives, Debbie King of Long Melford so perfectly sums up: "It's strange, but whenever we visit them we always feel 'lifted' and somehow inspired".

Ida Bird

When I first met Ida she was a mere strippling of 91 – and when photographed a spritely – 'bike riding' – 97. Born at Wickham St. Paul, she remained in the immediate area for her entire life, with the exception of three years in London 'in service'.

At the age of 88 however, she decided to visit her daughter in America – and despite having never flown or left the country before – proceeded to do so. Enjoying the experience so much, she then visited her other daughter in Australia, before – at the age of 90 – again flying to America!

Charlie 'Bommy' Martin

Born at Belchamp Walter in 1902, Charlie spent his entire working life on the land of the village until moving to Nash Court in Halstead shortly before his ninetieth birthday.

Consequently it took some perseverance to track him down, but when I did finally knock on his door, he instantly broke into a radiant smile: "Yes!" he declared, "there's heaps I can tell you!"

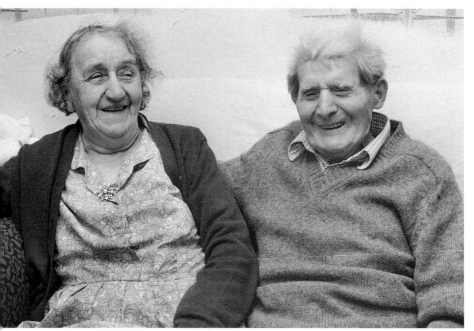

Alf and Maggie Finch

Ida Bird

Charlie 'Bommy' Martin

For rural girls domestic service was one of the few employment opportunities available. Man
eventually had to leave the area and seek positions elsewhere. Relaxing on the lawn of Goldinghai
Hall Bulmer about 1908 however, are housemaid Lottie?, parlourmaid Emily Rowe (Evelyn Reeve
mother), and cook Ethel Mansfield.

Sudbury's rural heritage. An old oast house
(near the Bus Station) tells of the town's bygone
maltings and breweries. A railway track can stil
be seen in the road near Cundy's old warehouse

George Harding-Payne who was Twinstead's
Church organist for over fifty years. From 1908
– 55 George's parents also kept the village's
'Waggon and Horses' public house.

The 'Kings Head' Pebmarsh. Note the advert for 'OLIVER BROS: ALES & STOUT'. Olivers were a Sudbury firm with a brewery along the Cornard road (near today's Solar garage).

The White Horse, Edwardstone. Olivers are still commemorated on the roadside wall.

The Bulmer 'Cock and Blackbirds'. The legendary 'tap room' was on the right. The pub's famous weather-vane – a metal cockerel also remains. During World War Two a hole was shot through the tail! (See Khyber Connection, p.162).

Tom and Bertha Bird of Wickham St. Pauls and now Bulmer. Bertha – who had earlier been 'in service' at Dynes Hall, Great Maplestead holds her war-time Ration Book. After discussing the Home Guard and Food Rationing, Tom and the author soon found another topic of interest – village cricket. On one occasion Tom shared in an opening partnership of 110 with his son Stephen on Wickham green!

After a hard day's work in factories and on farms a group of Wickham St. Pauls lads prepare for a 'Wednesday night' game in the early 30's.
(Back row, from left to right): Alfred Bird, Arthur Cornell, Ron Honeywood, Gordon Harding, Frank Marsh, John Watson.
(Sitting): Sid Brown, Charlie Weavers, Cecil Smith (farmworker who inspired 'The Khyber Connection'), Tom Bird.
(At front): Leonard Honeywood.

A Hundred Years of Gestingthorpe Cricket!

Gestingthorpe team members in 1953. (Back Row left to right): Hubert Meekings, Frank Nice, Joe Spillings, Sid Reynolds, Arthur Nears, Tony Self. (Front Row): Sid Beckett; Johnny Radley; Tom Elsdon; George Kemp; Les Rippingale.

A team one Sunday in 1969. (Back Row): Tom Elsdon (umpiring due to injury), Paul Cooke, John Hogsbjerg, Arthur 'Chubber' Laver, Alf Martin, George Carder, Frank Nice. (Front Row): Cyril Reeve, Kath Laver (scorer), Ken Elsdon, Nicky Stovell, Tony Self, John Hasler.

Gestingthorpe C.C., 1988 – in front of the new pavilion. (Back Row): Tom Elsdon, Andrew Self, P. Harding-Payne, Bob Skillicorn, Tim Stovell, Phil Stovell, Colin Padgett, Tony Self. (Front Row): John Hasler, David Self, Chris Moulton, Colin Ellis, Paul Elsdon.

Reminiscing the game in 1947 when Greenstead Green were dismissed for just five runs, are retired Gestingthorpe players Hubert Meekings, Johnny Radley (who took six wickets for four runs), George Kemp, the author, Joe Spillings and Dick Finch, together with Len Cook (on right). Greenstead Green's other wickets were taken by Arthur Nears who took 5 wickets for 1 run – both teams having twelve players. (Photo by kind permission of the 'Suffolk Free Press')

Chilton-Waldingfield Airfield. The gateposts – where the road was closed when the runway was in use – can still be seen beside the Sudbury to Waldingfield road. Chilton Grain's premises – erstwhile hangers – are in the background.

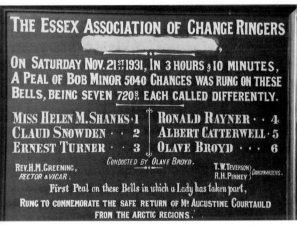

THE ESSEX ASSOCIATION OF CHANGE RINGERS

ON SATURDAY NOV. 21ST 1931, IN 3 HOURS & 10 MINUTES, A PEAL OF BOB MINOR 5040 CHANGES WAS RUNG ON THESE BELLS, BEING SEVEN 720S EACH CALLED DIFFERENTLY.

MISS HELEN M. SHANKS·1	RONALD RAYNER · · 4	
CLAUD SNOWDEN · · 2	ALBERT CATTERWELL · 5	
ERNEST TURNER · · 3	OLAVE BROYD · · · 6	

CONDUCTED BY OLAVE BROYD.

REV. H.M. GREENING, RECTOR & VICAR.

T.W. TEVERSON R.H. PINHEY } CHURCHWARDENS.

First Peal on these Bells in which a Lady has taken part,

RUNG TO COMMEMORATE THE SAFE RETURN OF MR AUGUSTINE COURTAULD FROM THE ARCTIC REGIONS.

To confuse enemy parachutists, sign posts were removed and village names obliterated from Post Offices, churches and village halls etc. At one local church however – not far from Gestingthorpe Village Hall – the name has still not been replaced!

PORTRAIT PHOTOGRAPHY BY ALASTAIR TUFFILL.

With thanks also to Dorothy Cornell, John Dixey, Brian Fleming, John Harding-Payne and Albert Rawlins for the use of other photographs and with special thanks to Paul Matthews of Photogrphic Partners, Sudbury for much invaluable assistance.

Bill and Kath Yeldham. A temporary 'dummy airfield' was situated on the fields between Gesting-thorpe and Little Yeldham behind them. (There were two rows of lights with flat cardboard aeroplanes).

Ford tractor mechanic – and later manager of Mann Egerton's tractor depot in Ipswich, Johnny Hart recalling early mechanisation and war-time agriculture.

The late John Frost of Halstead describes the structure of the local Home Guard.

Farmer Jim Ruffle of Wickham St. Pauls recalls parading with "broomsticks and farm shotguns!"

someone might bring an accordion. We'd start early and walk right round the village and come back about midnight. If there was no moon, we'd carry lanterns and finish off by coming across the fields from the sandpits. We walked for miles. On one occasion we got as far as Lamarsh *Lion* and we children had to wait outside...we seemed to be stopped an awful long time! But lots of other places gave us mince pies and a drink of some sort, and as for some of the 'big houses' – well, after our little cottages, they were like palaces!...Oh yes, Christmas was lovely years ago!"

Popsy's final remark was not only repeated on countless occasions but as farmer Wally Twinn – also of Alphamstone – explained:

"People spent weeks and weeks preparing for it; getting in logs, plucking cockerels, making wine and cooking the plum puddings with silver threepenny pieces in."

It really didn't matter that there was hardly any such thing as children's Christmas cards. "Although," says one source, "we might make them at school for our Mums and Dads."
Amidst the home-made paper chains and decorations of holly and ivy, there was also genuine munificence from some 'big houses'.

"At Hengrave Hall, near Bury St. Edmunds," recalls farmworker Frank Billimore, "Sir John Wood not only gave *four pounds* of beef to his employees but additionally another four pounds for each member of the family. Well there were ten in our household. Think of that! We got FORTY POUNDS of beef!"*

Yet the beef provided more than a well-appreciated meal; it also produced gravy:

"And do you know," exclaims Gladys Finch of Gestingthorpe, "I can remember people having beef gravy on their Christmas puddings!"

* Hengrave's generosity was exceptional. A more typical quantity (from the Auberies of 1882) was 3lb of meat to a married couple with smaller amounts for their children. (From *Bulmer Then and Now*).
At Gestingthorpe, however, the allocation was even less precise: "Although it was a joint of beef," retells Doris Pannell, "it was distributed in the Post Office. However, the men had to come in one door – but leave by another – so that no one else knew exactly what they'd been given!"

129

Surprisingly the practice was not that unusual:

"Lots of people did," exclaimed Edna Chapman, when the question was put to Cavendish Horticultural Society. "In fact I can remember one old man who quite simply refused to eat his Christmas pudding without beef gravy!"*

But with Christmas, we have also reached the dark, cold gloom of winter.

"Mother would take us up to bed with a candle," recalls Ruby Finch, "and then blow it out as she went downstairs. Most people could only afford a lamp in the room where they lived."

Where beds were concerned there was another difference:

"FEATHER MATTRESSES!" declares Lavenham farmer Dennis Holland. "They were lovely! You'd sink right into them and soon be warm. It was like laying in a nest… Trouble was, you had to shake all the feathers level again in the morning. That was a real palaver. You really did have to shake them as well – because if they were goose feathers they'd sometimes come through and scratch you at night."

Others spoke of the elementary bed-warmers:

"We used to put a brick in the oven," reminisces farmworker Cecil Cook "and when it was hot we'd wrap it in cloth and put it in the bed."
"But just occasionally," laughs Dick Finch of Gestingthorpe, "the brick would fall out – and thump on the floor. And you'd wake up and think 'what the devil was that!'."

"At Pentlow – where I was born," relates Wally Twinn, "we had a brass bed-pan which was filled with hot ash and cinders and then ironed all over the bed to take the chill off. One day, however, a catastrophe occurred. We left it in mother's cycling dress for too long – and a big hole fell out!"

* So too do two contributors to this book – Alf Finch and Sudbury's Claude Alleston. For the record, the majority of contributors would refer to their Christmas puddings as 'Plum Puddings'. (The plums have been slowly discarded in recent centuries).

"But, however cold the weather," recalls Ida Bird of Wickham St. Pauls:

"we never ever had hot meat except maybe a pigeon, and on the very rare occasions we had beef, it would be cooked and then eaten cold. We had sparrow pie of course. My brothers would 'have a fit' on catching them on certain nights – with a lantern and nets – and then the pie would be made inside pastry, in a cloth which would be folded up like a suet pudding."

Yet the winter did have its compensations. There was sledging and 'sliding' and snowballing – and for those who could afford the footwear, there was skating. At Wethersfield, Jack Wallace learned to skate by pushing a chair in front of him, whilst, "Between Earls Colne and Halstead," says Harry Gilbert, "there were <u>crowds</u> of people on the frozen meadows by Parley Beams."

"At Gestingthorpe Hall," reminisces 'Rover' Finch, "Mrs. Oates wouldn't allow us on to the main pond until a farmer had ridden his horse over it first. Then it would be lovely. There'd be braziers roasting chestnuts and lanterns hung up in the trees and it was wonderful. I remember one time when I went sliding though, I kept at it all day long…all day, Huh! Next morning I could hardly walk!"*

Then there were the games – possibly mischievous – that were played with snowballs.

"You'd go to the house of some grumpy old man," explained one 'anonymous' Gestingthorpe source, "knock on the door, then run to the hedge and when he opened it, start hurling snowballs like mad! 'Course we also made slides – either by pressing the snow down, or by pouring out a trail of water which then froze. But if you had any devilry in you, you'd cover them up with snow again – so people would slip over. We were rotten really weren't we? Tormented the living daylights out of some of them old people. 'Course," our contributor concluded sagely, "you knew who you

---

* "One very cold winter," recalls Wally Twinn, "my parents skated from Cavendish to Long Melford along the River Stour." Maggie Finch's mother had similarly skated from Melford to Sudbury, whilst Charlie Martin provides a similar memory of skating over the flooded valley beneath Belchamp Walter Church.

could play games on and who you couldn't!"*

At North End, Bill Yeldham described a variety of tricks suited to long winter evenings:

"A lot of cottages only had one door and so a couple of lads would tie the doors of neighbouring cottages together...then they'd knock on one of the doors. Oh dear! The poor devils would have to climb through a window to get out!"

It might not have been their only aggravation.

"Another old caper was this. You'd get a button and a pin and a long piece of cotton and hang the button over somebody's window and keep on, 'tap...tap...tap...' until they looked out...then after they'd sat down, you'd start again. Oh yes, we got up to all such games as that! But the thing was this. Nothing was ever stolen and nothing was ever broken."†

Village nicknames could also cause amusement. Bulmer's favourite correspondent remembers:

"There used to be a chap here called Bunn, but whose secret name was Pussy. We didn't half torment him. If he was working beside the road somewhere, we boys would walk about ten yards past him and then you'd hear someone go 'me-ow, me-ow!'. He'd turn round looking that roilled – but you may depend on it – we didn't hang about long after that!"

However, we should not forget the strict authoritarianism of those times:

* The impression prevails that anyone who was 'slightly backward', or a little bit 'slow', – or an older person who had grown a shade too idiosyncratic – was the butt of endless teasing, leg-pulling and practical joking. In turn, however, they were both accepted – and ironically – 'protected' by the village community. As one contributor put it: "God help anyone else – newcomers or strangers – who tried to take advantage of anyone a bit backward – Oh no! They'd soon have someone a little stronger to contend with!"

† Interestingly, both 'capers' described by Bill Yeldham were also recounted by several other contributors – from different parts of the area – and qualify as a genuine part of our folklore.

132

"In Gestingthorpe," says Leslie 'Luke' Smith (b.1921), "all the men had to 'touch their hats' to Mrs. Oates and all the women curtsey if they chanced to meet her in the street."

"In some villages," says another contributor, "we even had to touch our hats to some of the larger farmers, who were dreadful really, snooping round on their horses like lords and kings. I was given a real sharp 'telling off' by my Father – because I didn't say 'Sir' to the farmer he worked for."

It wasn't the only strict area. There was also the attendance of Church or Chapel. At Lamarsh Lettie Smith was typical of many contributors in:

"going to Sunday School *and* Church followed by Church *again* in the afternoon."

As Alf Finch explains: "Our parents wouldn't let us outside to play if we didn't go to Sunday School... So we had to go to get out!" Meanwhile in Bulmer, "The blessed school teachers also ran the Sunday School! So if we didn't go – oh dear – we'd cop it next day!" At Little Yeldham:

"The children who were required to attend Sunday School and Church were not even allowed to sit with their families at the latter. Instead they were positioned at the back of the Church...this also applied to the afternoon service."*

For the older boys and girls, there was confirmation to be considered. The impression prevails that through a process of reprimands and inducements, it was almost impossible to avoid, 'unless you were a staunch Chapelite'. Indeed in some villages, the candidates even received 2/6d after being successfully confirmed. "But it wasn't that simple," came a quick retort;

"because you had to go to one other communion first – before you got your half crown!"

---

* From *A History of Little Yeldham* by Adrian Corder-Birch, published by Halstead History Society. Another contributor commented that Sunday mornings – when the children were at Sunday School and Church – often provided the only time of the week when their parents could enjoy any privacy and quietness in their overcrowded cottages.

(Certain contributors with forenames like Dick, Chris and Jack made additional wry comments on the subject!)

But with confirmation we are moving from childhood to adolescence.

"And on Sundays," recounted Dick Finch, "all the Gestingthorpe lads would meet up together at the Foundry corner or in the 'Basin' [opposite Delvyns]," whilst for Jute Chatters, "it was a regular thing. Every Sunday before dinner, all us Belchamp lads congregated in front of Otten Church. Then we'd lay in the grass and have a good chat or get up to some pranks and games." Yet Sunday was still the Sabbath – "so if we wanted to play cards, we'd have to go and hide up in an old barn or some such place."

Doubtless many were like Wethersfield's Jack Wallace:

"My best mate would get his big brother to buy 5 Woodbine cigarettes for 1d. Then we'd sneak off and smoke them. 'Course, we made ourselves as sick as cats, although we thought we had enjoyed them!"

Yet if smoking was initially unpleasant, Dick Halls is one of many to comment, "It was wonderful how much you learnt from collecting the cards in cigarette packets". Sixty years later, his sister, Dorothy Cornell, still has her collections of *Birds, Kings of England, Dogs, Flowers and Film Stars*.

Then there was Sunday evening:

"When," reminisce Tom Bird and George Harding-Payne, "all us village boys would go for long walks together round the neighbouring villages – Twinstead, Pebmarsh, Maplestead and Gestingthorpe. But we didn't go in the pubs though. We boys hadn't got any money for that sort of thing."

"More to the point," quipped Jack Cornell, "everyone knew how old you really were – weren't a hope in hell of an 'under age drink'... well – not much under age anyway!"

Despite the fellowship and vitality that radiated from within the villages, we should not forget the harsh reality of those times.

134

'Jute' Chatters is one of several who slept, 'three in one bed; two of us one way and the middle one opposite'.* Gladys Finch described the rag rugs which slowly replaced sawdust and sand as floor coverings;† Ruby Finch remembered her mother, 'making all of our clothes with a hand-operated sewing machine', whilst Ida Bird poignantly described her childhood of nine decades ago:

"In the winter, before I was old enough to do needlework, I used to go to bed at five or six o'clock. You see my brothers would be coming in from their long day's farmwork and needed the fire and the food."

Bertha Bird of Great Maplestead similarly spoke of her mother, 'biking to Hedingham to do people's washing for two and sixpence a day'. Bert Surridge exclaimed of people's toughness:

"My Father never, ever wore gloves – I never remember it. He'd hold the handles of a wooden plough all day long – in the coldest of weather – but I never remember him wearing gloves," Bulmer's Horace Elsey agrees, "The only thing the old men might do, is perhaps put on an old leather mitten if they were cutting down blackthorns or something like that."

At Gestingthorpe, Dick Halls gravely observed:

"Time a lot of people got to about sixty, they were absolutely worn up. There were no end of cripples and hunchbacks in villages years ago."

* Large families with only one or two bedrooms were obviously faced with difficult sleeping arrangements. "The beds were fitted in just like dominoes!" recalls one. Interestingly both Claude Alleston of Boxford and Dick Finch of Gestingthorpe tell the same dry joke on how people coped:
"I asked one old man," laughs the latter, "where he put all his children at night and he say 'Huh boy! – what I do is this – I put two or three of 'em to bed – and then – when they're fast asleep and stiff as boards, I take them out and stand 'em up against the wall and put the others in the bed instead!'"

† This is not to be deprecating. Many were very colourful and deserve preservation. A typical comment came when speaking to Cavendish Horticultural Society: "Some of them were really lovely – but the dust they held!" The rugs were home-made and involved threading any waste material through a hessian base.

"Trouble was," continued Chris Felton, "once you were about sixteen, almost every single boy could carry – or reckoned he could carry – a coomb of wheat, and that was important, because it meant that you were a man...even if it did muck you up in later life." (A coomb of wheat weighs $2\frac{1}{4}$cwt – approximately 115kg).

But the hard work applied to both men and women.

"Think what a performance wash day was!" declares Janet Cooper of Elmsett; "There were faggots to be got in, water to be pumped up – and put in the copper, the fire to be lit and then all the clothes to be boiled. We boiled the white clothes for an hour and later put in a 'Recketts Blue Bag' which whitened them up beautifully."

Observing how much preparatory work needed doing before the washing could even begin, Dick Finch instantly commented:

Note the fire grate beneath the copper. This one held about six gallons, although some others were much larger.

"That's why everyone washed on Monday. When farmworkers did a full 'six day' week, Sunday was the only time they had to chop up the wood and bring up the water ready for their wives – especially if the pump was several hundred yards away... What's more you'd need a good barrow load of wood to heat up the copper."

Yet the copper had other uses. In many cottages it also heated the water for bath night – in addition to being used for cooking. ('Be like cooking in a washing machine,' I suggested to one contributor... 'Well, they were beautifully easy to clean,' came the reply). As Reverend Trevor Howard elucidates:

"When Mother cooked a ham in the copper, she'd have to clean it out before – and especially afterwards – otherwise when she next washed our clothes they'd get terribly greasy."

At Alphamstone, Rowena Twinn's mother made Christmas puddings,

"In a copper full of boiling water. She'd make about twenty like that, and they'd all be bobbing about in the water for seven to eight hours, and then after they'd dried out I'd take them round to old people in the village."

There is, in *A Christmas Carol* a very special moment – when Tiny Tim and his family wait with expectation – as Mrs. Cratchit leaves the room;

'to take the pudding up and bring it in... Halloa! A great deal of steam! The pudding was out of the copper. A smell like a washing-day! That was the cloth. A smell like an eating-house and a pastry-cook's next door to each other, with a laundress's next door to that! That was the pudding! In half a minute Mrs. Cratchit entered – flushed, but smiling proudly – with the pudding.'

Many cottages had a 'communal copper'. At Hengrave, Frank Billimore's mother had to share with two adjoining cottages, "So mum started washing at four in the morning and our neighbours took over about eight..." For wife Phyllis, the worst thing about a detached wash house was constantly having to go out in the cold. Meanwhile says Frank:

137

"when the sheets were being boiled they'd all bubble up – so when I was a little boy I'd have to stand there and keep on pushing them down with a stick!"

Others recall the big mangles – which were so heavy to turn – and the necessity for a girl to stand behind and hold the linen – together with the repeated instruction to 'watch your fingers!'...

"But I didn't watch mine," laughs Sudbury's Hilda Huggett, "and look! I've still got a bent one to prove it!"

Then there were the flat irons – with hot coals inside – that went 'clink – clonk, clink – clonk' as they went back and forth across the linen together with a recurring comment about the 'Tuesday ironing and mending'.

"You know its strange – because despite all the hard work, we got a tremendous amount of satisfaction from finally seeing a basketful of beautifully clean, nice white linen."

The sheer grind and exertion expended on housework years ago should never be forgotten.* As Phyllis Billimore says for all our contributors:

"When I was about seven, I started to help my mother. We really didn't get much time for playing. As for going to shops, that was unheard of."

In Twinstead Churchyard from which one has such lovely views, is a gravestone. It commemorates one Lucy Norman Gardener, who bore SEVENTEEN children, before dying, aged fifty three, in 1791. At Bulmer Tye, Alan Dixey showed me the enormous 20lb pot which was the only form of cooking for one farmworker's wife, whilst at Gestingthorpe, Bert Surridge told of his mother:

"Walking to Sudbury Market Hill in only an hour. She went on the footpaths mind – across to Wiggery Wood, then Upper Houses to Bulmer Church and Sandy Lane – but we children had to run to

* Cecil Cook recalls of bath night: "First, we had to carry up the water and then put it in large saucepans which were heated on the range. Next the tub was placed in front of the fire and that's where we had our bath. But I've thought about it since – it was hard work for our poor Mother."

keep up with her! She was the fastest walking woman as ever I knew."

Similarly Eddie Tuffin – whose own mother did a daily seven mile postal round from Henny, instantly remarked, "Huh! It made your legs ache to keep up with her!".
Doubtless the children – and mothers! – deserved a drink of water:

"But," laughs Eddie, "you didn't want to look down the well where I got my water. There were toads in the bottom! There again – it never harmed us."

Several contributors recount that turning the handle (or windlass) of a well was quite heavy work – even for men. However as Lavenham's Dennis Holland remarks:

"The water from a well was lovely. Even in the hottest of weather it was ice-cold. The only problem was if a bucket got dropped in! That caused a rare palaver because it stirred the bottom up. Oh yes – your water would be a bit sandy for a day or two after that!"

However, as Cecil Cook points out:

"Don't forget that no-one had flush toilets! Just a bloomin' ol' shed up the garden with a large bucket under the seat which needed to be emptied each week! It was a good job people had large gardens to bury it in."

"Worst thing about the privies," says Great Maplestead's Dolly Argent, "was walking down the garden on a windy night – and then your candle getting blown out... Besides, if it was a rough night, the wind would blow up the back of the privy – right where you were sitting!"*

How easy it is to forget these aspects of the 'good old days'. But what then about places like Sudbury and Halstead?

"In towns," explains life-long Sudburian, Alan King, "carts

* Another place where candles would 'blow out' recalled both Ruby Finch and Dorothy Turner of their draughty childhood homes was: "Going upstairs to bed. Even though you did put your hand round it. Oh, they were cold old places in the winter!"

would come round to collect the 'night soil'. But everthing was so different in those days. I can remember three dairies *right in the middle* of Sudbury! One was in Ballingdon Street, another in Weaver's Lane and the last in North Street – and *every single day* the cows were brought up from the meadows and through the town to be milked. Then there were horses pulling waggons on the roads' and sheep and cattle were driven along Friars Street to the market each week. The animals – especially the cows – made a mess wherever they chose but in those days these were quite natural and normal smells."

"In fact," says Claude Alleston, "in towns like Sudbury and Hadleigh people would actually rush out and collect the horse manure – to put on their allotments."

Similarly, when Bulmer's principal estate, *The Auberies*, was sold in 1806, the auctioneers' advertisement proudly announced that: 'POPULOUS SUDBURY SUPPLIES DUNG MANURE'.

Yet there were compensations. Something that everyone enjoyed were the 'sing songs' which were the high point in any family or social gathering. Many like Claude Alleston (b.1912) recalled those on Sunday evenings – usually of hymns, "when, mother played the piano and we'd all join in." Others like Dorothy Turner of Twinstead described their fathers leading the music with an accordion;

"It was more or less a Sunday routine. However, it had to be hymns! I mean if you even hummed a popular tune on a Sunday, Mother would soon be giving you 'scolding looks'. 'Don't you know what day of the week it is!' she'd rasp."

Also extolled were the 'Good Friday teas' at non-conformist Chapels before the Second World War, "They were a real Red Letter Day for Bulmer Street!" declared the late Hazell Chinnery.

Another long anticipated event was the annual 'Choir Treat'. (Nearly all the children were actually in the choir for some period). "You'd look forward to it for weeks and weeks", says Phyllis Billimore. For almost all, it provided, the first opportunity of visiting the seaside; of riding on a train – AND of seeing a small corner of the world other than one's home village and its nearest market town.

One such 'Choir Treat' to Clacton is described in the *Gestingthorpe Parish Magazine* of 1896. Actually arranging transport from the village, however, required considerable forethought...

"First our good old parishioner Mrs. Branwhite of *Moat Farm*, had to be approached for the loan of her Suffolk Punches, and then Mr. Malyon for the use of his light waggon, whilst Mr. George Finch sent his old grey mare – in the 'pot cart' – with Smith as 'charioteer'."* (The latter began its journey from Pot Kiln Chase at 6.30am – and presumably picked up passengers as it passed through the village, whilst the larger waggon departed from near *Crouch House* at 7.15...the train finally leaving Hedingham Station just after eight o'clock).

For many school children there were also the Big House 'treats'. At Bulmer for instance, *The Auberies* hosted a children's party in the harvest holidays. Years later Gertie Coe explained, "There were games, a lovely tea, a present for everyone and then a scramble for sweets." At Gestingthorpe, there was the 'Vicar's Annual Treat'. In July 1897, 110 children sat down to tea on the Vicarage lawn. The following year, schoolgirl Mabel Finch, wrote:

"After grace had been sung we had bread and butter, bread and jam, cake and also some nice tea to drink. Games followed until seven o'clock when Mrs. Oates presented the awards for attendance." (see page 111)

Hosting these events was a role the 'Big Houses' apparently enjoyed. Both *The Auberies* and *Gestingthorpe Hall* provided a similar 'Christmas Treat' with tea, games and a Christmas tree, complete with individually named presents ranging from 'a nice box of sweets to toys or maybe a diary'.†
As Evelyn Reeve put it: "Make no mistake – it was a real highlight of the year." Yet apart from these, half yearly bonanzas, there was one other event which is nostalgically remembered by those who were so truly 'Of the Furrow Born'.

* For more details of the Gestingthorpe Pot Works, see *Of the Furrow Born*, Chapter Two.

† The sheer novelty of the Christmas tree is revealed in School Logs and Parish Magazines. On 17th January, 1872 the Chelsworth schoolchildren: 'went to see Miss Cantleys Christmas tree which pleased them immensely' whilst in December 1895, the Gestingthorpe children were: 'invited to the Hall for tea and that never failing source of amusement, a Christmas tree.'

Quite simply it was Harvest. For as Edwin Partridge of Hadleigh explains;

"As soon as we heard that anyone had started harvest – well, we children would be falling over ourselves to report it to the teachers so that we could get our holiday... It was the general thing then you see, that the children should take their parents tea in the harvest fields or help with the gleaning."

Eddie Tuffin warm-heartedly continues;

"Harvest that time of day was full of children! They'd be jumping on the waggons and standing on the cart track calling out, 'Ride? Ride?', as you left the stack yard for the harvest field where they were loading sheaves. You were half your bloomin' time loading them into the waggon – and then half your time taking them out when you got there!"

When they arrived there was an additional attraction.

"Especially when the binder got towards the middle of the field," relates Charlie Martin of Belchamp Walter. "There'd be all these boys with sticks, and then as the rabbits came out they'd be after them – they'd run like buggery. But we were lucky because my father 'had' the rabbiting all year round on the farm where he worked, and you know we almost lived on them."*

And for some lads there was the first – gentle baptism into the heady world of adult work.

"The first job as ever I did," says Boxford's Claude Alleston, "was to sit on the 'trace horse' of a binder team, but that time of day, we boys only wore short trousers...and my goodness, it did make your legs itch. The horse was sweaty you see and you got 'suffen' sore sitting up there! But you had to watch your feet – if not, when you went round a corner they'd get caught in the chain. They would get nipped!"

* The 'day men' on a farm were otherwise usually prohibited from rabbiting – which was often the privilege of the head horseman, or sometimes 'let' to professional rabbit catchers.

But eventually the long hours of work – of 'shocking up' and of 'pitching' and of 'loading' and 'stack building' achieved their objective. The last fields were cleared; the final stacks built and the farmer 'settled up' with his men 'who had taken the harvest' – and now received their payment.

It was then that Alf Finch had bought his first pair of 'after-harvest boots', – "from a cobbler called Raymond on Finch Hill in Bulmer", whilst at North End, Bill Yeldham recalled:

"Every year after harvest, the farmworkers and their families from Little Yeldham, would go to Sudbury in a road waggon. The horses' brasses would be all shone up; the waggon would have been washed down, straw put in and sometimes decorated up with a few flowers or branches. It was a festive time and it would often be the children's only visit to Sudbury for the whole year. The waggon would be left at either the *Anchor* or the *Christopher* and then the purchases of 'after harvest' boots or clothes would follow. As they came home somebody would be playing the accordion and everyone else would be singing along."

Our chapter is again verging on adulthood and is nearing its natural conclusion. It has been difficult at times to maintain a balance between an idyll of the pre-television village, with its scampering children playing in 'flower-filled meadows,' and the reality of the stringent anxieties that prevailed on their parents.

Maybe from the children's viewpoint it is Harry Gilbert who should have the last word:

"You know, I can honestly say, that I can never ever recollect any of my life – or my childhood – as being dull or uninteresting."

His pleasures were truly, *'Of the Furrow Born'*.

"...round here the last sheaf in the field was called the 'Bobby shock' or 'the policeman'. Time that stood there you couldn't go gleaning – because the field hadn't been horse raked."
"The other thing was the Church Bell. At Raydon it rang at eight o'clock in the morning and then eight o'clock in the evening and the mothers couldn't go gleaning either side of those hours. But there was one lady here – Mrs. Dyer – and she was a wonderful gleaner. She'd regularly get enough to take to the threshing machine and then Layham Mill. But several of them would take a pram into the fields to put the gleanings in."

The late Edwin Partridge, (1893-1993).

"When I was young, Mother usually baked on Saturdays. The bread would keep for a week – and as the oven was hot, it was a good opportunity to cook anything else that needed doing – such as cakes or scones. A brick oven will stay warm for two or three days, so on Saturday evening, Mother would put in a pot of pears – to stew for Sunday dinner.
"In those days, people wouldn't <u>dream</u> of cooking on a Sunday – but this way we had a nice Sunday pudding. Then in the evening we would put our clothes in the oven – to 'air them' for Monday morning. And the other thing was this. The food from a brick oven had a most lovely – unforgettable – flavour all of its own."

Farmer's daughter, Janet Cooper, Elmsett

144

"In Wickham St. Pauls there was a shopkeeper who baked bread on Saturday mornings, and the women nearby would take their cakes or rabbit pies or whatever and put them in his oven – and he'd bake it for them for a halfpenny or three farthings."

Eddie Tuffin, Alphamstone

COPPERS

"Just before it boils, the water in a copper goes perfectly still – for just a few moments. The old men used to say, 'When you can see the reflection of your face in the water – that's when you should add the malt'. If the water gets any hotter it starts to boil and goes bubbly – and that's no good because it would kill the malt.'

Ken Partridge
(b.Monks Eleigh – now of Station Road, Sudbury)

"I don't think that Mum had even got a mangle to put the washing through. So if it was a wet day, she'd put all the wet sheets and washing around the fire on a linen rail. But we'd come in from school really cold and creep under this linen horse until she found us out – and then we'd get packed off to bed quick! You see people reckoned that they caught colds from the damp clothes drying near the fire."

Ruby Finch, Gestingthorpe

"I knew a wheelwright named Partridge from Belchamp when I was a boy and he was a wonderful carpenter too. He used to put the hubs of his waggon wheels in a copper to simmer – which made the wood soft – and then he'd take them out to put the spokes and fellies on, and do you know, they'd honestly look like they'd grown like that."

Tom Gilbert, Little Yeldham

145

PART FOUR

IN SERVICE AND
VILLAGE LIFE

*"When Gestingthorpe Hall was in its heyday, Mrs. Oates
had at least seven staff 'in the house'. There were four women
–a cook, parlour maid, house maid and laundry maid. Then
there were three men – a butler, a footman, and a coachman,
who drove her about in a pony cart. Additionally there was a
woman who went 'daily' together with two or three gardeners,
whilst Mr. Pannell occasionally went as part-time secretary
and carpenter!"*

Daisy Nice (1900-1990)

"I was only fourteen when I started at Henny Ryes. I had to pack my uniform, night clothes and other few possessions into a little tin trunk and then they came and got me in a pony cart.

"There were six of us 'in service' there and I was the servants' 'servant'. Every morning, my first job was to clean the kitchen range, unlock the doors and scrub the steps and then make the other servants' tea... Mrs. Barnardistan – my employer – was very nice really. 'Learn to control yourself, Dorothy!' she'd say. But the actual staff were a lot older than me. They were a bit hard on me at times."

Dorothy Turner, Twinstead

"At one time there were seven gardeners at Kentwell Hall. In the autumn they would all set about sweeping up the leaves beneath that lovely avenue of Lime trees. They'd do it every week and then the leaves would be taken away in a horse and tumbril to be made into compost."

Freddie Ruse, Long Melford

147

Chapter Fourteen

THE 'BIG HOUSE'
Gosfield, Kentwell and Borley

"Popsy Parker was my best frient. So when I was 'in service' at Countess Cross, Colne Engaine, and there was a dance at Alphamstone, I'd try and bike over. But first – before I could go – I had to help with the dinners, do all the washing up, and then 'turn the beds down', before cycling along those dark old lanes to Alphamstone – and no – I didn't like the dark much!

"Anyway, when the dance was over, I'd stay the night with Popsy. But next morning I'd have to be up pretty early – especially if I'd woken up Popsy's father when I'd come in the night before! – and then I'd have to bike back to Countess Cross in time to wake up the household AND get their breakfast ready!"

Dorothy Turner

If the farm were the backbone of the parish then the 'big house' was its 'exchequer' and cultural focus. Indeed,

"In an age before radio," declares Jack Cornell, "there was only one sort of time in Bulmer. And that was the time on *The Auberies* clock!"

It was an era of authoritarianism combined – at times – with well-intentioned paternalism. Of donations to the Parish Church, the School and of prizes for the children we have written elsewhere.* Yet it was not merely the young who benefited. For on December 8th 1895:

148

"25 old Gestingthorpe worthies made their way to the Hall and were regaled with roast beef, plum pudding and Foxearth Ale."

But even this pales beside the extraordinary celebration organised by Mrs. Oates to celebrate her son Lawrence's twenty-first birthday, and safe return from the Boer War, on 22nd June 1901.†

"A grand fete," records *The Halstead Times*, "was accompanied by a brass band, steam roundabout, swings, coconut shies, etc... To this jamboree, ALL of the village's hundred or so schoolchildren were invited to tea...whilst no less than TWO HUNDRED AND EIGHTY ONE Gestingthorpe residents sat down in the Hall barn and cartlodge to an excellent dinner. After dinner all proceeded to the Hall grounds to present an address of welcome to Lieutenant Oates as 'the young squire'."...(For the record some 381 people or 80% of the total parish population were entertained).

LOCAL DETAIL

Another vivid insight into the 'Big Houses' and their staff comes from census records.

In 1881 for example, the Rector of Belchamp Otten was not untypical in having just one servant who 'lived in' the house whilst at Assington Vicarage there was a governess, a cook, three domestic staff and a page boy to look after the Rev. J. Wilson Brown.

At Henny Ryes – with its enchanting views of the Stour Valley – dwelt not only the squire, Col. Barnardistan and ten relatives, but also nine servants including a page boy and a dress-maker. Between Middleton and Sudbury – at Ballingdon Grove – lived five servants under the roof of brickmaker and maltster Elliston Allen, whilst at Belchamp Walter Hall, those residing with the Raymond family were butler Joseph Corder, housemaid Rosa Smee, cook Susan Bullock and kitchen maid Emma Hardy.

* Another worthwhile activity several 'big houses' encouraged was Scouting. The latter not only provided village boys and girls with their first (and often only) holiday but was also a first step into the armed services. Local Scout and Guide troops were inspired by the proprietors of the Auberies in Bulmer, Henny Ryes, Gosfield Hall and especially Musette Majendie of Hedingham Castle.

† Later to become Captain Oates – 'the very gallant gentleman' who walked out into the blizzard – in the hope that his comrades might live, on Scott's ill-fated expedition to the South Pole 1911-12.

At *Kentwell Hall,* Eliza Bence had no less than twelve staff on the premises, whilst at neighbouring *Melford Hall,* Sir William Hyde-Parker was recorded with nine family and FOURTEEN staff, together with a coachman in nearby accommodation. Interestingly, some of his staff derived from Hampshire, Scotland, London and Paris, whilst at Kentwell the senior positions of governess, butler and footman came from Surrey, Wiltshire and Cornwall respectively.

It was the last age: by the nineteen thirties, the continuous decline in farm rents combined with 'capital taxation on death' had resulted in the 'big houses' manifestly pruning their expenditure. Outlying properties were sold off and the droves of housemaids and footmen, grooms and gardeners, were slowly reduced. Yet so important had domestic work been – particularly to girls – that of all the women interviewed for this book, all but a handful were once thus employed.

Gosfield Hall (above) is about 3 miles from Halstead (just off the Hedingham to Braintree road). The property is now a Home for Ageing Gentlefolk and is open to the public on certain days each summer. It has over eighty rooms and was visited by both Queen Elizabeth the First and Louis XVIII, (who lived there from 1807 – 1809 during his exile from France). At the time of Louis' residence, the property was owned by the Marquis of Buckingham. The latter's most important local achievement was to introduce 'straw plaiting' to our area (about 1800) which created work and vital income for village women until the mechanisation of the industry in 1879-81.

One of them is Edith Hurry. Born in 1898, she worked at *Gosfield Hall* – the second biggest house in Essex – where a staff of SIXTEEN looked after the two occupants, Mrs. Lowe and her son Willoughby. Today Edith still lives in the nearby village and it was here that I visited her one unforgettable afternoon shortly after her ninetieth birthday.

"When I left school," she vividly recalls, "Mother wouldn't let me work in a factory but replied to an advert from *Gosfield Hall*. About a week later the Housekeeper visited our home in Braintree – and luckily I was accepted."

A few days afterwards a 'dog cart' was despatched to collect her:

"As we approached *Gosfield Hall*, I simply couldn't believe my eyes. It was enormous! Some of the rooms were far bigger than our entire house! It was like a palace! But I was very happy there. I was fifteen when I arrived and I stayed for ten years. It was strange really. You weren't ordered about. It was just your job to do certain things."

"Is there anything you particularly remember of your first days?"

"Yes. As soon as I arrived I had to 'put my hair up' (a ubiquitous resentment!), also we had to change our uniforms every day after lunch. To begin with I was the 'third housemaid' – the lowest of the low – and all I did was clean the other servants' bedrooms! But something I shall never forget is that they had a parrot, and I had to clean its cage out .... but he was a rascal! He would call out my name and then pretend to bite my finger and go 'Oooh!'."†

Edith's day began at 6.30 with the ringing of the bell on the clock tower by the 'Odd Job Man'. Breakfast was at eight with lunch at one o'clock whilst the bell was finally tolled at 9pm by which time all the servants had to be 'in'.
Yet there was more to the day than this. There was 'house sewing' in the afternoons and then tea in the servants hall at 4.30. Later there was the lighting of the gas lamps in the interminable passages, whilst in the evenings:

---

† Edith soon became a second housemaid and eventually climbed the ladder to become housekeeper. Sadly she passed away in 1993.

151

"There might be a little job pop up – such as make up a fire somewhere or fill a hot water bottle...there wasn't a lot of work but you had to be 'on call'. And then in between times we would sit in the servants' hall or sitting room and play whist or dominoes or draughts – in front of a lovely fire."

However, there were some frustrations. One was the limited amount of 'time off'. (Over two and a half *months* passing before Edith could make her first visit home).

"But there was no telephone or anything so I couldn't warn my mother. Luckily she was at home when I arrived and we were both so excited, but I couldn't help thinking 'how tiny this house is!'"

(Not surprisingly, every other contributor to this chapter said something similar).

"I'm sure my parents must have thought that I was swollen-headed. Later my father bought me a bike. But riding it back to Gosfield for the first time was an adventure! The roads were all rutted – and there I was, falling off and getting on that bike all the way back to Gosfield!"

This then was Edith Hurry's life within the self-contained community of the Mansion – with its stretching lake and surrounding 3,000 acres of estate; with its grand staircase – there were twelve staircases in all, classical statues, alabaster urns, ballroom and rows of chandeliers. Her days were governed by the bells which hung in a row near the housekeeper's room and it was impinged upon by the strictness and the prejudices of the time ("originally we weren't allowed out on Saturdays because the 'factory girls' were out and we were meant to be 'better'!"). Her uniform was a starched cap, blue dress and white apron in the morning, with a cap, black dress and white apron in the afternoon. Black shoes and stockings were mandatory all day. Yet she repeatedly refers to those days as being happy. Happy perhaps because of the sense of friendship and warm-heartedness amongst her fellow servants; possibly also, because it was one of them, coachman and later chauffeur, Leonard Hurry, whom she married in 1924.
Whilst Edith Hurry was able to find employment comparatively close to home, others were less fortunate:

"When I left school," recalled the late Daisy Nice (b.1900), "there wasn't any work at all, so I had to go to London – as a lady's maid – at Ashley Gardens in Westminster. For a country girl like me, it was just unbelievable. I'd hardly ever left the village before – and never ever been to London!"

(Another of our contributors was also in 'service' in London. The remarkable Ida Bird of Wickham St. Pauls. Like Daisy, she also remained for about three years until the Zeppelin raids of World War One).*

How one can imagine the complex emotions of shyness, excitement and homesickness, that must have faced these fourteen or fifteen year old girls from isolated rural backgrounds when they first arrived in London!

Many applied to agencies for their placements. Bulmer's Ann Finbow went to:

"A grey-haired lady in Sudbury who wore a dark dress, sat very straight and was very judging and superior in her manner. She spoke in a very aristocratic way about 'gels going into sarvice' [sic] – but most of us went to her to further our positions."

Like Ann, (whose first job had been in Bulmer) the majority of girls got their initial training locally.

Farmworker's daughter, Bertha Bird (b.1913) vividly described her first days at the magnificent *Dynes Hall* in Great Maplestead – with its lovely wooded views, across the hills and valleys beside the River Colne. Here she was a kitchen maid:

"Doing all the vegetables, skinning the rabbits, plucking and drawing the pheasants and so forth... I learnt the lot!"

"But if these were your duties at work, what about your time off?"

"Every Sunday we had to go to church for morning service then once a fortnight we were allowed home for Sunday dinner, provided we were back by 2pm. The following Sunday we could go out

* After returning to the safety of the Suffolk-Essex border, Daisy, (who was born at Balsham), obtained a position at Gestingthorpe Rectory, where she met her future husband, blacksmith Dick Nice.
  One penetrating, poignant insight into a local girls move to London can be found in *The Polly Leeks Letters*, by Richard Deeks and Elizabeth Wigmore of Long Melford Historical Society.

from 2pm-9pm."

"Was that all you were allowed out each week?" I wondered quietly.

"Oh no! We were also allowed out one afternoon a week as well."
(In the winter from 2pm-8pm. In the summer 2pm-9pm).

"So you never really had a whole day off?"

"Well," Bertha answered, "once a month we could go at 10am
and didn't have to be back until 9pm."

"Eleven hours in one go," I calculated.

"Scandalous," muttered husband Tom dryly, "whatever was the
world coming to!"

But if Bertha Bird's hours of freedom seemed short, they were – as
we have hinted – a dramatic increase on those before World War
One.

"At Gosfield," explains Edith Hurry, "we were only allowed out
on *either* Sunday afternoon *or* evening and one weekday afternoon
or evening."*

Moreover there were no allowances for Christmas Day:

"None of us servants ever went home," records Gosfield's third
housemaid Evelyn Reeve. "It was reckoned it wouldn't be fair on
the others. However the house was beautifully decorated with
greenery, everyone got a present from Mrs. Lowe, and on
Christmas Night the entire household – servants and aristocracy –
ate a cold supper together in the servants hall."

---

* It has been suggested that from these strictures arose the concept of
Mothering Sunday – the day on which all domestic servants could visit
their parents. As early as 1900 however the *Gestingthorpe Parish
Magazine* included the following warning:
   "It is lamentable to find the growing dislike to service. This is attrib-
utable, broadly, to a resenting of control and a determination to pass
evenings chiefly in pleasure seeking and in outdoor freedom which frequently proves the quick road to ruin...this danger is too often fatally
ignored by parents and employers." (Reprinted from the *Derbyshire
Association for the Help and Protection of Girls*)

Inevitably there were problems when courting. At Belchamp St. Pauls, Rose Chatters reminisces of her teenage days as a housemaid at *Foxearth Hall*:

"It was a 'real event' to be sent to post a letter – to be allowed out onto the street – and maybe bump into some of the boys. And if there was a dance at the village hall, you would quite honestly have to go on bended knee to get permission to stay out late, otherwise we had to be back by 9.30pm. And then next morning, if you were polishing the letterbox on the front door, or crossing the road on some errand and someone called out, 'Hello Rose', it wouldn't be long before your employer would mutter curtly, 'And who were you talking to this morning, Rose?'"

As Ann Finbow says of her days at *Kentwell Hall:*

"Occasionally I was ordered to go to Melford Railway Station to collect the fish from the East Coast that arrived in those big, plaited straw-bags. But it was like an enormous treat to do that job – to be allowed out – to FREEDOM – out of the house!"

Other contributors – and their husbands – similarly recalled that, "there wasn't much time for courting – but you might get half an hour against the back door if the old people weren't looking!"

For Frank and Phyllis Billimore – like many others – private meetings were only possible in the "coal house, the wood bunker or some such place as that". Perhaps it didn't matter. For the romance which began at *Stanchells Farm*, Flempton, where he was a horseman and she was the cook, has led to over fifty years of happily married life.

The restrictions on social life were not the only grievance. From a wage of 5/- a week, Bertha Bird had to purchase her own uniform, whilst Rose Chatters remembers:

"Often being up until midnight – washing up after a dinner party – but still having to be at work by 6.15 the next morning." During the winter months when she worked at Greyfriars, Friars Street, Sudbury: "the whitening would freeze as I put it on the steps and then the Brasso would freeze on the door knocker."

"At Borley Rectory," recalls Maggie Finch, (b.1904), the Rector's wife, (Mrs. Bull) would come down the stairs *backwards* to make sure that the carpet had been thoroughly brushed and dusted." In addition to her normal duties, Maggie also helped clean the now famous Church. "The cook received 2/6d extra, but, as I was the maid, I was expected to do it for God!"

Similarly at *Kentwell Hall*. Here Ann Finbow had to:

"Clean both of the kitchens, all the utensils and 'range' and then scrub the long wooden passage to the side door – and as for the stone steps outside – yes they were my responsibility as well!"

"Did you also have to help with the washing up?"

"No! I didn't help with the washing up – I DID ALL the rotten awful washing up – and then helped prepare vegetables! I must have washed thousands – hundreds of thousands of knives, forks, plates – and I didn't break a single dish!"*

Yet however obliging and willing, the staff were still very much treated as...servants.

Kentwell Hall, (Long Melford). On summer weekends the property has now become the venue for a fascinating exploration and re-enactment of Tudor life.

* As Ann is keen to point out: "All we had was hot water, washing soda and soft soap. And there were all the copper pans, saucepans and moulds to do as well. The moulds were for fish, jellies, pies and so forth and had to be cleaned with salt, silver-sand and vinegar."

"Oh no. They didn't worry how much they grumbled at you" exclaimed one source. "They knew that if you left, they could always get someone else". As Gertie Coe put it, "No one ever dared answer back – if they did, well, they'd never have got another job."

"Some of them held you down," recalled another contributor, "almost for the sake of it. Like if you'd forgotten to put out a handkerchief or something small, they'd still press the bell and make you come and do it – just to show you up."

But despite the invariable reservations, there was – equally – a recurring comment, summed up by Rose Chatters: "When we were 'in service' we learnt to turn our hands to anything. I've reaped the benefit since." Gestingthorpe's Daisy Nice, reiterated what was possibly a paramount thought:

"Everyone reckoned," she recalled, "that girls who had been 'in service' made better wives than those who had been in shops and factories." (No! I don't want 150 angry letters on this subject!). Ida Bird continues the theme:

"After I left school I spent a few months helping my grandmother and then went to *Gentry's Farm*, Little Henny, as a maid for a farmer, Eddie Nott. There was only the housekeeper there apart from myself, and so I used to prepare all the vegetables, light the fires, clean the house and maybe do a little cooking... if you had a good housekeeper you'd get a really good 'grounding', and later on start to 'climb the ladder'.

"Were there any men to do the heavier work?"

"Usually. At Wickham St. Pauls Rectory where I worked later on, there was a gardener/coachman, who had a lad to help him. It was their job to bring in coal and wood and to pump up the drinking water and so forth."

Many male contributors recalled their own days of being the 'backhus boy' at a local farm or 'big house'.

"Even when you were still at school you tried to get a back-hus job of some sort" states Sudbury's George Cresswell. "When I was eleven I did my very first job in Station Road."

157

At Gestingthorpe Rectory, 'Rover' Finch became a full time 'back-hus boy' after leaving school – and earned three shillings a week, whilst farmworker Ernie Lott (b.1899) describes his own days of being 'in service' at Henny Ryes for the Barnardistan family.

"It was my job to clean the boots, polish the cutlery, chop the wood, get the coal in and generally run any errands. After ten o'clock, however, I had to work outside in the garden."

This itself provides an amusing memory:

"When we cut the lawns we had a donkey to pull the lawnmower. My father drove it and I led it in front. It had leather pads on its feet to stop it cutting the lawn up. But it could be a stubborn old devil! It would stop and be as awkward as anything in front of the windows – where we couldn't hit it; but it was jolly well nimble enough when we went to catch it on 'the meadow'!"

Inevitably, the workings of the 'indoor' and 'outdoor' members of the household provided other opportunities for amusement.

"At Borley Rectory," remembers Maggie Finch, "we had to go into the study at about 8.30 whilst Reverend Bull read from the Bible and said prayers. But the gardener would look through the window and pull funny faces and try to make us laugh, whilst we knelt beside the chairs!"

Another memory concerns timeliness... It was always expected – but not always adhered to – as one time Gestingthorpe bellringer, Reg Rippingale tells of the nineteen twenties:

"Although Mrs. Oates always expected everyone to be punctual for her, she was often a little bit late arriving for morning service – so if we were ringing the bells, we just had to keep on ringing them – until she finally arrived!"

Yet although the aristocracy enforced their position, there were also examples of genuine thoughtfulness – and irony. We leave this chapter with a story, recently repeated by the Rev. Trevor Howard, and which comes from *Belchamp Walter Hall*:

"In the late nineteenth century the butler – a man named

158

Pannell, attempted to join the full time ministry. Unfortunately, he wasn't accepted for the clergy in England – where it was still largely the preserve of gentle folk – so his employers, the Raymond family, 'enabled' him to travel to America where he was not only ordained – but after many years, became a Bishop.

"In the fullness of time he returned to England and visited *Belchamp Hall*. Here he had tea with Mr. and Mrs. Raymond in the same room where he had previously served it. However, when he made his departure, he momentarily slipped back into the terminology of his 'service position' calling Mrs. Raymond 'My Lady'.

"'Ah,' she replied quickly 'in those days you had to call me 'My Lady'. But now – you are a Bishop. And it is I who must call you – 'My Lord!'"

✤ ✤ ✤ ✤ ✤

Chapter Fifteen

BUTLERS AND ICE HOUSES
Behind the Scenes

"When Sir Connup Guthrie lived at Kentwell Hall there was a dazzling assortment of winter dances, hunt balls, shoots, summer balls and garden parties. Sometimes Mr. Purnell – the butler – would allow me to go up to the gallery and peep through the door and look at the beautiful gowns and gorgeous ball dresses. For an unsophisticated country girl from Bulmer it was just overwhelming – enchanting! Compared with what I'd been used to, the wonderment of it was just indescribable.And no – it's strange, but I was never jealous or affronted by it. And the reason was that the housekeeper, Mrs. Clarke was so very, very good to me – and so considerate to my parents. How ever hard the work, I always knew she cared."

Ann Finbow, (now of Cavendish)

We have written of the 'odd man', the 'backhus' boy and the gardener, but what of the most august of male servants – the butler?

It is time to return to *Gosfield Hall*, whose final butler, Horace Reeve, latterly lived in Gestingthorpe.

I must confess however that I found the idea of visiting him a little daunting. Thinking of the self-righteous 'Hudson' in *Upstairs, Downstairs*, I did not particularly expect to enjoy my evening.

In fact, as I drove past Gestingthorpe Church to his low-beamed cottage I consciously prepared myself for several hours of smug pomposity. There was only one thing that puzzled me. For Butler Reeve had married third housemaid, Evelyn Cornell...sister of practical joker and arch rural humorist, Jack Cornell...

Parking on the grass verge opposite *Moat Farm* I walked across and knocked on the door.

"Come on in, Ashley," called Evelyn. Stooping slightly, I entered and was introduced to a fine-built, dark-haired man in his early eighties.

"Pleased to meet you, sir," he rumbled warmly. After we sat down and he nestled a delightful Dachshund on his lap, and I seriously – and a little deferentially – explained my mission.

"When and where were you born?" I asked, trying to 'cross off' my routine questions.

"Nineteen hundred and two. At Stanton, near Bury St. Edmunds."

There was a pause as I opened my notepad, took the cap off my Biro and began to write down the details. In the interim, Horace continued with a few remarks about his early life. For the next two hours I didn't stop writing and when I did, it was to wipe away the tears from my eyes and to feel almost ill – from laughter.

He told me firstly of his early life. Of the schoolboy prank when he and Jeff Baker had put a wet bag on top of the butcher's chimney at Stanton – resulting in the shop being completely smoked out. He continued by telling of his dreadful mischief after being coerced into the Stanton Choir – of cutting the cord off the organ pump to terminate the practice night. ("I was soon turfed out; but I didn't cry much over that"). And he described also how his father, (a harness maker), had made a goat cart for him to ride about in, but how too, the goat had been induced to butt their neighbour's 'posterior' as he bent over his garden. "Oh dear! I was wholly jawed at! I got in the wrong for that."

At the age of thirteen the irrepressible practical joker (and I began to realise why he was Evelyn's husband and Jack Cornell's brother-in-law!) left school and became a page-boy for Sir Walter Green at *Nether Hall*, Pakenham.

Here he was given a special uniform – with a cockade in his hat – in which he would ride on the top of a horse-drawn carriage to Society Balls at the Bury St. Edmunds *Athenaeum* or *Angel*. Then:

"after jumping off and opening the doors, helping everyone out and being 'generally available', we servants would be given a

161

supper of our own and enjoy ourselves as we waited for the function to end."

In time Horace found a position as an under-footman, before coming to *Gosfield Hall* as 'Head Footman' in 1919, eventually being appointed Butler a few years later.

When he arrived, the proprietor, Mrs. Lowe, was already a frail invalid of 75 and the 'great' days of the mansion with its gracious living and spectacular socialising were over. Mrs. Lowe lived another twenty years and Horace remained until her son Willoughby passed away during the Second World War. Yet despite the quiet phase in the house's history, the full regalia of pomp and service was still minutely adhered to.

The servants 'calling bells' Horace learnt, were rung once, twice or three times, depending upon whom was required. The butler and head housekeeper ate their meals separately from the other servants, and the butler officiously inspected the footman's hair – to ensure it was neat and tidy. As Head Footman, Horace's uniform was, "a blue double-breasted tail coat with a short front and brass buttons", whilst as butler, he had to change his suit three times a day finally serving dinner , "in tails with a white bow tie". Yet irrespective of it all, his good humour and impish sense of fun, could not be restrained.

"On one occasion," he recalls, "Doctor Harrison from Braintree was staying at the Hall. Now, I enjoyed fishing and one morning, I got up at 4 o'clock and went to the lake and caught a pike. When I came back about 8 o'clock I was met by this doctor, who asked me if he could have the pike – to take home. Well, I didn't have much option did I? But I thought to myself, 'You wait, I'll suck him in for this'.

"Now as I was washing it down, I chanced to press the pike's back with my hand – and its mouth opened up to a huge size. Just then I spied an *Adams Ginger Beer* bottle... Well you know what I did, don't you! Course, eventually the Doctor's cook opened up the pike...discovered the bottle inside and told Dr. Harrison. And he was so astonished that he wrote a very serious letter to the local newspaper! ...'Anatomical prowess of a pike' or some such thing!".

But it wasn't only fish that provided opportunity for entertainment.

"While I was there, the vicar became interested in rare birds.

Now one of his special birds was a parrot. But occasionally this parrot would get away and then the parson would get on the phone and worry us all silly. Well we got fed up with this, so one day after he'd rung up yet again, I said to Eric Swan (the Head Footman), 'I reckon we could 'help' this chap...' Anyway, upstairs there was a glass cabinet full of stuffed birds. Course, you can guess what we done can't you! Put a stuffed parrot on top of a fir tree just outside the Hall!

Then I rang up the vicar and told him the 'good news'.

'Well done!' he said, 'I'll come across right-away.'

But the best thing was this. It was just getting dark – so he really was convinced that it was his bird! So, he got it some bread and nuts – and kept talking to it – and then asked us to keep watch.

Next morning, he came back again, full of expectation, but during the night, it had mysteriously 'flown away'.

'I'm sorry,' I said, 'I don't know what's happened to your pet parrot. We kept our eyes open – didn't we Eric – but it must have gone away during the night.'

'What a pity. But thank you for trying,' he said, as he slipped us half a crown each... Oh dear, we had some fun and games in that old house!"*

As Evelyn plied us with scones, mince pies, Cherry and Christmas cake, the memories continued:

"I remember one time, when Mrs. Lowe was ill and we were all in the room next door. We often had to hang about like that – sometimes for hours on end – because if she wanted moving, four of us had to carry her on a litter. Anyway, I was cutting the hair of one of the other Footmen, when she suddenly rang the bell. Course, we all sprang into action. But this chap jumped up whilst I was holding the hairclippers and a big tuft of hair came out of the back of his head. Cor, he looked painful! As we went into her room, Mrs. Lowe rasped out, 'I say! I do believe you've got ringworm!' We had a DEVIL of a job not to laugh!"

"Whatever did the other servants make of you when you first arrived at Gosfield?"

"I don't know. It was a long while ago. But I do remember two

* As Edith Hurry commented, "Oh dear, Ashley. If you've been to see Horace you must have had some laughs!"

163

old kitchen maids. You see, every afternoon they used to sit down in the servants hall, throw their aprons over their faces and have a cat-nap. Now in those days women wore those great big, laced-up working boots. But one time, when they were both fast asleep, I was 'egged on' by the other servants. So you know what I did, don't you? I crept up and tied their bootlaces together. Then I got behind a door and crashed an old tin tray on a radiator. Cor! They wholly jumped! ...And being as they were tied together, they fell right over – onto the floor! They didn't half curse! Needless to say, having done it once, we thought we would do it again. That's how luck goes though. They found me out next time.And I got a rare dose of their tongue!"

They weren't the only ladies to have jokes played on them. For as Evelyn who arrived 19 years later recalls:

"I was just 15 when I started at *Gosfield Hall*. About my third night there, I had to walk along the 'Statue Hall' on some errand. Oh, that was a creepy old place. It had a long row of those big marble statues and just a couple of gas lamps in the entire passage. There were more shadows than light! I was petrified. Then I thought, 'I bet there's someone hiding somewhere'. There was, as well. Guess who!"

A few days later, another 'induction' took place in the library.

"The others had told me about the secret door, which looked just like several shelves of books, but then they tiptoed out and locked the proper door! So there I was, searching around all these books and making a proper fool of myself, whilst they watched me through the window! Weren't they awful!

It would be easy whilst reading the memories of Horace, Evelyn and Edith, to think that being 'in service' was unmitigated fun – almost reminiscent of a tale by P. G. Wodehouse.

Obviously it wasn't. The frustration caused by the limited free hours, the resentment felt after an unnecessary reprimand and the meagre remuneration must have created a rankling grievance. And yet, as with so much from that era, the corrective balance – the soothing tranquilliser – came from within. It came from the humour, the practical joking, the dry ironies and the amiable leg-pulling that is the oil of life, wherever people are together in a common situation.

At some 'Big Houses', humour – or at least cheerful acceptance was needed in the winter. Ann Finbow continues:

"I slept in the top of the left-hand tower at *Kentwell Hall*, and shared a room with the nursery maid and house maid. But it was freezing up there in the morning. There were icicles <u>inside</u> the window!"

In the master's quarters at least, the 'big houses' were often pioneers in the use of both gas and electricity. Edith Hurry elaborates of Gosfield:

"There was a gas plant at the back of the stables with a gasometer and a 'gas man' who filled the retorts with coal and so forth. The gasometer would slowly go down and then about twice a day you'd see smoke coming out of the chimney as he made some more."

At Belchamp Otten Rectory:

"They made the gas from carbide," recalls Rose Chatters, "but when I was first there I didn't know what this thing in the garden was. 'Course, I went wandering over to look at it with a naked light. I really did get a 'telling off' for that!"*

It was not only gas and electricity which were not on the mains. Neither was water.

At Gosfield it was pumped up by two horses on a circular horse-works, whilst in less grand houses it was done manually. Yet local underground water is notoriously hard.

"And so at Wickham Rectory," explains Ida Bird, "all the 'soft' rainwater from the rooves was channelled into a special tank – beneath the kitchen – and every day the 'backhus' boy would pump it up into the 'washing tank' whilst the hard water from the well (which was used for drinking and cooking) went into another".

Another requisite was ice. Many mansions such as *Culford Hall*, *Belchamp Hall* and *The Auberies* at Bulmer, cut ice from the ponds during winter and then stored it in subterranean 'ice houses' – which were insulated with wide, thatched, cavity walls.† Latterly, others had it delivered when required.

"We obtained our ice," says Long Melford butcher Freddie Ruse, "in half hundred weight blocks from the Colchester Ice Factory on a lorry covered with tarpaulins. As a lad however, it was my job to deliver it – by bicycle – up to *Kentwell Hall*. I remember one Saturday afternoon though. I was anxious to get done and I went pedalling up that drive flat out. Oh dear...flat out! I hit one of those

---

* At Kentwell Hall Mrs. Phillips explains that the carbide plant was actually used until the late 1960's when there were still only two rooms with electricity. (The carbide was obtained through Dixon and Scott of Sudbury). Interestingly some underfloor heating was installed in 1827. A boiler was positioned in the cellar and steam was circulated in large iron pipes.

† Peter Minter says that the ice houses were about 12 to 15 feet square; ten feet beneath the ground with a dome over the surface. The walls were up to four feet wide whilst the ice, he believes, would last for up to twelve months.
    Freddie Ruse relates of the Melford Hall ice house:
    "It was made like a well and the staff could climb down into a fair-sized 'cool' room at the bottom".

166

huge tree roots and tipped the whole lot out. Then I had to go back and arrange to get some more... That was my Saturday afternoon!"

These then were our 'Big Houses' of which *Gosfield Hall* was the epitome. As such, it was almost totally self contained, with its own laundry, gas plant, dairy, vegetable garden and farm. It had its own builders, carpenters, plumbers and estate workshops; it was a community – like a luxury liner at sea – from which only occasional excursions were allowed and from which contact with the 'outer world' was maintained – but once a day – when Len Hurry took a pony and trap to Halstead to collect the newspapers and mail.

In its heyday the Big House was the centre – 'the jewel in the crown' of the village – around which the smaller planets of farm and school and cottage revolved. It was, the Buckingham Palace of parish life.

✣ ✣ ✣ ✣ ✣

And finally there is a happy – if surprising twist to this chapter. It concerns Ann Finbow, the lowly scullery maid at *Kentwell Hall*, who for two years had daily scrubbed the long stone passages and washed up "thousands – no hundreds of thousands, of knives, forks and plates – AND all the other utensils they used in the household's cooking!"

For just over half a century later, Ann was to return. Much had happened in the interval. She had been married, raised a family, become a senior Social Worker and attended a course at Trinity College, Cambridge. Some years later she had been widowed. And the reason she returned? On 20th December, 1986 she re-married. And KENTWELL HALL was hired for the reception...

"It made me feel so happy, it made me laugh, I wanted to cry with joy! I had never ever been there before – except as a scullery maid. But now! Oh yes, I really did 'sweep in – where once I'd swept out!'"

✣ ✣ ✣ ✣ ✣

Chapter Sixteen

PUBLIC HOUSES RESEARCHED
An Evening with Jack Cornell

"I went to a harvest horkey at the Wethersfield 'Dog' when I was a lad... You see those days, once harvest was done, the head man on the farm would go round to the harness maker, the miller, the blacksmith and the wheelwright, and ask for a donation – or 'largesse' as he called it – and he'd get a shilling here and a shilling there, and then we'd have this meal in the middle of the day and drink beer in the afternoon and sing songs in the evening."

Jack Wallace (1894-1986)

At the Easter Quarter Sessions of 1628 one Frances Cornhill of Gestingthorpe was, "charged with keeping an alehouse without a licence." She was by no means alone for "in Elizabethan Sudbury," states Edith Freeman, "TWENTY EIGHT alehouses were suppressed in one go!"

Indeed in 1577 (the middle of Queen Elizabeth's reign) there was approximately one alehouse in England for every 144 inhabitants. By 1700 however the ratio had dropped to one for just eighty seven people.*

---

* By comparison, in 1935 there was one public house for every 719 inhabitants. From *The English Alehouse – A Social History 1200-1830* (Published by Longmans). In considering the statistics, we should remember that 'clean' water was not easily available in many towns, (because of the effluents from dyers, tanners and animals that contaminated the water-courses). 'Second beer' was often the labourer's only drink.

168

From 1769 it becomes comparatively straightforward to trace the development of hostelries in Essex – for a register of licences is preserved at Chelmsford Record Office.

PUBS REGISTERED 1769 (landlords' names in brackets)

Ballingdon .... *Kings Head, White Horse* (Sarah Spink)
Birdbrook .... *Swan*
Belchamp St. Paul ... *Half Moon* (Martha Jay)
Belchamp Otten ...... *Dog* (in 1770 was recorded as *Bell*)
Bulmer .... *Cock* (John Paine)
Bures (in Essex) .... *Eight Bells, Swan*
Colne Engaine .... *Five Bells, Compasses*
Gestingthorpe .... *Compasses* (Robert Pannell)
Gosfield .... *Green Man, Kings Head*
Halstead .... 29(!) including *Old Bull* and *New Bull*
Henny .... *White Horse*
Castle Hedingham .. *Castle, Swan, Cock, Falcon, Bell, Kings Head*
Lamarsh .... *Bell, Lyon*
Little Maplestead ..... *Cock* (William Knott)
Pebmarsh .... *Kings Head*
Ridgewell .... *Kings Head*
Stisted .... *Dukes Head, Black Lion, Crown*
Toppesfield .... *Green Man*
Wethersfield .... *Red Lion, Bull, Dog, Cock*
Wickham St. Paul .... *Two Brewers* (also Sarah Spink)
Great Yeldham .... *White Hart*
White Colne .... *Red Lion*

LOCAL DETAIL

Yet if this was the situation in 1769 what of their subsequent evolution? For interest we have examined three neighbouring parishes.

At Wickham St. Pauls, Sarah Spink kept the *Two Brewers* until 1777, after which no alehouse was licensed until 1795 – when a Richard Ginn opened *The Fox*. By 1802 however, it was no longer listed and Wickham 'theoretically' remained dry until the 1830's.

Meanwhile in Bulmer another pub – in addition to the *Cock and Blackbirds* – was opened in 1783 with John Bruce registering *The Plough* (which was situated on The Tye, close to the Turnpiked road), whilst in Belchamp Walter *The Eight Bells* was first licensed in 1786 – with surety for publican Edward Digby being offered by the landlords

169

of the Belchamp St. Paul's *Half Moon* and Otten *Green Man.**
In 1830 was passed 'The Beer Act' – enabling premises to obtain 'beer only' licences. By 1848 there were legitimate beerhouses in Ashen, Ovington, Twinstead, Little Yeldham and Wickham St. Pauls, whilst at Alphamstone *The Windmill* was now 'fully' licensed with Samuel Nott as victualler.

Thirty four years later, in 1882, the Gestingthorpe *Compasses* had disappeared although the village did have four beer retailers – each with a truly local name – Henry Corder, Susan Felton, Peter Finch and Thomas Rippingale. At Bulmer Tye, the *Plough* was no longer registered although Wickham had a *Ship* and Ashen a *Red Cow*. By the end of the century John Pearson was operating a beer house in Belchamp Otten – later to be known as *The Red Lion*, whilst at Ovington, John Murkin was similarly listed at premises, to be nostalgically remembered as *The Kicking Donkey*.

By the beginning of the twentieth century the population of our local villages was falling. Agriculture and the brickfields were in decline. In turn came a reduction in licensed houses.

On 21st December 1907, the *Halstead Times* reported that *The Prince of Wales* in Belchamp Walter and the Bulmer *Greyhound* had relinquished their licences.†
Other pubs to have disappeared in more recent times include:

The Waggon & Horses: Twinstead	*The Bell:* Lt. Maplestead
The Eight Bells: Belchamp Walter	*The Rising Sun:* Sudbury
The White Horse of Kent: Gt. Maplestead	*The Angel:* Pebmarsh
The Christopher: Sudbury	*The Windmill:* Alphamstone
The Green Man: Belchamp Otten	*The Bell:* Sible Hedingham

---

* All dates have to be regarded as approximate. These outline details could well be 'honed up' with further research. Additionally, many places – like 'Bulmer Tye, doubtless had hostelries before 1769 – although none was listed there between 1769-1783.

† The *Prince of Wales* was on Chapel Hill whilst the *Greyhound* stood near to the Sudbury-Halstead road at the turn to Henny – near *Gentry's Farm*. The Gestingthorpe *Compasses* was situated close to *Moat Farm*, on the Hedingham road.

Additionally there were numerous village 'off licences' of which Evelyn Reeve – who kept an 'off licence' in Gestingthorpe's Moat Street – wryly explains:

"'Officially', no one was allowed to drink inside the premises of an 'off licence'," then she pauses, "...course you can imagine thirsty farmworkers obeying that law down a remote country lane, can't you!"

But our final comment – on the number of hostelries – comes from Sudbury's Edith Freeman:

"At one time," she laughs, "there were so many pubs and ale-houses in Ballingdon that it was said, 'if you fell out of one – you'd fall straight into another!'"...Today only the *Kings Head* remains.

As recorded one of those to disappear is *The Bell* at Sible Hedingham. It is particularly sad since the inn held a singular record. The licence was held by one person – a lady – Rose Harrington – for no less than SIXTY SIX years! (from 1894 until she died in 1960).
Throughout much of this time however Rose had been assisted by her daughter Lily (b.1911). Today the latter vividly recalls the vibrant hostelry of her youth with its stabling facilities, guest rooms, and:

"sales 'reps' who would arrive from London on the train, and then stay for a few days whilst they travelled round in a pony and trap."

Later she described the atmosphere of the public bar.

"The humour of some of the customers was just out of this world! And believe it or not, I never-ever-closed. Not one single night of the year! There were at least half a dozen of the customers for whom *The Bell* was their 'home' on Christmas evening. I never even thought about closing. And you know, there were other occasions when people would come in, full of trouble and worry and just pour themselves out to you."

Now we go to the Bulmer *Cock and Blackbirds.** We will imagine it is the early nineteen thirties; for from 1920-36 the landlord was one John Cornell. Do I really need say more? We are once again with his son Jack (b.1918) whose enthusiasm, interest and humour has inspired so much of this research.

"I remember one time in the *Blackbirds*. This pompous old farmer came stumping in and chancing to see his shepherd said, smarmy-like 'What'll you have then? Beer? Whisky?' You can guess the reply can't you. 'Huh,' say the old shepherd. 'Seeing as it is you then... Both!'"

After leaving Bulmer, Jack moved to a small-holding at Little Maplestead. It was here, just after 8.30 one February evening that my investigation continued.

"Father took the *Blackbirds* in 1920. Course, the layout was different then; so for that matter was the type of mugs that they drank from. When Father started they were all pottery mugs – platter mugs I think they called them – trouble was that when you were serving you couldn't see when the damn things were full! In fact I can clearly remember my father buying the glasses – and all the old men saying that the beer didn't taste right!"

"Did you do any food?"

"Not really. Mother might make up a bit of cheese and pickles if someone specially wanted something, but it wasn't a regular thing like today. You see food was perishable in those days and you couldn't keep a supply on the 'off chance'. There were occasional dinners though. Lacy Scott, the estate agents, who managed Belchamp Hall, used to give one for the farmworkers instead of a horkey; and there might also have been one for the Football Club. But there wasn't a lot of it done. Still, I expect it brought in a few more shillings."

As the conversation continued, I observed that many landlords in remoter villages now depend on a second income to make ends meet.

* The pub's famous weathervane (as described on page 162 of *The Khyber Connection*) is still there for all to see. Further along Bulmer Street there is some fascinating architecture – note especially the lovely detail on the brick Chapel.

"At least in your father's day," I said knowingly, "there was enough local trade to make a village pub pay."*

"Tain't so likely!" came Jack's swift retort.

"Really?" I replied – slipping another cassette into my tape recorder.

"I mean, there might have been in the towns and beside the main roads, but no; a village pub has never been a full time living. I'll tell you this. When Dad kept the *Blackbirds*, he would go biking off to his threshing tackle at six o'clock in the morning, do a full days work and then keep the pub until 10 o'clock at night. No, there was nothing in a pub if you didn't enjoy doing it. I reckon he just about got enough to pay his rent and rates and perhaps a bob or two on top – but not a great sight more. He'd have been a long while getting very rich without the threshing!"

"And most other small village pubs were the same?"

"Oh yes. Some publicans ran brickyards; others did black-smithing – one or two of 'em might have had a windmill⁵ and a lot of 'em would do an odd days threshing or something of that sort. Tom Mansfield at the Otten *Windmill* was a regular helper when we worked over there."

"In the last twenty years," I commented seriously, "the Belchamp, Gestingthorpe and Bulmer pubs have all changed hands about once every six years. Was it the same when you were young?"

"No. People used to stay in pubs for years and years and often keep it in a family for generations. Things were different in those days; it really was something to have a good roof over your head and most of the 'brewery houses' were well kept up."†(see page 174)

"But you had a good regular trade in those days?"

"I don't think it was much different from now. In the winter a

* At Alphamstone for example, Samuel Nott is recorded as being the landlord of the *Windmill* public house in 1840, whilst also owning the village's corn windmill. (From *White's Directory* and also *Essex Windmills* Vol. 3, by Ken Farries).

village pub would be almost deserted on weekday nights. Apart from a couple or three in the 'tap room' there was hardly any trade at all. Course, Friday and Saturday nights were much more lively".

"What was the 'tap room'?"

"IT WAS THE BEST PLACE IN THE WHOLE BLOOMIN' PUB! Least that's where we had the most fun. If you were coming home straight from work, it is where you could go, without taking off all of your 'clobber' and hob-nailed boots. It was only a small room with a wooden floor and wooden forms along the sides where you could sit."

The sparse furnishings led to an amusing memory:

"Makes you laugh to think of it though, but on a Sunday night in the tap room, Uncle Harry Rowe would cut some 'bacca' up with a shut knife and there would be him and two or three old men with these 'ere clay pipes on the go! Well, talk about the smoke! It was enough to cackle you! You could hardly see from one side to the other. God alive!! You didn't ever need to fumigate it!"

Observing that there seemed to have been more different rooms in a pub years ago, (at the Blackbirds there was a 'tap' room, public bar, smoking room and club room or lounge), Jack provided the following explanation – as the hands of his mantelpiece clock touched 10.15.

---

† Jack believes that the Pearson family were at Belchamp Otten *Green Man* for three generations, whilst, "at Bulmer *Fox* the landlord, ol' Foster had been there – well – for all living memory!"

Similarly in *A Pictorial History of Sible Hedingham* Adrian Corder-Birch reveals that; "At the *Half Moon*, the landlords were successive members of the Finch family. Arthur Finch held the licence for more than sixty years, taking it over when he was only twenty and retaining it until his death in 1938 at the age of 81 – being then followed by his son, for another twenty years until itsclosure in 1958."

In Sudbury, the Scillitoe family kept the *Ship and Star* for over 120 years, whilst another 'great' family of local publicans were the Weybrews. A Roger Weybrew was at the Bulmer *Cock* in 1790, then in the nineteenth century, Ann, and later Sarah Weybrew, kept the Gestingthorpe *Compasses* until at least 1848. In 1882 a James Weybrew kept a beerhouse in Greenstead Green whilst a Woodford Weybrew kept the Sible Hedingham *Sugar Loaves*.

"There was a lot more class distinction amongst working people in those days.* A head gardener, or the head carpenter or Hayes the ex-policeman, would sit by themselves in the 'smoking room' *all night long* rather than mix up with the others; and the gamekeeper was a bit the same. He couldn't abide anyone knowing where he was! AND AS FOR WOMEN!

"It was *unheard of* to take a girl into the tap room or public bar! It was very, very unusual to see a woman in a pub at all, and if someone's wife came in, she would sit by herself in the lounge with only Mother to talk to. But the War changed all that.

"I think the men liked to 'let off steam' and be a bit boisterous and of course, other things were different. I mean, in those days, no-one would ever swear in front of a woman – so I think they felt it would put 'the damper' on things if women came in.

"It would have been the height of scandal if a girl went into a pub – even though it was quite acceptable for a woman to run one. It is curious really – because I very much doubt whether mother had ever been in a pub before she became a landlady!"†

Despite what today would appear to be a singular lack of female company, many older contributors reminisced nostalgically of, 'some of the good ol' times we had at the pub in the hard ol' days before the Second World War'.

Many recall the sing-songs; accompanied by an accordion which was usually the only instrument – and which an intriguing number of people could play. Not surprisingly, at a time when farmworkers had no annual holidays, the 'bank holiday' evenings such as Easter or Whit Monday, were particularly memorable and both the singing and all-male company suggests something of a 'stag night' or rugby club

* As David Tuffin says of the Henny *Swan*: "My father was a rare clever man at 'pitch penny' – which they did in the 'tap room'. But by rights – being as he was a 'tradesman' – he shouldn't really have gone in the 'tap room'."

† Despite the attitudes concerning women visiting pubs, the list of those who ran them is legion. From Lily and Rose Harrington of the Sible Hedingham *Bell* to Sarah Spink of the Wickham *Two Brewers* or Frances Cornhill of Gestingthorpe the impression emerges that possibly half our local pubs were either run – or assisted by women who were on their own for much of the time. Perhaps the most famous of all is Martha Blewitt, landlady of the Birdbrook *Swan*, who had nine husbands before dying in 1681.

atmosphere.*

But apart from the raucous singing there were also the more moderate pub games which brought a little amusement at the end of a hard day's work.

As usual however, my ignorance was soon manifest.

"I expect the old men sat by the fire and played dominoes and there would be a dart board, but what about the other traditional games?" I asked.

"What's all this about a dart board?" demanded Jack.

"Surely they had darts...?"

"Not that I know of! In fact, before 1924 we'd never heard of darts. And I can well remember the first dart board we ever had. It was made of elm and every night it had to be soaked in water. Later on there were others which had something like plasticine on top – and every evening they had to be rolled flat again."

But Jack is not alone in remembering the introduction of darts. As Bert Surridge of Gestingthorpe explains:

"Our first elm board only had scores of five, ten, fifteen and twenty on it. Eventually however, we got a cork one, but then it got that we weren't allowed to play on Sundays. In fact we weren't allowed to play cards or dominoes on Sundays either. Imagine that! What's worse, our blessed police sergeant used to come into the *Red Lion* to check up. Course you know what we did don't you? – Went and played out the back instead!"

Other pub games which Bert recalls playing in what is now *The Pheasant*, include, skittles, shove ha'penny, spin a penny, and 'ringing the bull'. Of the latter he recalls:

"You played the best out of twenty one throws; Dick Finch and I could often get 21, but a lot of the others only got 3 or 4. The secret

* The need for 'men to be men' and let off steam is particularly understandable when we remember the desperately overcrowded conditions in which people lived.

176

was to have the ringle returned to you the same side up as it landed on the hook – otherwise the string got twisted."

All local pubs provided improvised versions of these 'fete' type games.

"At the Belchamp *Cherry Tree*," reminisces Jute Chatters, "there were table skittles. But we also played 'nicky brick' – or 'spin a penny'... The head place for that was the Otten *Windmill* because there were a lot of little bricks in the floor. You see to 'score' the penny had to stop spinning and land on a joint".

Similarly, there was 'pitch penny' – which was played at the Alphamstone *Windmill*.

"There was a hole about the size of a milk bottle top," explains Eddie Tuffin, "which was bored through the wooden form which went round the tap-room walls. You'd stand on the other side of the room and try to pitch a penny or a halfpenny through it. You generally played the best of nine throws. Oh dammit yes! Some of these old men could pitch them in just anyhow."

In some pubs (such as the *Saracens Head* at Newton, Belchamp *Bells* and possibly Otten *Windmill*) there was even a little box to catch the coins in. At Long Melford there was a 'skittles alley' beside the *Black Lion* and outdoor quoits at *The Hare*. By comparison Lily Harrington spoke of the less usual snooker table, bagatelle and two-rinked bowling green at the Sible Hedingham *Bell*.

Yet amidst these refinements we should not forget the ubiquitous shove ha'penny for which some pubs had tables marked out – whilst in others there was a 'proper board'.

"But as the board filled up," explained Jack Cornell, as his clock chimed eleven-thirty, "one of your mates would say dreamily, 'I want my coin to stop about there' and then place his finger on the spot. Well, if he was a crafty old codger like ———, he'd have licked it first to make the coin 'stick' when it got there. Then you'd hear shouts of 'HOLD YOU! Bring out the duster!! Dirty old cheat!' Course, the other thing was to very slightly jog the table. Oh yes, there were all manner of capers!"

Yet for those who laboured in the drudgery of digging clay for the local brick-yards, or trudging over puggy fields with horse and corn-drill these simple games were the SINGLE moment of distraction from the endless grind of daily work. The grim reality is, that in an age of six days work each week, and holidays unheard of, no other recreations actually existed.

Yet if I thought my enquiry into local public houses was almost over, I was soon reminded of its incompleteness. For as I rose to leave Jack's sitting room – with the time approaching midnight – he thoughtfully observed, "'Course, we ain't said much about local breweries yet."

Historically all alehouses brewed their own beer; as such it was truly, 'Of the Furrow Born'.* In the Hedinghams and Maplesteads, hops were grown until at least the eighteen fifties and in 1848, a James Rippingale of Gestingthorpe, was still listed as a 'beer retailer and hop merchant'. (As already noted, in earlier years a Hop Fair – or market – was held by local growers at the Castle Hedingham *Bell*). Even today, wild hops can be seen growing on the 'stays' of telephone poles in local villages whilst there are occasional remains of oast-houses in the Maplestead/Hedingham area. Meanwhile in Sudbury, at least ten maltings were operating in the eighteen nineties and during the nineteenth century, 'at least forty licensed houses brewed their own beer'. (From Grimwood & Kay's *History of Sudbury*).

How inspiring it is to think of those earlier times when both the barley for the malt, the hops for the flavouring and the water for the liquid came from within sight of the very public houses where the beer was eventually consumed. But who then actually drank it?

Why, the same steady men who had 'dibbled in' the barley seed and later scythed and shocked and threshed and flailed the ripened grain. And with them – as they drank – were their friends and neighbours who had picked the hops or done the malting of that truly local beer.

* However, as early as 1700, one third of publicans did not brew their own beer. By the 1820's the figure was less than half – although in Suffolk there were still about 200 brewers. (From *A Directory of Nineteenth and Twentieth Century Suffolk Brewers* by C. R. Bristow, Salient Press, County Hall, Ipswich 1985).

Wild Hops. Although imported during the previous century, they were not cultivated in England until about 1524. Their addition produced a more refined drink called beer. By the late sixteenth century, beer had completely replaced ale – 'which often had a thicker consistency like soup'. Today's 'ale' is only a name and bears no resemblance to traditional ale. (From *The English Alehouse – A Social History 1200-1830*, by Peter Clarke, published by Longmans 1983).

LOCAL DETAIL

Of especial significance are OLIVERS of Sudbury, who brewed on the Cornard Road and had a maltings near today's bus station*, WARDS of Foxearth who, we believe, employed upwards of 50 people and supplied around 40 pubs from that isolated village; MAULDONS of Ballingdon whose earlier premises still remain (almost opposite Ballingdon Post Office) and whose traditional 'real ale' was revived after an absence of some twenty four years in 1982.

In Halstead there were ADAMS and COOKS – the latter still continuing, although never having pubs of their own, whilst further afield were THOMAS DANIELS of West Bergholt and GOSLINGS of Braintree and Wethersfield.

However not all is historic. Following the resurrection of Mauldons, another local firm – the Nethergate Brewery of Clare – began production in 1986 committed to, "real ales containing all malt

* The chimney of an oast house or maltings can still be seen nearby.

and no artificial flavouring."

Neither have all the old brewery names have been entirely expunged. For at Edwardstone in Suffolk – and tenaciously emblazoned on the outside wall of the village's *White Horse*, is the historic proclamation:

OLIVER BROS:
FINE ALES AND STOUT

(Happily MAULDONS name is also preserved – in the frosted windows of the Sudbury *Angel*.)

Yet even when the 'Olivers' or 'Mauldons' beer had been skilfully brewed and safely delivered, the weight of the barrels could still cause problems:

"Talk of a struggle," laughs Jack, as I stand in the door of his kitchen 'well after midnight'. "At the *Blackbirds* we had to push those eighteen gallon barrels UP a five foot ladder from the cellar and then over six or seven steps to the bar. They must have weighed at least 180lb (80kg)... well, you jolly well wanted a pint or two time you'd done that sort of work!"

"What about la..." I was just about to ask.
"What about what?"
"Lager?" I suggested contritely.
"Never been heard of. Not that time of day. And precious few shorts were ever drunk because no-one could ever afford them."

✣ ✣ ✣ ✣ ✣

Others also recall our erstwhile village pubs – with their oil lamps, smoke-stained, yellowy-brown walls and customers who would have been related or known to each other from childhood.

From Belchamp Otten it is the memory of, "farmworkers calling in at *The Red Lion* for a pint of 'second beer' as they trudged to work at half past six in the morning".* At the *Cherry Tree*, it was the spellbinding sight of Joby Cutmore, "step dancing on two bricks" – to a mouth organ or accordion and the reminder that, "if anyone came in who

* The Sible Hedingham *Bell* and Cavendish *George* were similarly open at 6.30 am.

180

could play the piano – well – then you were well away!" Of the Alphamstone *Windmill* Frank Turner declares:

"It was a smashing place. We had some wonderful times there. 'Course it was only a tap room and lounge but it was very popular and at weekends, crowded... But I do remember one old man though. He was a queer hawk! You see he didn't like to be beat by anyone. Well one year he had a really long Runner Bean... But the next night a farmworker brought one in that was even longer... He went nearly scatty!!"

Tom Gilbert of Little Yeldham recalls *The Stone and Faggot*:

"The landlord would buy a box of 'bloaters' (dried-salted herrings) off my father, scatter them on the fire and then say 'help yourself boys!' And those herrings were salty as well. Oh yes! He knew they always pushed up beer sales!"

At Little Maplestead, Cecil Cook described the 'old' *Cock* public house:

"It was a long, low building with a rail in front for people to tie their horses to. And then at mid-day, farmworkers would come into the tap room with half a loaf of bread and a quarter of a pound of cheese and have a pint or two of beer and that would be their dinner."

But there was one particularly memorable customer:

"The person I shall never forget is old Henry Cook. He had lost *both* his hands in farming accidents – one in a reaping machine – the other in a chaff cutter. However he had had hooks fitted to his arms (hence his nick-name 'Hooky' Cook), and despite his disabilities could still do a full day's work – using a pitch fork with a leather loop on it. But he'd also mastered the knack of drinking a pint of beer – because he'd pick the glass up with his teeth. In fact in *The Cock*, strangers would buy him a pint just to see him do it!"

Meanwhile the Twinstead *Waggon and Horses* was kept by the Harding-Paynes for some forty seven years. Intriguingly, the adjoining building was originally used by a 'pig killer and sausage skin maker'. As son George sardonically commented: "Country life was different years ago."

From Twinstead to Gestingthorpe. Here in 1918 the *Red Lion* was advertised as having "stabling for four horses and an excellent supply of drinking water." And if beer drinkers are amused at the 'supply of water', it does emphasise its importance for horses. Indeed as Bert Surridge explains: "That time of day pubs like *The Lion* often hired out horses and wagonettes."

Quite possibly a wagonette was hired to visit Sudbury in July 1872. For 'Blondin' the legendary tightrope walker performed that month in the *Anchor* yard. Half a century later the *Royal Oak* was proudly boasting:

"Exclusive sparkling ales, comfortable lounge and a WIRELESS CONCERT NIGHTLY." (July, 1924)

Yet despite the temptation to trivialise, we should never forget: the hostelries have been a cornerstone of local life. They have been, through many centuries, a meeting point for strangers; a forum for relaxation; an environ for making friends; a refuge for the sharing of anxieties and a catalyst for therapeutic humour.

At the larger inns stage coaches stopped on their journeys to and from the capital.

From Sudbury in 1844, there were two departures to London each day from both the *Rose and Crown* and *Swan*, and another from the *Christopher*. The *Black Boy* was the venue for a daily coach to Bury St. Edmunds, whilst others went from the *Rose and Crown* and *Swan*.*

'Carriers' also left from the public houses on their regular runs from Sudbury.

From the *Royal Oak* in 1844 went E. Salter to London on Sundays, Tuesdays and Fridays.
From the *Bear* (now *Harlequin*) travelled W. Mann to Hadleigh on Tuesdays and Saturdays.
From the *Black Boy* journeyed W. Ruggles to Ipswich on Mondays and to Bury on Wednesdays.

* But the hostelries were not merely the embarkation points for passengers. For as Dorothy Hartley points out, "The hay and water provided for the horses by inns and coaching houses, made them as important as petrol stations are today". (From *The Land of England*).

From the *Anchor* went D.Bray to Colchester on Fridays.
From the Angel departed I. Snazell for Hartest each Monday
and Friday.

(All from *White's Directory*, 1844).

In some, justice itself was administered. Within our Colne/Stour countryside fortnightly Petty Sessions – presided over by the local J.P.'s – were held at the Clare *Half Moon*, Long Melford *Bull*, Hadleigh *White Lion*, Braintree *White Hart*, and Castle Hedingham *Bell*.

Yet invariably I am drawn to the pre-war era. It is now well past 1am and I am standing in the porch of *Mosses Farm* cottage, close to the cabbages and brussels sprouts, the raspberry bushes and pea sticks of Jack's impeccable garden. A magnificent full moon lights up the surrounding fields and the nearby water-tower which supplies Little Maplestead's needs. Inadvertently yawning but frantically scribbling down notes in the semi-light, I weakly suggest that we ought to 'call time!'

"Like a good landlord," quips Jack. " 'Course," he continues, "pubs used to shut at ten when I was a lad and it wasn't a bit unusual for the village policeman to come and sit on his bicycle outside and start pulling his watch out. And that was it! You had to be moving! 'Course I remember one time…"

It is almost two o'clock. Jack is telling me of the *Blackbirds* and an

evening after harvest when he was still a boy.

"It hadn't been a proper horkey – not in the traditional way, but they had an almighty good booze up!

"Anyway, the old copper came at ten o'clock and everyone had to leave. But poor old 'George' was pretty much the worse for wear. He swayed out singing and laughing and then staggered up the avenue to Bulmer Church. Well, the ol' bobby was good enough to follow him at a distance. Anyway, George kept hollering and lurching about and just about made his way up to the graveyard. But that was it. He just couldn't go a step further. He just collapsed – there and then – and laid down amongst all the graves and tombstones. So, the ol' policeman walked up and shook him on the shoulder. 'Come on,' he said, 'you can't lay here all night.'

'Who says?'

'I do.'

"George just raised himself on one shoulder – and very weakly pointed to the gravestones. 'Tell some of them other buggers to move,' he said. '...they've been here long enough!'"

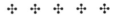

COWPAT – CRICKET – COWPAT!

A brief summary of sport in our parishes

Especially to commemorate the hundredth anniversary of village cricket in Gestingthorpe, this chapter is dedicated to:

TONY SELF, TOM ELSDON and JOHN HASLER

– who have done so much to keep the club going – and in respectful memory of the late George and Fanny Cooke who provided the parish's beautiful playing field.

"I was captain of Gestingthorpe at the age of nineteen, up there on Tin meadow – between cow pats and tufts of grass...and my goodness, when Mr. Prior asked me to play in his Farmers' team at Sudbury – well, it was like going to Lords!"

Arthur Nears

"It was either hit or miss years ago – much more sporting. None of this block, block, blocking. You either hit it or got out!"

Bert Surridge

"When I was young farmworkers didn't get holidays. I'd lose a day's pay to go and watch county cricket. I once biked to Colchester to see Hutton but when I arrived he was injured, however I did see Maurice Leyland and then O'Connor – the Essex captain – who scored 140. Another time I saw Wally Hammond of Gloucestershire"

"Do you remember Hutton scoring his 364?"

"I remember him overtaking Bradman's record of 334. We'd just got our first radio and when I came in for dinner I heard the crowd burst out singing 'Ol' Langs Ayne' and all such as that. When I went back to work – at Wickham Hall – I met an ol' horseman and he say, 'they hully done some singing!'"

Tom Bird
Stockman and brickmaker

"Men were tougher in those days. Blacksmith Dick Nice would often cycle to Wickham St. Pauls or Park Gate Farm and 'cold shoe' two or three horses when the farmer hadn't got time to send them to the forge – but he'd still play cricket the same day!"

The late Douglas Hasler
Gestingthorpe

186

Chapter Seventeen

THE VILLAGE AT SPORT
Cricket, Football and Gamekeeping

"The best thing ever invented," declares Alf Finch, "was the Saturday afternoon holiday for farmworkers. . . as soon as we had it we formed Borley Football Club."

Until World War One farm labourers worked six 'full' days each week. In 1918-19 hours were reduced. Work ended at Saturday lunchtime. Henceforth it became possible for farmworkers to play village cricket and football. But why had there been no sport on Sundays?

"The Church round here was too strict for that," says Bert Surridge, "right up to 1945. Gestingthorpe never played cricket on Sundays – not until after World War Two!"

Yet team games in our area can be traced back for at least three hundred years. In 1643 it was alleged that Samuel Brinsley, Rector of Alphamstone:

"played at 'bat and trap' with the boys of the parish – on the Sabbath!"*

By 1787, 'all day' games of cricket were being played locally. Some occurred on Bulmer Tye – then a stretching twenty three acre 'green' or 'common'. In the following year John Bruce, landlord of *The*

---

* From *Annals of Evangelical Non-Conformity in the County of Essex*, by T. W. Davids, published 1863.

Plough advertised:

"A match of cricket on Bulmer Tye, when the company... will be esteemed in favour by their humble servant John Bruce... Stumps to be pitched at ten o'clock. Dinner at two..."

Cricket's popularity was increasing. In 1836 Dickens' celebrated account of a match at 'Dingley Dell' appeared in *Pickwick Papers*. In 1844 Clare had a *Cricketers' Arms* public house, whilst the squire of Bulmer – Captain Caledon Alexander of *The Auberies* – formed his own 'country house' team. Apart from inviting some of the best available players he also engaged a leading professional.

And who did he engage in 1848?

It was a cricketer whose name we still commemorate. Founder of the famous almanac – referred to every single day on Test Match commentary – the immortal John Wisden. With Wisden's help, the *Auberies* team actually beat the M.C.C. and gained a mighty reputation.*

Gosfield, Bures and Steeple Bumpstead similarly had 'gentleman's' teams. And by the end of the century many other villages such as Bulmer, Gestingthorpe and Great Yeldham had more representative sides – although still it would seem without farmworkers.

The earliest reference we have to cricket in Gestingthorpe comes from the days of W. G. Grace and C. B. Fry. (Although further research may reveal an earlier date). For on 24th May, 1893 the *Suffolk and Essex Free Press* reported:

'CRICKET MATCH BETWEEN
BULMER-CUM-BELCHAMP AND GESTINGTHORPE'

"Played at Bulmer on Whit Monday. Bulmer scored 125 in their first innings. Gestingthorpe replied with 24 in their first innings and 37 in their second."

Three years later, in July 1896, Rev. C. D. Bromwich, revealed in Gestingthorpe's *Parish Magazine*:

* From *East Anglian Sporting Days* (O. Johnson, East Anglian Magazine). See also *The Cricketers of Sudbury 1787-1987* by Alan Cocksedge, and *Bulmer; Then and Now*.
An Essex County Cricket Club existed from 1864-65 and was reformed in 1876 and 1886.
Alexander also built Bulmer School (page 102).

"On June 13th we played Wickham St. Pauls on their own ground. Gestingthorpe went in first and got 98 ... Wickham St. Pauls were all out for 48.

"The second match was played at Bulmer on June 20th. The Bulmer team went in first and were disposed of for thirty runs. Our team then batted and ran up the score to 255!"

But who were Gestingthorpe's players – and what did they do? Almost a century after the match against Bulmer occurred – and after much painstaking research – village history recorder Doris Pannell has kindly unearthed the teams' professions:

Alfred Abrams 27
    labourer ?
James Flitton 48
    coachman for Mrs. Oates
L.E.G. Oates 18
    schoolboy, later Inniskilling Dragoon
Patrick O'Sullivan ....70 not out
    Inland Revenue officer
Jeffrey Ruffle 12
    farmer at Hall Farm
Charlie Downs (Capt.)..45
    'Agricultural Implement Agent' in 1891 census –
    later semi-retired
Fred Finch 0
    labourer?
Fred Hunt..11
    groom from Revd. Bromwich
Arthur Pannell..6
    wheelwright and carpenter
William Hunt..1
    gardener

Total: **255**

(Among Gestingthorpe's players in the earlier match were gardener Arthur Surridge and baker Joseph Felton.)

✣ ✣ ✣ ✣ ✣

189

It was a time in our villages of both transformation and solidity. Beneath the Victorian sunset squire and parson were firmly ensconced and the imperial flag held sway over a quarter of the globe... Yet in Sudbury and Halstead the workhouse stood open – appalling and grim.

But change was afoot. In 1885 farmworkers were enfranchised for the first time; in 1893 the locality was rocked by the labourers' strike at Belchamp Walter; in 1894 the old 'Vestries' were finally replaced by democratically elected parish councils. In almost every village independent 'non conformist' chapels were proud beacons of freedom of worship. And schools in every parish were raising expectations and standards.

It was also a decade of depression. Village populations were plummeting. Gestingthorpe itself was fortunate to be partly 'industrialised', boasting not only two brickyards, a pottery, wheelwrights and blacksmith, but also an iron foundry. The parish benefited also, when the incoming squire William Oates, arrived in 1891, 'bringing money with him' to finance repairs to the Church, the building of a village room and other acts of benevolent paternalism.

Cricket-wise however, it was his eldest son – L. E. G. Oates – later Captain Oates – who was to gain parochial renown, "as a great hitter".

Eight decades after his death in the Antarctic wastes on Scott's ill-fated expedition to the South Pole, the story is still repeated – by Paul Cooke, Basil Radley and others – of:

"One gigantic – enormous six – hit from the south end of Tin Meadow right over the far boundary to an elm tree – where an oak post was driven in the ground to commemorate the feat."

After his father's death in 1896, Oates as 'the young squire' assisted the Gestingthorpe lads. Our next glimpse comes from the accounts of a Boys Cricket Club dated 1909-1910. The ledgers provide an intriguing insight into both expenses and village self-sufficiency.

From: Mr. J. FELTON *(baker)*
Nether Hill, Gestingthorpe
August 27 1909, for 'Boys Cricket Club'

3 doz. buns............................1s	6d
1 doz. lemonade 1s	0d
1 doz. ginger beer................1s	0d
3s	**6d**

From: DAVID COE
Gestingthorpe Boot stores *(near today's Pheasant)*
August 28 1909,

Bat bound & ball repaired 1s	0d
Bat bound..............................1s	6d
Cricket ball stitched up.............	4d
2s	**10d**

From: PERCY DOWNS *(Ironmonger, later Bicycle Shop proprietor)*
Nether Hill, Gestingthorpe
1909-1910

1 pair youth's leg guards.......6s	9d
1 cricket ball..........................3s	3d
scoreboard 1s	0d
11s	**0d**

Football was also encouraged. On November 3rd 1909, Percy Downs
(known by some as 'ol' Wire and Nails'), sold the Boys' Club:

1 Bussey's Football 720A 7s	0d
1 Inflator...............................3s	0d
10s	**0d**

The last invoice was settled by a single donation from Captain
Oates – who had also donated five shillings to the Boys' Cricket Club.
Was Gestingthorpe's 'most famous son' more interested in football
than cricket! At the time ten shillings represented an astronomical –
unimaginable expense for the lads themselves, since their fathers –
who were mostly farmworkers – earned barely thirteen to fourteen

shillings a week.

A month later however, another Downs invoice records:

"For repairing burst in football and blowing same up.....9d"

But we must never isolate village life from the wider international scene. On 29th July 1910, Bulmer Boys were host to the Gestingthorpe lads – who won by nine runs. Yet of Bulmer's eleven players two were to be killed in World War One. (Ernest Weavers and Frederick Raymond). Five others were also to serve in the trenches. (Archibald Barrell, A. Smith, Fred Bunn, Ernie Lott and Willy Gardiner). So too did Harold Blye who played in the return fixture.

It is then, with humility and respect that we progress to the conclusion of the Great War. On 19th May 1919 a minute was entered in the Gestingthorpe year book:

"A meeting was held in the School Room to re-open the old Cricket Club..."

It initiated the most genuine, vintage, years of village cricket. When men with sunburnt arms and swarthy faces, more used to pulling mangolds, building stacks or hoeing corn met up with those who laboured in the village brickyard, or the joiners shop at 'Rippers' in Sible Hedingham.

On July 5th, 1919, a Gestingthorpe score sheet reveals not only a match against Wickham St. Paul, but a poignant comment scribbled on the base of the page:

"First match after War. Very little gear and no funds. No bus service, could only pick members who had cycles. One player, Flitton, walked via Oakley Wood."

It was the beginning of the halcyon era: of matches on Wednesday nights and Saturday afternoons: of practice nights "when," says Arthur Nears, "enough for two teams would turn up from the village alone", whilst of the boisterous home games Dick Finch declares: "half the bloomin' village would turn up to watch – it was a real social occasion!" Douglas Hasler continues:

"There was a tremendous atmosphere. The spectators partici-pated far more in those days. If a player dropped a catch – however difficult – shouts of 'Butterfingers!' would come from all

192

round, whilst when we were batting they would always want us to run more than was possibly safe."

Then there were the outfields:

"But the grass was sometimes knee high!" declares Ernie Lott of Bulmer. "The ball would never roll through it! If you didn't hit it up high – you hadn't a hope of getting a boundary!"

"At Hawstead near Bury St. Edmunds," exclaims Rev. Philip Wright, "there weren't any boundaries! You could run a four, but the only way to get a six was from a 'lost ball'. The ball itself was used until it was almost shredded – and then the boot-maker would repair it for us to practise with!"

Inevitably the pitches affected performance. As a farm student in 1924, Philip had played for Great Maplestead against Sible Hedingham. The latter scored eighty. For Great Maplestead Philip had the distinction of being top scorer. His total? . . . was just two – the village being all out for nine!

Jack Cornell continues the theme:

"On many meadows you were only allowed to mow a strip twenty two yards long – and just a couple of yards wide. Most of the time you were buggering around in grass a yard high!"

"On Tin Meadow at Gestingthorpe," chuckles Bert Surridge, "the batting area was cut with a scythe – but it was often the only area that was cut! There have been balls land in 'cow pats' and splash the 'slips' – and other times they've stopped in cow pats on the outfield – and then been hurled back to the slips!"

But where was the legendary Tin Meadow – on which Gesting-thorpe played its matches?

"About 300 yards down the path from *Hall Farm* towards Little Yeldham in the valley behind *Gestingthorpe Hall*," explains the late Daisy Nice, whose husband blacksmith Dick Nice was often captain in the 1920's and 30's.

"And I ought to know!" she continues. "I've been down that track hundreds of times to do the teas. But first we had to take the tables and crockery down there! We took the 'crocks' down in baskets and then someone would carry a couple of pails of water from Pump Yard and we'd boil it up on a thing like a vallus stove for the tea."*

The cricket is always fondly remembered – despite occasional contretemps.

"I remember playing on Tin Meadow for Little Waldingfield," says Peter Rowe, "and one of our players, farmer Billy Bedford had a huge hit, but the ball just clipped the leaves of a tree as it landed – so he was only allowed a four. That caused quite a controversy!

"But as far as cow mess was concerned, Waldingfield's ground was no better than Gestingthorpe's. I've picked up wheelbarrows of cow muck on Sunday morning ready for cricket in the afternoon!"

Other pitches provide equally nostalgic memories.

Farmer George Jackson (1884-1983) recalled playing for Long Melford against Edwardstone in the early twenties and:

"lobbing a ball up which then rolled down a rabbit hole! Well we started running...and carried on running! But why ever didn't they block the hole up properly? They knew it was there – because they'd stuffed a bit of grass in the end!"

Thirty years later Tom Elsdon also played at Edwardstone and remembers:

"running seven or eight – but the ball was only a few yards from Square Leg umpire in a clump of ox-eye daisies!"

"At Belchamp St. Pauls," recalls George 'Jute' Chatters, "we played on a little meadow behind the *Green Man* pub and used to cut the pitch with two horses and a grass mower. Charlie Offord

---

* Ladies could however take part – occasionally. In June 1933 a team of Gestingthorpe Ladies challenged some of the younger men – who included such stars as Lennie Martin, Douglas Hasler, George Vickers, Basil Radley, Fred Rippingale and Dick Finch. The men are believed to have bowled and batted left-handed and recalls Dick, "it made a bit of fun! Whatever fun you had in those days you made yourself – didn't you?"

usually had Red Poll cows on there – although he took them off when we played – so if you had white trousers you had to watch out! But a lot of players just wore what they could."

One typical Belchamp St. Paul's team – which played Gestingthorpe on 14th May 1930 – was recalled by Jute, on a cold December afternoon, sixty four years after the match occurred. As I sat in his warm sitting room – not far from Belchamp St. Paul's Church – his bright twinkling eyes and cheery smiling face lit up with infectious enthusiasm as he recalled his team mates from long ago.

Chris Golding b Reeve 5
farmworker at Woodbarns Farm
Georgie Gibbons b Felton...0
Sexton's Son
George Bartram b Felton 0
farmworker at Upper Farm, Ovington
Alf Golding run out...1
farmworker at Woodbarns and Paul's Hall
S. Sargeant run out 4
from Clare
Arthur Mann b Felton..0
worked at Woodbarns Farm, later on roads
Jack Mann c Clark b Felton..6
farmworker later at Gestingthorpe
J. Martin b. Felton..0
farmworker at Shearing Place? and Butlers Farm?
George 'Jute' Chatters c Martin b Reeve.....................1
farmworker, Fowes Farm, later Paul's Hall
Bob Catton not out...0
haulier. Father was local rabbit catcher

Extras   8

Total: **26**

Reeve 2 for 6, Felton 5 for 10
Gestingthorpe's innings totalled 49. Alf Mann taking five wickets.

195

But as Jute explains:

"We weren't 'over-stocked' with good players. In fact getting a side was always a headache. The trouble was, if you had to leave someone out, the following week they'd say – 'Oh! You didn't want me last week – I shan't play next!'"

Meanwhile Belchamp Walter played at *Waits*, and later *Clarkes Farm*, and it was here, that contributor Charlie Martin once took "five wickets for seven runs". Arthur Pannell recalls, "Someone trained a dog to retrieve the ball – it ever it went in the hedge – that was really convenient!". "At Pebmarsh," says Hazell Chinnery, "the pitch was originally opposite *Le Mote* farmhouse." Later however, remembers Tom Bird, "it was near Tom Notts – at *Oak Farm*. I've bowled there and had over twenty Wickham lads cheering me on!" At Bulmer reminisces Tom Hastie:

"They played on the meadow between the Church and Bulmer Street – almost opposite the *Cock and Blackbirds*. But Hazell Chinnery would often hit a six right out of the ground and over the road into the yard of *Brickwall Farm* where Spencer Coe's pigs and chickens were!"

Hazell himself recalls facing, 'under-arm bowling' in village games – "and it was surprisingly awkward to play. There was one bloke at Wickham St. Pauls – a horseman called Howard – who was particularly tricky." (A memory corroborated by the late George Jackson). Hazell however also provides a memory of Gestingthorpe's most famous son when:

"Captain Oates came over to Bulmer – in a pony and trap – to play against us with a team from Gestingthorpe. I always remember him walking across the pitch to us. He was a fine, upright looking man."

Yet although the squire may have travelled by pony and trap, many others recall, "doing a full day's work and then biking to a Wednesday evening match at a neighbouring village with a pair of pads or a bat tied to the crossbar."
Quite obviously when the motorised transport of Harry Rippingale's bus arrived it was highly appreciated. (We recall the comment made by Dick Halls and Christ Felton:

"CRICKET EVENINGS on the bus were FANTASTIC!".
Douglas Hasler continues, "We'd play pontoon on the journey and
then after we left the pub, sing all the way home!"

For in those years – before World War Two – before motor cars for
working people, and before telephones and television, the village
cricket was – for sportsman and spectator alike – a joyful distraction
from the unremitting hours of manual labour.

From the daily work of pitching sheaves or threshing stacks, from
ploughing – with a horse – a 'summer fallow', or from 'turning hay'
or 'chopping-out' the endless rows of sugar beet or mangolds…
Enjoyment was paramount! As Dick Halls tells of a game at Ashen:

"I was batting at number ten or eleven – and doing rather well I
thought – when suddenly someone hollered out from the boundary: 'HURRY UP AND GET OUT DICK! THE RED COW'S
ABOUT TO OPEN!'"

✢ ✢ ✢ ✢ ✢

Yet who were the players – the other 'great names' of our local cricket in the decades when Bradman and Larwood, Hammond and Hutton were viewed on the Pathe Newsreels at Sudbury's Gainsborough or County Cinemas with awe and admiration?

The following scorecard records the Gestingthorpe team who played against Gosfield on 24th August, 1929:

Dennis Felton not out...15
worked at Rippers joinery factory
Charlie Downs b Williams.............................1
descendant of iron founder semi-retired
George Pannell b Williams............................0
wheelwright and carpenter
Dick Nice (Capt.) c Williams b Wegg 5
blacksmith
Dick Felton b Williams 7
baker, with 'off licence' and grocer's shop on Nether Hill*
Jack Finch c Humphries b Williams 4
farmworkr
Bob Emburson b Barker...............................11
shoemaker
Lennie Martin b Barker................................1
cobbler, later postman
Harry Catterwell run out..............................2
worked at 'Rippers'
A. 'Razor' Finch b Williams...........................0
brickmaker and smallholder of 'The Homestead
Stan Surridge run out.................................0
farmworker

                                                    Total: 55

Gosfield – who included two members of the Lowe family – won by five wickets.

---

* "Dick Felton," recalls Douglas Hasler, "regularly got up at 4.00am to bake the bread and then take it round in his pony cart. But when he batted he swung at every ball as though to hit it out of the ground. Often he was out first ball, but sometimes he connected and hit some spectacular sixes. He wore neither pads nor gloves and often the bat slipped from his hands. It was an exciting time when he batted!"

When Gestingthorpe visited Wickham St. Pauls, during the tense summer of 1939, the Wickham team consisted of:

Tom Bird b M. Francis 22
stockman, later brickmaker
Arthur Pannell b J. Overill...0
farmworker, later engineer
Charlie Moore b. J. Overill 0
farmworker
Tom Wiseman c Francis b Overill 4
farmworker
Ron Honeywood b Overill 0
egg collector?
Bill Percival c Francis b Overill 0
farm and threshing worker
Leonard Honeywood c C. Honeywood b Overill........0
worked at Whitlocks (agricultural engineers)
Ted Barnes b Francis..13
builder
John Cattermole c Honeywood b Francis...................0
council employee
Jackie Mayes not out 0
worked at Rippers
Gordon Warren b Francis 0
farmer

Extras   6

Total: 39

Farmworker Jack Overill, of *Hopkins Farm* taking 6 for 15, and Francis 4 for 3.*

* Amongst Gestingthorpe's younger players were some of our contributors – Dick Finch, Douglas Hasler, Joe Spilling, Stanley Surridge, and Cyril Reeve – the latter scoring 21 in Gestingthorpe's total of 95. For Wickham, Tom Bird took 5 wickets for 34 runs and Ron Honeywood 4 for 15.

The stong family names – which once predominated in certain villages – are quite naturally reflected in the scorecards. Belchamp Walter's for example, frequently included several Theobalds, Pearsons and Overills together with Charlie 'Bommy' Martin and farmer, countryman and past landlord of *The Eight Bells*, George Chatters. Great Maplestead's team of the nineteen thirties predictably contains Bockings, Spillings and Jeggos, whilst one Pebmarsh team of 1933 included Messrs. C. G. and J. Rust; G. B. and D. Page; L. and C. Turner, A. Harrington and A. Weavers.

199

✤ ✤ ✤ ✤ ✤

Yet it is not just about names – or statistics. For village cricket teams – like pubs, shops and chapels have been sadly declining for the past four decades.

In 1932 Gestingthorpe's fixtures included:

Ridgewell	Belchamp St. Paul's
Stoke by Clare	Bulmer
Greenstead Green	Sudbury Y.M.C.A.
Belchamp Walter	Ashen
& Blackmore End	

– none of which now have teams. Other village teams 'to fall by the wayside' include Colne Engaine, Great Maplestead, Foxearth, Alphamstone Poslingford and Pebmarsh.

It is this that makes the survival of Gestingthorpe, Wickham and Twinstead (founded circa 1950), so worthy of note.

The clubs have been able to continue only because of the immeasurable commitment and dedication of a hard core of devotees.

Yet even arranging matches in the early years presented real problems – for most fixture secretaries could only be contacted by mail or telegram. Yet in 1930 Pebmarsh succeeded in arranging THIRTY TWO games and Gestingthorpe thirty.

There are other memories of the pre-war years. "Charlie Downs gave any of the young lads 'half a crown' – if they scored over ten," is one recollection. Lennie Martin similarly recalled:

"If farmer Frank Nott rode past on his horse when the boys were practising he'd sometimes put a shilling on top of a single stump – and he'd take the bat – but if they could bowl the stump down, they could keep the shilling!"

Yet they were also years of depression. The parish's population continued to decline. From 1928-32 it could not even muster a parish council. Eventually one resident, farmer Everton 'Toffee' Halls placed an advert in the *Halstead Gazette* exclaiming:

"WAKE UP GESTINGTHORPE!"

200

For a few weeks even the cricket club was racked with dissent. However on 17th June, 1932 an extraordinary meeting was held – and harmony was soon restored. Agriculturally the village was also to make national news headlines. For in May 1933 an outbreak of the 'Tithe War' occurred at *Delvyns Farm*.

Six years later the World was plunged into a very different, uglier conflict. Village cricket was again suspended. Thirty one young Gestingthorpe men served in the forces. One occasional player Don Meeking was killed in action.

The baton was picked up in 1946. At Bulmer the first season was played on a meadow at Goldingham Hall – then a dairy farm – before returning to the pitch opposite the *Cock and Blackbirds*.

Gestingthorpe's players resumed on Tin Meadow. With them in 1947 came a new proprietor – the late George Cooke.

Unassuming, and committed to the newer, fairer post war society, he was also, totally devoted to cricket. Tom Elsdon continues:

"I'll never forget the matches he organised against teams in London. In those days – before many people had cars they were real 'events'. And then on Whit Mondays he would get up a team to challenge the village, and after the match everyone – all the players and spectators – were invited up to the Hall for beer and sand-wiches... Lovely times!"

In the late nineteen forties and early fifties came new regular players. Nicky Stovell – later to represent the English Deaf Team, Ken Elsdon – dependable opening batsman, his brother Tom – fast bowler and mighty hitter, wicketkeeper George Kemp – whose family name con-stantly recurs in local research – and 'all rounders', Arthur Nears, Tony Self and Cyril Reeve. All were born in, or lived close to the parish itself. It was still an utterly, genuine, village side.

So too were those of neighbouring parishes. The Bulmer and Wick-ham St. Pauls teams which played on July 19th, 1953 consisted of:

F. Barnes b Day...0
D. F. Barnes c Weavers b Day.....................9
T. Bird c and b Day 11
P. Minter b Day..1
B. Pryke b Coe..0
D. Barnes c Weavers b Day 3
S. Brown not out.......................................10
T. Brown b Radley..4
M. Raymond b Radley 0
P. Rash c East b Radley..............................0
N. Bird b Radley 5

Extras   6

Total: **49**

Day 4 wickets for 15 runs, Radley 4 for 11.

(Three weeks later F. Barnes scored 107 not out against Yeldham. In that game Wickham totalled 185, with contributor Bill Yeldham taking 4 of their wickets for 47 runs. Today, the latter's grandson Ian, plays for Gestingthorpe).

In reply to Wickham's total the Bulmer Scorecard read:

Peter Weavers c Raymond b Rash 4
R.A.F.
Ted Radley b F. Barnes 4
worked at 'Rippers'
Ivan Stowe b Rash...5
builder
Arthur Day lbw b Rash..4
farmer at Upper Houses
Lawrence Coe lbw b Barnes..1
*farm and threshing contractor, smallholder
at Brickwall Farm*
Norman East b Rash 1
plumber
Jack Cornell not out...12
threshing contractor, smallholder

Harold Bettinson b Barnes   1
farmworker later at brickyard
Desmond Younger b Barnes 0
fitter with 'Eastern Tractors'
Alan Dixey run out 1
gardener
Chris Bettinson b Rash 0
schoolboy, son of Harold, now university lecturer

Extras   1

Total: 34

Bowlers: P. Rash 5 for 14, F. Barnes 4 wickets.

(With thanks to Evelyn Reeve for occupations).

How I wish this entire book had been devoted to village cricket! The scorebooks and anecdotes reveal so much of our human history.

"I was stockman at Wickham Hall when I was younger," says Tom Bird now of Bulmer Brickyard, "and did I love cricket! I played for Wickham for nearly forty years! But I still had to do the pigs and bullocks – morning and night! On one occasion I took nine wickets for five runs against Waldingfield – but then I had to go back and do the animals... You didn't get many moments of glory!"

Years later the ageing scorebooks tell of similar deeds. Against Alphamstone in 1947 Gestingthorpe's Cyril Reeve scored 63 not out and then took five wickets for ten runs. In the same year another history enthusiast and contributor, farmworker Cecil Cook captured five Gestingthorpe wickets for twelve runs in Maplestead's defeat of the village. Nine years later it was Foxearth farmworker Jim Hastie who wreaked havoc on Gestingthorpe's batting when he claimed six wickets for five runs – Gestingthorpe being all out for seven! A year later the tables were turned and Foxearth were defeated by 72 runs (Tony Self taking 5 for 7).

Foxearth's scorecard in the victorious game – which they won by 33 runs, reads:*

21st July 1956

Ken Coleby b Seward 3
A. Garner c Radley b T. Self 9
B. Reeve b Seward 0
Jimmy Whittle b Self 0
Jim Hastie c Catterwell b Self 0
Gordon Hastie c & b Self 0
F. Cutmore b F. Nice 20
Melvynne Grainger lbw b F. Nice 3
Jack Sargent not out 1
Alan Chinnery b D. Hasler 1
R. Gooding b F. Nice 0

Extras   3

Total: 40

Yet there were also exceptional innings. One occurred amongst the buttercups and bumble bees of Tin Meadow in a game against Cornard in 1959. For on the balmy afternoon of August 16th, Arthur Nears hit an extraordinary eleven 'sixes' and nine 'fours' in a quite 'Bothamesque' innings of 135 not out.

* Other exceptional bowling feats include Gestingthorpe's dismissal of Greenstead Green for just 5 runs in 1947. (Arthur Nears taking 5 wickets for 1 run and Johnny Radley 6 for 4 – both teams having twelve players). On 27th July 1929, Bulmer were bowled out for a mere 8 runs, with Jack Finch taking 5 wickets for 6 runs and the late Stanley Surridge 5 for 1. About 1912 George Pannell took ten wickets for Gestingthorpe against a Halstead team – and son Arthur still has the ball. More recently there are records of Les Rippingale taking all ten wickets against Stansfield and Brian Seward capturing nine against Gosfield. Elsewhere Derek Pearson once took all ten wickets for Pebmarsh, whilst Tom Bird recalls the late Bill Yeldham doing the same for Yeldham against a Sudbury team.

Since the move to formal 'playing fields' in the 1950's the average scores attained by village sides have increased several fold. However noteworthy bowling performances can still occur and on 24th June 1990, club captain Keith Shortland took an extraordinary 7 wickets for 1 run against Sudbury Institute.

204

Yet change was afoot. Gestingthorpe's last brickyard had closed in the mid nineteen fifties. And mechanisation had come to agriculture. The parish's last 'working horse' had been 'put out to grass'. Livestock were being concentrated on fewer holdings. The farm labour force was declining. Employment was increasingly sought at Rippers in Sible Hedingham, Whitlocks at Great Yeldham and C.A.V. in Sudbury.

Expectations were rising. And there was a national drive to encourage Playing Fields and Community Centres.

Gestingthorpe Parish Council first discussed the issue in 1958. On the evening of August 18th, farmer Robert Nott formally proposed that, "the Planning Authority be approached for permission (and advice) to develop a Playing Field."

The following year Mr. & Mrs. Cooke kindly offered Bird Meadow on a 99 year 'peppercorn' lease.

To pay for the conversion work a 'house to house collection' ensued. The field was drained, levelled and seeded by Ernest Doe and Sons. On the afternoon of 11th June, 1962, (the Whit Monday Bank Holiday), the Playing Field was officially opened with a game between a George Cooke's team and Gestingthorpe.

The village scored 142 for 4 declared. Tony Self – who has devoted so much of his time to the cricket square since – appropriately making 55 not out and Brian Seward 62. Watching from beneath the chestnut trees on the boundary – as they would on so many occasions in the future – was our local hero 'Bluffy' Rippingale, 'tithe war' celebrity Marjorie Gardiner and erstwhile butler Horace Reeve.*

With passing seasons the baton has been passed to younger generations. Few now are involved with agriculture, several live in local towns – although some still have Gestingthorpe connections with a

---

* A team of twelve players represented the village for the official opening game viz: Nicky Stovell, Ken Elsdon, Tony Self, Frank Nice, Brian Seward, Arthur Nears, Alan Beal, Tom Elsdon, David Jeggo, Alf Martin, John Radley, Hubert Meeking.

The following Saturday Brian Seward scored a remarkable 146 (a club record?), at Halstead against the town's Portway Tortoise works.

Other century makers we know of include Nicky and Phil Stovell, John Butcher, Chris Moulton, Alan Wright and Robert Gardiner.

205

grandparent or uncle resident in the village. For others it is *The Pheasant* which has lured new blood to the team.

Yet happily there is still a perceptible thread which links contemporary players with those of yesteryear. In 1965 John Hasler – whose father, Douglas, is quoted earlier – played his first game – and still continues playing today. In the 1970's and 80's came a new generation of Stovells and Selfs to revitalise the club anew. In more recent years Richard Nice and Mark Prior have become 'third generation' players. Even more exciting is that batsmen Phil and Tim Stovell are actually the GREAT GRANDSONS of groom Frederick Hunt who played in the legendary game against Bulmer in 1896!

Happily a Football Club also continues. Amongst the leading lights is Gestingthorpe born and bred Chris Moulton, whilst mid-field player Peter Nice is another grandson of blacksmith Dick Nice recorded earlier... And the lad with the bright twinkling eyes? His name is Colin King. He bears not only a striking resemblance to our heroic Borley schoolboy and horseman Alf Finch – but is indeed his look-alike grandson!

Today both sports – together with the 'indoor Carpet Bowls' at Bulmer Village Hall – continue to foster community spirit, 'bring people together', initiate friendships and serve as wonderful catalysts for enriching human life through competitive fellowship and understanding.

At the time of writing – at least a HUNDRED AND ONE years since cricket was first played in Gestingthorpe the Club's fortunes are buoyant again. On August 28th, 1994, a record FIVE HUNDRED AND THIRTEEN runs were scored in one memorable day's cricket. Appropriately the opposition were a team brought from London by Paul Cooke. The latter batted first and scored a staggering 256. Gestingthorpe's innings began after tea. The scorecard of their exceptional – and spirited reply reads:

206

Tim Stovell st Bird b Garrow...35
Tourism graduate, great grandson of Fred Hunt,
son of Nicky, lives in Acton
David Self c Bird b Garrow...51
Bank Manager, born in Belchamp Walter,
lives in Earls Colne
Ben Hulbert c Wollheim b Garrow.......................................8
Schoolboy, lives in Bulmer.
Russell Leggett c Gee b Garrow..0
Business student. Parents kept 'Cock & Blackbirds' in
early 1980's. Lives in Bulmer.
Alan Wright not out..73
Structural engineer, lives in Clare, recently moved
from Gestingthorpe
Robert Gardiner b Garrow 21
Farms in Gestingthorpe and Little Yeldham – lives in
latter. Descendant of J. S. Gardiner – see manorial
courts p.16
Ian Yeldham not out...51
Farmer. Grandson of contributor Bill Yeldham. Lives in
erstwhile parish of Northwood – now Little Yeldham.

Did not bat:
Keith Shortland *Herbal Life salesman. Lives in Sudbury*
Mark Prior *Farmer. Lives in Gestingthorpe*
Nicky Harrington *Schoolboy. Lives in Little Yeldham*
Phil Scillitoe *Carpenter, lives in Halstead*
John Butcher *Past landlord of Bulmer 'Fox',*
 now Gift Shop proprietor, lives in Sudbury

(12 players each side)   Extras   18
Garrow 5 for 54

TOTAL: TWO HUNDRED AND FIFTY SEVEN!

(Scorer: Teresa Long; Ground Preparation: Tony Self, John Hasler
and volunteer players; Umpire: Mike Prior).

Yet, as the auburn rays of the sinking sun lit up the red brick tower of
Gestingthorpe Church and the shadows lengthened across the impeccable

207

square, there was one, last statistic which might so easily have been over-looked.

After ninety eight years – which have seen so much change and transformation – Gestingthorpe had finally overtaken the total of 255 – which was scored by Captain Oates and his friends – against Bulmer – in 1896!

As scorer Teresa Long commented, "It was a wonderful, unforgettable game to watch!"

FOOTBALL, GAMEKEEPING & POINT-TO-POINTS

Space alone does not allow us to investigate other sports so fully. Let us remember however, the disproportionate cost of the Boys football in 1909, reinforced by a comment from Jack Cornell (b.1918):

"I just don't know how me and my mates got our first football – but half the time it was probably flat!"

Alf Finch – who so rejoiced in the abolition of Saturday afternoon farmwork about 1918 – recalls the subsequent inception of village football:

"To start with Borley had a team of its own – although later we had to go in with Foxearth to make the numbers up. We used to play Lavenham, Acton, Clare, Cavendish and Sudbury Swifts and travelled in one of John Palmer of Melford's 'brakes'. It would be pulled by a pair of horses but it wasn't covered in – so you hoped it wasn't raining! For 'home games' we used a meadow at the back of the Church. Something else we used to play though – on week-day evenings were quoits. I've seen a dozen men on Borley green playing at quoits!"

At Alphamstone, reports Eddie Tuffin, "a bowls club was formed by the Reverend Butler – and very enjoyable it was too." At Borley, "a 'club room' with a billiards table, cards and dominoes was opened three nights a week."

"At Gestingthorpe," says Bert Surridge, "if the men had a race at a fete or on a farm, they'd do it 'yards for years' to give everyone a fair chance – whatever your age." (i.e. Deduct a yard for every year over a certain age).

There were also challenges for those more muscular in arm than leg. In 1838 for example, the South Suffolk Agricultural Association

208

offered prizes:

"to the labourer who performs the greatest number of rods of land draining between 8am and 2pm, on November 12th at *Houghton Hall*."

First Prize £1   5s   0d
Second Prize.........................£1   0s   0d
Third Prize 15s   0d

Although the first prize was equivalent to three weeks wages, what about the competitors who won nothing despite having done six hours heavy digging?

With thoughts of the land – and the adjoining hedges and woods – we briefly remember our 'countryside sports'. Fortunately part time gamekeeper and encyclopaedic fund of rural knowledge, Harry Gilbert of Colne Engaine spent a couple of afternoons recounting his observations of the countryside he loved so dearly.

Initially he spoke of the traditional 'keepers' who 'gave a shilling' for every partridge nest found beside the roads – and who could then:

"lift an English partridge off its nest, take out the eggs, put stone ones in their place and then put the bird back. These eggs were then put under a broody hen – almost until they were ready to hatch – when they were returned to the partridge. You see that way they avoided predators.". However young partridges need insects to feed on, "and so," explained Harry, "the keepers would often put a shovelful of ant eggs beside a newly hatched nest."

There are fundamental differences too.

"There are no more really dark nights in the countryside now. Electricity has changed that. But years ago, if we went out at night with rabbit nets – which were five or six hundred yards long – then it really was important to have noted all the gates and trees in day-light so you could keep you sense of direction."

"I remember one night, at Parley Beams, we 'clean killed' over 50 rabbits with long nets... but all the time we were doing this, we were also listening and watching. That is how the most skilful old countrymen knew how to 'call' stoats and weasels. The way to call a fox is quite commonly known, but it is also possible to call a rabbit. But there's a lot less that can do that."

At Wickham St. Pauls, farmworker Toby Rash recalled that his own ferreting record was an extraordinary ONE HUNDRED and THREE with Cyril Toatley in a single day at Fenn Farm, Henny. However, for Jack Hunt of Bulmer Street the memory is of formal shoots and:

"the distances we beaters had to walk! Perhaps we'd go from the Auberies right down to Middleton Hall to start with, and then traipse everywhere else on foot for the rest of the day – such as back to Brakey Hill and then down to *Kitchen Farm*. We did miles!"

Yet the pheasants which were so beloved by the gentry also caused damage to the working farmer. So great were the losses incurred by George Jackson at *Bridge Street Farm*, Long Melford, that it necessitated the ultimate remedy...he gave up his tenancy and moved to Red House Farm, Foxearth.
Not all memories are so serious.

"In Bulmer," relates one youthful truant, "I'd go biking round with my mate and every now and then fire a 'starting' pistol. Then we'd hide up and watch the 'keeper pedalling about like mad, trying to catch the person who was 'shooting' his pheasants!"

By comparison, several spoke of the days when, "hunting was a genuine farmer's sport" and told too of the pre-War 'Point to Points' – which were often held locally. At Alphamstone Rowena Twinn describes the charm of those pre-motorised times.

"We made our own fun in those days – and we jolly well enjoyed it! So if they had a Point to Point on John Nott's land at Kings Farm, we would look forward to it for the whole year. And it was lovely. Farm waggons were drawn onto the field and we would climb aboard to get a better view. The course was two miles – but for some races they went round twice. But everything was so friendly. A lot more farmers hunted in those days – just riding on a cart horse – or possibly a half-bred light cart horse that normally pulled a pony cart. It was fun! A real get together."

Another venue was *Butlers Hall*, Bulmer – of which smallholder

Rover' Finch nostalgically declared:

"It was ideal wasn't it. You could stand at the top of the hill and watch all the riders going round. What's more they used to sell pears and hot chocolate and all of your friends would be there. We didn't have many highlights years ago – but that was one of them!"

PART FIVE

DEFENCE
OF THE
FURROW

"Threshing machines dusty? Should think they were! I remember one time in the War when we had some Land Girls helping and Doe came from Bures to do some stacks here and he say 'Eddie, this barley's got smut'.

'Smut?' I said. 'I've never seen that before'...

Anyway we started threshing and all that smut-dust came off and we got as black as coal, but that was worse than coal dust because it stuck to you so... we were covered in it!

Well there was a land girl with me and she kept looking at a mirror and then ol' Bob Seadon came stumping down the road and said something to she – about this dust – and that didn't quite suit – and I thought she was going to clout him!"

EDDIE TUFFIN,
threshing near Alphamstone Church
during World War II

"We had some smashing times in the L.D.V. Oh yes, it was good fun. But the Home Guard though – that was different. That was a different kettle of fish."

FRANK TURNER, Twinstead

"The Agricultural Clubs at Bures, Stanningfield, Burwell and Long Melford were all started about 1943-44 by the Ministry of Agriculture to encourage better, more productive farming in this area... to tell the truth, I think the farmers also got a little more 'petrol ration' for attending!"

DAVID TAYLOR-BALLS
Chairman, Bures Agricultural Club
Brunnings Farm, Nayland

"I remember one time with the Home Guard. It was just before harvest. Talk about hot! It was enough to roast you! But they'd given us these 'molotov cocktails' and we had to practise ambushing this bridge – in case 'Gerry' came. Anyway the officer told us to throw these things at the road – to pretend we were blowing the bridge up – but it was such a bloomin' hot day that everything caught fire! The road tar was all runny anyway and that soon caught hold and then all the grass and rubbish round about got on fire – and made a HELL–OF–A–SMOKE! Come the finish, the fire engines had to come rushing out... Talk about blowing it up – we jolly nearly burned it down!"

FRANK BILLIMORE, now of Bulmer
recalling one 'H-G' exercise at
Hengrave near Bury St. Edmunds.

213

Chapter Eighteen

HOME GUARD MEMORIES

"In the event of an invasion, the preservation of this kingdom
must depend upon the unanimity of the people...
We are resolved to unite our efforts against the common enemy...
We will contribute by every means in our power to the defence
of the country."

One could be forgiven for thinking that the above was broadcast in 1940. In fact, it dates from Napoleonic times. But it was uttered locally. At Wethersfield's parish Vestry meeting. On 25th July, 1803.* And it well sums up this chapter.

During the First World War the threat of aggression became reality. Airship raids took place over East Anglia. On the night of 31st March, 1916, Sudbury was attacked. Thirty bombs were dropped on East Street, Constitution Hill, Newmans Road, Melford Road and on Brundon Meadows. Five people were killed.†

Meanwhile innumerable young men left local villages to join the army. Stark memorials record those who did not return. Of our own contributors, Edwin Partridge, the late Ernie Lott, Harry Gilbert and Hazell Chinnery saw service in those awful days, the latter also being

* From the parish documents lodged in Essex Record Office. Closer to home, Basil Slaughter records that, "in readiness for a Napoleonic invasion, warning beacons were positioned at the top of Ballingdon Hill near *Armsey Farm*." (*Bulmer, Then and Now*).

† Apparently some thirty Zeppelins took part in the raid with one being hit by anti-aircraft fire as it approached Stowmarket. Damage from Zeppelin bombs is also believed to have occurred between Sible Hedingham and Halstead.

a Prisoner of War in Germany.

In turn German prisoners came to England. Some were temporarily billeted at Halstead workhouse, and whilst here built the early silage silos at *Brundon Hall* and *Fowes Farm*, Belchamp Otten.

Significantly, Hawstead farmer's son, the Rev. Philip Wright (b.1908), recalled his father's horses being commandeered for the war effort, whilst on one occasion:

"We had a threshing machine come to my Father's farm – but you know, there were so few men left that it was almost entirely staffed by 'land girls'."

We now move forward. We blithely skip some two decades of peace time's quiet living, as the steady farming seasons came and went along our Colne-Stour countryside, until, in 1939 the clouds of war burst open once again.

Early in the summer of 1940 was formed the origins of the great 'Dad's Army'. A close relative provides a typically humorous memory.

"The day they called for volunteers," exclaimed John Cooper (b.1916), "your father and I walked down to Hadleigh to join the L.D.V."

"Ah, so you joined the – er – Local Defence..." I began hesitantly.

"NO!" he stormed. "L.D.V. stood for LOOK! DUCK! and VANISH!"

Initially there was not very much equipment to do the defending – or vanishing! – with.

"All we actually got was an armlet with L.D.V.* marked on it and our own shotguns from the farm. But about half the volunteers were ex-soldiers, so the first thing we had was drill training and 'Rocky'† started up with, 'Pull your shoulders back! Quick March! Quick March!' He used to work for us at the time, so next morning

* The initials did of course stand for Local Defence Volunteer.

† Stanley Pinson-Roxburgh; see also *The Khyber Connection*.

I'd come out of the house and shout, 'Morning Stan! Quick March! Quick March! ... What a game! But at the beginning we all mucked in together and had a laugh. We all enjoyed it in the early days."

John was not alone in experiencing a reversal of roles. At Little Maplestead Hall, Joe Blomfield recounts:

"Oh yes! Everything seemed topsy-turvy. One night we actually did a duty at 'The Hall'. But my cowman had been in the First World War and so he sat in my chair beside the fire and close to the telephone, while I shivered in the porch outside!"

Meanwhile the first armaments were arriving. At Elmsett it was five rifles with five rounds each, whilst at Bulmer recalls Jack Cornell, "we got this 'ere arm band; then a few months later we were given some denim suits and finally ten rifles arrived... course, they all went to the ex-servicemen." Farmer Jim Ruffle adds:

"We used to parade about Bulmer with broomsticks and pitch-forks... Huh! broomsticks and pitchforks. Anyway, after a while they sent us some special cartridges to use in our twelve bore shot-guns. They were special as well!! The cartridge contained just one big ball. They were terrible. Frank Marsh shot one and it blew up the dust 250 yards away. I'm surprised it didn't split the barrels really."

At Colne Engaine, 'old soldier' Harry Gilbert was actively involved as Corporal and then Sergeant.

"Our job was to get to know our own countryside. That way if paratroopers landed or an aeroplane crashed, we could get there in the quickest possible time – especially as all the signposts were removed."

But there were also amusing moments. Some have become part of our folklore:

"We were building hay stacks one day at *Munns Farm*," continues Harry, "when the siren suddenly went to warn us of a raid. Course we all scrambled away to the air raid shelter. But after a few minutes someone said 'Where's your father-in-law? Oh dear! He was still on top of the stack wasn't he! No-one had thought to put a

216

Thomas Gainsborough's painting of 'Cornard Wood' was completed about 1748 when the artist was just twenty one. The picture provides an intriguing glimpse into the flora and fauna of the Suffolk-Essex border at the time. (By kind permission of the National Gallery)

The late Harry Gilbert of Colne Engaine. Retired gamekeeper, station master, smallholder, World War One veteran and countryman, Harry was a veritable oracle on all aspects of bygone rural life. A fuller account of his life has recently been published by Colne Engaine History Society.

"Greengage, Bullace and Walnuts! We bought bushels of them as we went around!" Tom Gilbert – who was born in Little Yeldham – reminiscing about his Father's horse-drawn 'fruit and vegetable' business.

For over four hundred years the Suffolk-Essex border was a vigorous centre of non-conformity – ar freedom of religious worship. Ridgewell's brick Chapel (above) is a feature of any journey along t A604 to Cambridge. Like many independent Chapels its congregation's origin can be traced back to t 'Act of Uniformity' in 1662.

Even isolated Little Maplestead had an elegant chapel – with seating for 400 people! It was situat not far from the 'Cock Inn' beside the Sudbury to Halstead road.

Enid and Trevor Howard. For over thirty years Trevor was the rector of Belchamp Otten, Belchamp Walter and Bulmer. Having farmed in his youth he was ideally suited to the area of which he later became Rural Dean. As Basil Slaughter wrote, "he succeeded in inspiring a vigorous church life and lovingly ministered in a meaningful way".

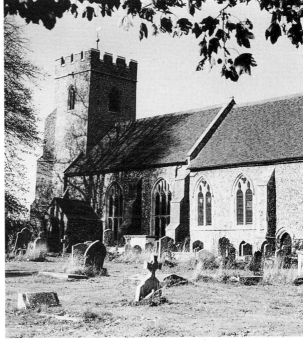

Father Aidan Harker, rector of Belchamp St. Pauls and Ovington, believes that churches dedicated to St. Andrew were often some of the first to be established by Christian missionaries in the Saxon era. Left: St. Andrews Church, Halstead. Right: St. Andrews Church, Bulmer.

A photograph that always brings a smile. Bulmer Home Guard 'on manœuvers' in Sandy Lane!

*The high 'box-pews' of Brent Eleigh Church, are typical of those which were once a standard featur
in most local churches.*

After Radio Four, "had breakfast at Hill Farm" – to discuss 'The Long Furow' – the author was invited to give lectures by the Mayors of both Bury St. Edmunds and Sudbury.

The most memorable evening however was spent in the tiny Village Hall at Alphamstone where a packed audience – including contributors Dorothy Turner, Popsy Parker and Rowena Twinn – were shown slides of the old countryside. The real 'star' of the evening however was retired shepherd Eddie Tuffin – aged 90 – who at the merest hint would spontaneously interject another sparklingly vivid memory. Later chairman Desmond Bridge of Goulds Farm wrote – "it was amazing. The Eddie and Ashley double-act was like something off the London Palladium!"

ladder up for him... No! He didn't forget about that for a day or two – I can tell you!"

With the start of daylight bombings and the evacuation from Dunkirk, the 'real' war had begun. Some months later The Home Guard was formed to replace the L.D.V. and it became compulsory for those in reserved occupations to assist with Britain's defence. Nevertheless I was still somewhat mystified by the structure of the Home Guard ("So were we!" quipped one source). Fortunately, retired engineer John Frost of Halstead was able to help. Today he lives at North Mill – where his ancestors have been millers for over two hundred years, and it was here, one summer's evening, that he helpfully explained:

"In North-East Essex the Home Guard were part of the 15th Battalion of the Essex Regiment. The Battalion consisted of five companies together with a full complement of officers – similar to the regular army. In time, full uniforms, boots and a rifle for every 'private' were issued. Later, a certain number of Tommy guns; Browning automatics and Sten guns were also available."

As John described the duties of the 'H.G.' and also the role of its officers – who were responsible for weapons training, camouflage, intelligence gathering and medication – I had to confess my humility. Whatever its reputation, the Home Guard had obviously been far more professionally organised than I had ever imagined.*

Yet despite the improved organisation, status and equipment there were also aggravations. "There wasn't quite so much of being hollered and yelled at in the L.D.V. – when we were all volunteers", was a comment made by nearly every contributor. Another – very real – irritation is recounted by hurdle maker and shearer Tom Rowe:

"The thing was this. We country boys weren't supposed to know anything. One of them instructors told me for a certainty 'that vacuum was pressure'. No, it got on your nerves really."

* As an Intelligence Officer, John felt he was on duty the whole time. "It was my job to keep in touch with people; to organise 'look-outs' and 'observers', to monitor any unusual comings or goings and to keep an ear to the ground for reports of 'suspicious or doubtful people'".

217

Almost invariably however the dry East Anglian humour worked its revenge on the pompous and officious. Farmer Jack Wallace provides an example from Chadacre.

"We were having target practice when the rifle instructor bellowed at one of my old mates. 'Don't you know what a 'fine sight' is yet!' 'Yes,' came the grunted reply, 'a bloody good dinner'."

Maintaining seriousness could be equally difficult. During a 'mock' battle, recalls Halstead's Tommy Letham, a little message was discovered pinned beside a tree. It read:

"HAVE RECOVERED FROM MORTAL WOUND... GONE HOME TO TEA"

At Bulmer, one exercise provided some genuinely rural humour.

"We were spaced out in a long line," says Jack Cornell, "and had to 'push forward' across the top of Lemon Hill from Gogum Hall to attack the road. Well, some of 'em were getting on for sixty or more. Course, they couldn't keep up with us boys, so it wasn't long before the line had a big old kink in it! Now one of the oldest was Sid Rowe and every two or three minutes, the sergeant would bawl out, 'Man next to Sid Rowe get back a bit! Man next to Sid Rowe get back a bit!

"Oh dear, it made you curl with laughing, because it was the beet hoeing season and they were 'chopped out' in a line as well. Course, Sid couldn't quite keep up there neither. So all that summer on the beet fields, there were young lads imitating the officer's voice with: 'Man next to Sid Rowe, get back a bit!'*

"Oh yes, we had some games! The best capers were the ones we got up to ourselves. Like when we had to capture a light in the middle of Church Meadow or some such place. Well, they generally left the less nimble ones to guard it, so if we boys had a grudge against any of them older men – well, that was good opportunity to settle a few old scores..!

" 'Course, half the time no-one really knew what was going on. I

* Sid was actually a veteran of World War One. Whilst in the trenches he made a beautiful miniature desk of drawers from old shell cases – a photograph of which is included in *The Long Furrow*.
The 'Lemon Hill' referred to in the story is between Lower Houses, Bulmer Street and Goldingham (or 'Gogum') Hall.

mean, the very first time we had to capture this 'ere paraffin lamp, the damn thing went out. Then it got so blessed windy that they couldn't relight it. Next thing was it started to rain... Well you can imagine what happened, can't you. With all us lot on our hands and knees naneking about in the dark. And then you'd suddenly hear someone whisper '...psst! ...psst! Is that you Jack? We're over here! Come and capture us quick! *The Blackbirds* is going to close in twenty minutes!"

Irrespective of whether the exercises were held in village halls, farms or meadows the irony of the situation was never lost.

"I remember one winter," re-calls Alf Finch of Borley,"when we went to Bull Lane in Melford to do an exercise in Fire Control. Do you know what we had to do...? We had to crawl about on the floor of this 'ere derelict house pretending there was a fire on. Pretending there was a fire! It was a cold as hell!"

On occasions the 'all night' exercises were no more explicable.

"We had to stay out all night guarding the top of *Seven Forms Hill*" (between Borley and Belchamp Walter).
"What were you guarding?" I asked curiously.
"What? I don't know! I've spent 50 years wondering and I still don't know!"

Despite the reservations, the Home Guard did provide a basic training in weapons and explosives. Eddie Tuffin had his first machine gun practice at Bures pits. "My poor ears!" he declares, half a century later. George Cresswell was not alone when his first five rounds went off – simultaneously – at Ballingdon Chalk pit. Yet the impression prevails that for many countryman the rifle practice and shooting competitions were one of the most rewarding features of 'H.G.' duty.*

Yet there were sad and shattering moments as well.
On Sunday, 23rd April, 1944 a devastating tragedy occurred at *Rectory Farm*, Gestingthorpe. Six men lost their lives in an awful

---

* Jim Ruffle and Tom Bird for example, remember using the chalk pits at Goldingham Hall, Bulmer; the sandpits at Alphamstone; the brick yards at Maiden Ley, Castle Hedingham; and the army ranges at Middlewich and Fingringhoe near Colchester.

accident during explosives training.

Captain John Philp *(aged 41)*......Gestingthorpe
Sgt. Thomas Firmin *45*..............Sible Hedingham
Sgt. Herbert Cousins *33* ....Sible Hedingham
Cpl. Cyril Halls *31* ....Sible Hedingham
Cpl. George Chambers *29* ....Pentlow
Cpl. John Partridge *36* ....Belchamp Walter

Three N.C.O.'s were also injured: Sgt. S. Wallace of Great Maplestead, Sgt. Frederick Lock of Gosfield and Cpl. Ernie Lott of Bulmer (and contributor to this book).

The Gestingthorpe disaster reminds us of the serious side of the Home Guard. We will continue with a brief resume of the vital work which was undertaken.

"At Colne Engaine," explains Harry Gilbert, "a post was maintained. Every night there were two of us from the Home Guard, one from the Red Cross, an A.R.P. Warden and perhaps a chap from the Fire Service. We had a hut right against the church with a few utensils and a primus stove.Directly we had news of an air raid, we were on alert. It was a very worthwhile thing to do."

Other crucial Home Guard duties included manning road blocks and checking identity cards. At Sudbury, the late George Cresswell had to guard the town's telephone exchange. "There were about six of us. You did an hour 'on guard' and the rest of the time you could sleep."

"On one occasion however," recounts George, "an officer tried to catch us out – by creeping up on us. But my old mate slammed a magazine in his gun. That shook him up! 'You're meant to say, 'who goes there' yelled the officer. 'Last time I said that was in 1916 – and I got taken prisoner!' came the reply."

All of our contributors did night duty. In the early days of the war Fred Chatters was a 'spotter' at Bulmer (doing aircraft observation etc.). At Alphamstone Eddie Tuffin was sent:

"To guard Bell Hill," [a lovely vantage point over the Stour Valley between Bures and Lamarsh]. "During the night we took it in turns. Two men did 10pm to 2am and two more did 2–5am. In the summer we could lay on the grass, but if it rained there was an old shed we could go in. But it leaked like a sieve. It was worse than useless!"

"How often were there Home Guard duties to do?" I wondered.

"At Halstead," explains John Frost, "the Home Guard met every Sunday morning and one evening each week for training. Every week to ten days, you'd be 'on duty' from 10pm to 6am But remember this, as soon as you came 'off duty' you had to go and do a full days work… oh yes! You probably would start to feel drowsy by the afternoon!"

Another vital role of the Home Guard was recalled by Wickham St. Pauls farmworker, Tom Bird.

"During the invasion threat, two of us were detailed to be out from 4 to 6am We had to walk around the roads and report anything suspicious. What's more, if a plane crashed we had to stand guard over it until the 'regulars' arrived."

Indeed in the Wickham St. Pauls – Gestingthorpe area, Tom recorded no less than five crashes – all within a mile of where he lived. (The exact locations can be gleaned from Dave Osborne's definitive *Halstead and Colne Valley at War*).

Yet even these, more serious, incidents provide some humorous recollections. One has been told time – and time again.

"Oh yes," laughs Freddie Ruse, "us lot in the Melford Home Guard used to tease the living daylights out of the Sudbury unit. You see a Gerry pilot baled out of his plane one night and so the Home Guard went rushing off to look for him – but simply could not find him…so finally the poor chap had to 'give himself up' to a postman!"

John Dixey remembers another night when…

"A German plane dropped a string of bombs over the Bulmer area. Naturally, the A.R.P. wardens went round to check that there were no direct hits and that no-one was hurt. When they'd finished, they went back to George Thompson's house [near

Gentry's Farm] for a cup of tea, just in case anything else should crop up. Well as it began to get light the others left and George happened to look in his garden. I know it sounds corny but you know what he saw don't you? A bloomin' great hole with an unexploded bomb in it!"

With this story, we have returned once more to Bulmer, where, declares Jack Cornell, "The best thing about the whole of the Home Guard was the boots they gave you!" (Again corroborated by almost every other contributor!). Indeed it wasn't long before Home Guard boots were being worn seven days a week. However...

"Right at the very end, old ——— came to an inspection wearing his farm boots. 'Have you still got your army boots?' the officer snapped. 'Well, Sir,' came the honest reply, 'I've still got the upper parts left!'"

There were other amusing exchanges.

"If the parade was for 7pm," continues Jack, "then you did actually have to be there, spick and span, by seven o'clock. Well there were lots of times when I might have been threshing until six o'clock at somewhere like Foxearth – and then I'd have to bike home, have tea, jump into my uniform and bike down to Gogum Hall. Trouble was that threshing wasn't an excuse. In fact, the only excuse that 'stuck' was if you had any animals to milk... Needless to say, it wasn't long before one of my relatives bought a goat on purpose. 'Why are you late?' the officer would bark out *every single parade*... 'Been milking my goat, Sir,' came the inevitable reply'."

Then there is the folklore. Tom Gilbert tells of searching through wet corn for a parachutist, "when ol' matey challenged a water pump in pitch darkness." From butler Horace Reeve, there came the gleeful memory of:

"checking identity papers near the Hedingham *Swan* and finding that old ———, who had always been a cut above himself anyway – hadn't got his on him."
"How do we know who you are?" we kept saying.
"You've known me all my life!"
"Sorry," we replied, "orders is orders... Oh yes, we got our own back on him that time!"

(As did several other contributors from different villages. "Oh yes! We made ol'———swear! He went ahead at us!" laughs Twinstead's Frank Turner of a different occasion).

Eventually, however, there was a little – just a little – financial recompense.

"After we'd done several night time spells," explains one gallant and illustrious Bulmer private, "we were all given 'one and six' [i.e. one shilling and sixpence] 'Course, that was a proper military performance. The officer sat at the desk and we had to go up, salute, be given the money, take a step back, stamp your boot and salute, all over again. Talk about a pantomime! Well, for some reason I was one of the last to go up. So I saluted and got my money and took a step back. But the officer wasn't looking, so I thought I won't bother about saluting again. When the parade was over my mate said, 'You only saluted once Jack'."

"Yes," I replied, "and that's plenty enough for 'one and six'!"

And finally, from Sir Robin Day who, interviewed on *Desert Island Discs*, commented of his own days with another platoon of the Essex Home Guard – at West Mersea:

"I've always thought that the T.V. programme *Dad's Army* was actually more of a *documentary* than a comedy."

Time and again in the research for this chapter the author was told, "Yes. That's about exactly how it was!"

Chapter Nineteen

RATIONS & RATION BOOKS
The Housewife's War

"We were threshing up at Borley one day when the bloke on the stack spotted the dray going to the 'off-licence' on the green. 'Look sharp!' he shouted to the boy, 'Be off and reserve some quick!'"

JACK CORNELL

As part of the research, I visited the Imperial War Museum in South London. Entering the gallery devoted to the Second World War I noticed a display on Food Rationing. Inside a glass cabinet was a plate of food. Although the allowance of butter, cheese and meat was by no means excessive, it was quite adequate for a normal day. Then I looked again.

It was a WHOLE WEEK'S ration

With the run down of British agriculture since World War One, food was suddenly a vital commodity. One propaganda poster declared:

B R E A D
Every time you eat bread remember
– One quarter of all the British and Allied Seamen
are permanently engaged in carrying grain for our bread
…at the table of every bread-waster
sits the spirit of a dead merchant seaman.

To take a lead and 'show the way', the Royal Family grew their own vegetables. Queen Mary was seen to have a Ration Book, Women's Institutes organised mammoth 'jam-making sessions' and 'Digging

224

for Victory' became a crusade that even involved rural schools.

"The afternoon session is put forward a quarter of an hour," noted Wickham St. Pauls School Log for June 16, 1941; "as the farmers are employing the children at singling sugar beet in the evenings and requested that they might go as early as possible. Eight of the senior children are helping."

At Henny school – two miles from Sudbury, the afternoon of 6th October 1941, was spent 'gathering hips for jam' – as were several others. In the following May, 'the vegetable garden was dug by the boys, and on 7th September:

"the tomato crop was picked and sold at ruling prices."*

In July 1943, the tiny school became NATIONAL NEWS. For the Minister of Food, Lord Woolton, had announced 'on a radio broadcast', that a typical school dinner was "roast beef, potatoes and cabbage, followed by chocolate pudding".

"WHAT!" exclaimed Henny's pupils, "NOT HERE IT ISN'T!!!"

"Consequently," reported the *Daily Sketch*, "the teacher, Mrs E. Paul, 'allowed' the thirty six children to write to the Minister and tell him of their meals." And they told him! Their lunches were actually 'bread and jam, bread and meat or bread and (etc.!)'

The Minister replied by return of post and:

"on July 5th," declared the triumphant teacher, "we commenced hot dinners under the emergency feeding scheme; the meals being sent from Hadleigh depot."

The first day's menu, reveals the *Daily Sketch*, was actually, "roast beef, potatoes, cabbage and chocolate pudding". However, we can't

---

* Cavendish School's log for October 6th, 1941, also records that, "the children gathered hips this p.m. – being part of War effort". Three weeks later however, when, "representatives of the Ministry of Agriculture called, asking permission to employ boys in agriculture owing to the national emergency," the request had to be referred to the Education Authority.

help wondering whether – if Lord Woolton had then asked the pupils were they satisfied – they might, just possibly have answered, "...Yes Minister!"

Rationing itself had commenced on January 8th, 1940 with local announcements in both the *Halstead Gazette* and *Suffolk Free Press*. Needless to say confusion, contrivance and straightforward practical ingenuity soon developed. There was the "boiling up of sugar beet to extract the syrup for sweetening," says Phyllis Billimore; "the shaking of creamy milk in a Kilner jar," relates Maud Lott, "to make butter for Sunday tea"; and the "sheer determination," states Foxearth's May Cresswell, "to make every inch of your garden provide food".

Many like Gertie Coe of Brickwall Cottage, Bulmer kept a pig:

"Although you had to give up your bacon ration, you were still much better off... But the evening after it was slaughtered was a busy time! All the fat had to be processed, you'd also cook some fresh pork and then the hams and bacons were salted down and eventually hung up in muslin bags so that the flies couldn't get to them."*

Bananas disappeared for months.

"But if a Fyffes lorry did go by," recounts Rose Chatters, "I'd bike down from Paul's Belchamp to Sudbury and queue up for ages...'course, when my turn came they'd usually have just sold out!"

It was the same with sausages. Although not rationed they were often difficult to obtain. "I've biked to Halstead and back – an eight mile round trip – for just half a pound of sausages," remembers Bertha Bird, whose consolation might have been another tin of Spam or corned beef.

* The 'salting down' lasted for several weeks. Additionally, the fat was boiled down to make lard and the head was made into pork brawn.
    One long term consequence of sugar rationing is explained by Heiti Lawson: "A lot of people had to give up making home made wine, and unfortunately never restarted when rationing was lifted – and many of the old skills and recipes were very nearly lost."
    For the record, there were extra allowances of sugar for the making of marmalade and jam. Beekeepers were allowed 10lb of sugar per hive of bees; whilst saccharine could substitute sugar in tea and coffee.

However, there were *some* variations. During the particularly stren-uous tasks of haysel, harvest and beet lifting, agricultural workers could obtain slightly increased rations of cheese, sugar, tea and mar-garine.

"But even so," declares Frank Billimore, "we were still basically hungry all of the time. We had a young child and although these rations might have been sufficient for office work, they weren't for manual."

Inevitably, a feeling soon developed that the system was never com-pletely fair. "The better-off could always afford more and buy stuff that was 'under the counter'," was a recurring comment. Not surpris-ingly 'little dodges' soon developed into a widely accepted black market.

"If anyone had been totally straight," remarks one contributor, "then I don't believe that they could have got through the war without starving. Oh yes, there was all manner of jiggery-pokery! We used to call it 'lease-lend' – Churchill's term!"

"It was like this," elaborates Wally Twinn, "during the War farmers were meant to sell ALL their eggs through the official Marketing Board. But our policeman soon discovered that he could just get six in his helmet! Oh dear, we soon had the entire U.S. army trying to get eggs off us!"

Another source remembers:

"You were only allowed to slaughter one pig – for private use – every six months. Now to prevent you selling others on the black market, you had to produce a 'Private Slaughter Licence'. Anyway, I had several good mates who said they could get silk stockings and chocolates, but wanted some hams and bacons. So I put this pig in my old car and went off to the slaughter house in Ballingdon. But just before I got there a policeman stopped me. "Where's your slaughter licence?" he asked.
"Oh God. I'm in a muddle now," I thought. Anyway I fumbled about in my pockets for a minute or two and then said, "Oh dear...I must have left it at home."
"Uhm...really," he said, drumming his fingers on the roof of the car.

"Yes," I thought to myself, "and I know what you bloomin' well want!"*

At Long Melford, butcher Freddie Ruse had the responsibility for allocating meat out to other butchers.

"It was a very trying time for us all – but especially for the smaller shops. Although they might get the same 'allowance per customer' they did not get enough to provide any variety."

But it was not just food that was rationed. Clothes were obtained by the accumulation of weekly 'points'.

"So what I did," explains Dorothy Turner, "was to make flour bags into pillow cases and tablecloths. That way you could save your 'points' for something you really needed."

Phyllis Billimore similarly saved bedsheets by putting 'the outsides in the middle'. After the birth of a first child however a grey 'utility blanket' was issued. Many are still in existence. And pregnant women were allowed more milk – "so the milkman," laughs Bertha Bird, "was always the first to know if anyone was 'expecting'!" For life went on. "Before you went to a dance, you'd paint a line on your legs – to look like the seam of a silk stocking", was a frequent memory, whilst at Halstead, Rene Cross nostalgically remembers:

"When Albert and I got married, we were given loads of coupons! Everyone 'chipped in' to help us make a start."
Other things – although not rationed – could be difficult to obtain.

"At furniture sales," recall one couple who married in 1942,

---

* A variation of this story – told to me in all seriousness less than two miles from Gestingthorpe – was of replying, "'Why ever should I want a slaughter licence? I'm just taking my pet pig for a ride!' But do you know that ruddy policeman followed me all the way home – right round by Long Melford and Belchamp Walter just to make sure I kept my word!"
At Borley, farmworker Alf Finch had a different experience.
"I kept this pig for six months but then the paper work got muddled up and I missed the chance to slaughter it – so I had to wait another six months to get a new licence. Well that bloomin' pig went over fourteen score (i.e. about 130kg) when it was finally slaughtered!!"

"there was a fixed price and if you wanted something you put your name in a hat. When we got married we bought our bed – or rather our name was pulled out of a hat – at an auction in Castle Hedingham."

It's a good job they got it. The contributors are the author's parents. Three years later Jack Cornell was married – and had to buy a suit. "But it took over a year to collect enough bloomin' clothing points!" he quipped four decades later. But perhaps Jack's greater concern was that the coal – upon which his traction engine depended – was also rationed, and often came from open cast quarries.

"There were lumps of wet clay in it and some of it was almost useless. Quite often we had to burn coke and wood at the same time... But that was terrible because 'it all went together' and you couldn't get any air through it. Then we got some other rare old stuff and God alive! It smoked Bulmer Street right out! We weren't very popular then I can tell you!"

When the threshing was completed, a form had to be filled in indicating the quantity of coal left over; the number of sacks threshed and the amount of tail corn dressed out. (To prevent 'fiddling' the tail corn was not allowed to exceed a certain percentage). Needless to say, "there were always those who wanted to 'wangle' the tail corn. (So that it could be fed to their chickens...to produce more eggs...to swap for something on the black market!) Oh yes, you had to be a bit careful with some of 'em."*
Meanwhile, tyres were 'difficult to come by' and petrol was rationed.

"In Sudbury the worst time for petrol," says Jack, "was after Dunkirk, when – for a while – only Dursley's Garage in East Street had a supply. What was really aggravating though, was that you weren't allowed to buy it in a can. So if you had any coupons 'left over', you had to go up Ballingdon Hill, let a gallon out of your motorbike – into a can – and then go back and get another gallon!"

* Maggie Finch explains that, "you were only allowed half a dozen chickens – you couldn't get food for any more. But we could go gleaning. I always used to look where the sheaves had been 'shocked up' (i.e. stood up in groups) – because it was a good place to find 'heads' which had fallen off."

Petrol however was also required to start certain agricultural tractors (e.g. the Case Model C and Standard Fordson). This was coloured red to prevent it being used for private motoring.

But late one night, as the research for this chapter reached its conclusion, and I sat in the comfortable lounge of a retired farmer – who is not otherwise a contributor to this book – it was explained that, "by putting ten gallons of 'red' agricultural petrol in 'a certain ingredient', the dye could eventually be distilled out". With this memory of the 'ingenuity' of the furrow, we are possibly crossing the amorphous boundary between the 'illicit' and the 'illegal'. But I couldn't resist the temptation to ask what other 'legal dodges' there were.

"It was quite a regular thing," came the reply, "to mix one part of paraffin in with three or four parts of petrol. It might bring the octane down from say, 98 to 90, and it would soon soot up the spark plugs and smoke something terrible – but it would give you a few more miles. Oh yes! You'd see cars going by looking like steam trains! It wasn't at all unusual! But the thing was this, we were young at the time and if I'm honest we just delighted in getting things that people said were unobtainable."

As David Tuffin of Henny so well sums up:

"Rationing! Cuh! If they'd known what was going on in the country then I reckon half of us would have been locked up!"

But if food, clothes, petrol and coal were rationed, and agricultural machinery restricted, were there any totally essential items which became very short.

"BEER! FAGS! AND BACCA!" came Jack Cornell's lighthearted retort. "'Course, I know it's nothing really but there were times when they completely dried up in some villages round here."

Fortunately, however, there was one legendary pub – the Belchamp *Eight Bells* – which was owned by a small brewery and nearly always managed to have some beer.

"In fact, when word got around that they were in good supply, and they'd serve non-regulars, it's been so damned full that we've had to stand outside – and drink it out of 2lb jam jars! To tell the

230

truth, you couldn't quite get a pint in a two pound jam jar – but that didn't over much matter!"

A couple of miles away one shortage at the *Cock and Blackbirds* produced an inevitable quip.

"This 'ere stranger came in and the landlord told him there wasn't any beer but he'd got some cider.
'What sort?' asked the disgruntled stranger.
'*Bulmers Dry*,' replied the landlord.
'...B_____right, Bulmer's dry!' came the response."

The enormous influx of billeted troops and airmen naturally compounded the problem. Amusing stories are told of both the Tilbury *Fox* and the Ovington *Donkey* where; "The demand was so brisk from the newly arrived Americans that – while it lasted – the beer was scooped out of a big bath to serve them quicker!". Lily Harrington similarly tells of her own days at the Sible Hedingham *Bell*.

"The beer got very short. It came in on Friday – and by Monday it had all gone. I didn't actually shut on the other days, but it was pretty much the same. I'd keep the door open – just in case someone wanted a bit of mineral water or something. But it was a job with the beer. You had to try and ration it a bit to non-regulars."

More surprising is the duration of rationing after the War. Several contributors presented me with their final ration books. To my amazement they were dated 1953-54. (Indeed it was not until after hostilities ended that bread was actually rationed, although it has been suggested that this was only to make people more careful). Moreover, the Ministry of Food continued to issue announcements in local newspapers on a WEEKLY BASIS until the early nineteen fifties.

In the *Halstead Gazette* of March 26th, 1948 for example, an advertisement exclaims:

FOOD FACTS
Recipes which are not hard on your rations.

It was followed by the exhortation:

YOUR EMPTY JAM JARS ARE WANTED
...milk bottles too please.

The following year, on 16th August, 1949, page ten of the *Suffolk Free Press* was completely devoted to a weekly series of articles – dramatically headlined:

FIGHTING NORTH EUROPE'S
BATTLE FOR FOOD

Nearly every contributor to this book – the men and women of our farming countryside – have helped to win that struggle. The spectre of food rationing has been removed from Western Europe.

Chapter Twenty

A MEMORIAL IN A WHEAT FIELD

To the Citizens of Sudbury
for their
Fellowship, Understanding and Hospitality
The Officers and Men
486 Bombardment Group
418 Air Service Group
U.S. Army Air Force
1944-1945
(from plaque on Sudbury Town Hall)

Question: What do Chilton, Earls Colne, Gosfield, Lavenham, Ridgewell and Wormingford all have in common? Lovely views? Beautiful churches? Productive land? Fascinating histories?

There is something else. If we include Boxted (near Colchester), Great Dunmow, Rattlesden, Raydon (near Hadleigh), Great Saling, Great Sampford, Stradishall, Wattisham...and Wethersfield, the picture becomes clearer.

Every single one of them was a wartime air base.

Astonishingly, no less than NINETY TWO air bases – each accommodating over 2000 servicemen were built in East Anglia in World War II.*

The pace of work was phenomenal.

---

* From *Action Station, Wartime Military Airfields of East Anglia 1939-45* by Michael J. Bowyer, published by Patrick Stephen, Cambridge.

Gosfield, Ridgewell and Earls Colne Airfields were ready in 1942 (effectively becoming operational in the following year). Wethersfield opened in January 1944 and Chilton in March 1944.

"On some days in Sudbury," says one contributor, "there were just hundreds of lorries with sand and stone, *continuously* rumbling through the town from morning till night."

For many old countrymen – born in the 1870's, the descent into their villages of bulldozers, cement mixers, trench diggers and finally pre-fabricated housing, must have seemed unbelievable.
Whilst clearing the countryside, laying the runways and erecting the Nissen huts and hangars was an enormous task, obtaining the sand, gravel and cement was another.

"Around Alphamstone sand pits," declares Eddie Tuffin, "it was almost impossible to get along the road with a horse and waggon after seven o'clock in the morning. There were lorries everywhere. You might just as well stop in the stable!"

Numerous other villages experienced something similar. At Cavendish, Glemsford, Liston and Long Melford, gravel was extracted from the valley beside the River Stour. "Although it wasn't perfect," explains Peter Minter of Bulmer Brickyard, "it was good enough for short term concrete".* By comparison hardcore was often obtained from the bomb damaged rubble of London.

"However," continues Peter, "where the ballast lorries were concerned there was a typical 'war time racket'. You see some of the drivers were absolute rogues. At Waldingfield they'd drive in one gate – go right round the perimeter and then 'come back in again' without ever tipping so they got paid twice for one load!"

Yet it is Dave Osborne's definitive *Halstead and Colne Valley at War*† which most enables us to grasp the overwhelming logistics of airfield building with his statistics of Ridgewell.

"Some 1,170,000 man hours were needed for its construction and no less than a million cubic yards of concrete were used...six

* The holes come to within about twenty to thirty yards of the actual river. Pebbles were similarly removed from the sea shore (e.g. at Thorpness) whilst there were also pits at Acton, Bures, Cornard, Edwardstone and Great Yeldham.

† Recently republished and available in Halstead bookshops or from Adrian Corder-Birch, The Maltings, North End Road, Little Yeldham, Halstead, Essex CO9 4LE. (Price £4.50 + 50p postage and packing).

miles of 4" and 6" water mains were laid, 12 miles of French drains, and seven miles of foul drainage. On the site were more than 500 buildings and a sewerage plant to handle a population of TWO THOUSAND FIVE HUNDRED."

(At a time when the entire population of Sudbury was approximately 7000, Halstead 6000 and Hadleigh 3000, the air fields represented a population increase in our area of quite staggering proportions).

By mid 1943 the majority of airmen in the locality were Americans. Memories of their presence are legion.

"They were EVERYWHERE" was one comment. "And as for towns like Sudbury – well the pubs were full of them! Of course, they were all young...and at times a little bit crazy. If you went to Ipswich or somewhere it wasn't at all unusual to see two or three American jeeps driven through hedges, upside down in ditches or stuck in fields beside the road!"

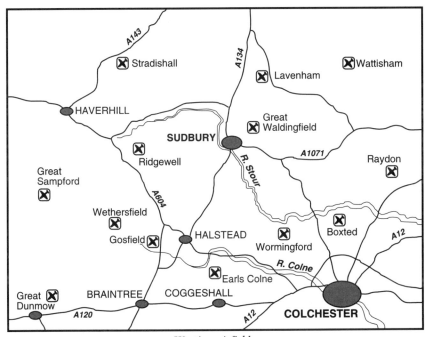

Wartime airfields

Within the intense pressure of 'live today: gone tomorrow', which surrounded the aircrew, there was the inevitable thirst for life – 'while you had it'. From Little Yeldham comes an amusing memory:

"If ever an American looked like being late back to the base, he'd just swipe a bike and then about a hundred yards from the gates he'd throw it into the pond by Mashey Corner – not far from Ridgewell Airfield. When summer came, the water began to drop and someone saw a bike beginning to emerge – so they fished it out. But as the water continued dropping they finished off getting about 50 others out as well!"*

Yet the flamboyance and 'letting off steam' was a vital therapy. For each airfield produced its heroes and sobering statistics.

*Of the 2800 servicemen based at the
Chilton/Great Waldingfield airbase,
an estimated 400 are believed to have paid
the supreme sacrifice.†*

At Ridgewell, where the 381st Bomb Group replaced the 296th in June 1943, there is still an atmosphere of stark solemnity.

Enhanced perhaps because one can quite legitimately drive across the old airfield.

Today there is a stretching length of black tarmac. Beside it an expanse of wheat field. A solitary hangar. And a memorial.

---

* There was of course the inevitable jealousy towards the young Americans who had never experienced rationing and had 'rather too much money to spend'. As one source put it, "If ever you went to an auction and they came in – well quite honestly you might as well walk out – you didn't stand a chance!"

† The 486th Bomb Group made 188 missions between May 1944-45 with Liberators and Fortresses. Horrifyingly, thirty three aircraft were lost in combat and 24 in accidents. The worst occurred on May 20th 1944, when two aircraft from Sudbury and one from Lavenham collided after take-off.

Those who died from the airfield are commemorated on a plaque opposite St. Gregory's Church in Sudbury and also on a memorial stone near the entrance to 'Chilton Grain' who now occupy the airfield.

About a hundred yards further along the road to Great Waldingfield are the old concrete gateposts, – where the traffic was stopped when the planes were taking off or landing.

On one day alone, a hundred young Americans lost their lives. (On the raid on the Schweinfurt ball-bearing factory on 17th August 1943). On average <u>one</u> in <u>four</u> aircrew failed to return; Yet two hundred and ninety seven missions were flown and 22,000 tons of bombs were dropped. Sadly two aircraft which did return collided coming in to land. All twenty aircrew were killed.Twenty four others lost their lives when loading bombs into an aircraft. In total, an estimated SIX HUNDRED servicemen based at Ridgewell paid the supreme sacrifice in twenty three brief months.

Every other local airbase – be it Lavenham, Rattlesden, Raydon or Earls Colne – has a similar story to tell.

One American to be based at Ridgewell – and who survived the 25 missions which permitted home leave – was John Comer. His harrowing, stirring, account of those days, entitled *Combat Crew*, has recently been published. Reviewing it in *The Suffolk Free Press* retired editor Geoff Brown wrote:

"*Combat Crew* is one of the most moving and at times, disturbing stories of the war in the air. It is a story of bravery without heroics, of appalling hardships and at times of disastrous blunders by the men who led them... All in East Anglia should read *Combat Crew*"*

Whilst John Comer was based at Ridgewell, this author's Father was living in a 'Land Settlement' house, close to the Camp's perimeter.

Nearly half a century later, on a Sunday evening in June, I slowly drove him back to Ridgewell airfield – with its views over Ashen, Tilbury, Yeldham and Ovington. Further in the distance, one can see Stambourne, Toppesfield, Castle Hedingham, Belchamp St. Pauls and – on a far horizon – the giant T.V. mast at Little Cornard.

A skylark sang overhead. For some moments we stood in silence; the breeze gently swaying the ears of wheat; around us nothing but quiet, tranquillity and peace.

* *Combat Crew* by John Comer, published by Leo Cooper, 1988. Another book on Ridgewell – and which also refers to the unveiling of the monument on 28th August, 1982 – is *The Mighty Men of the 381st* by Chaplain James Good Brown.
For information on Gosfield, see *The 410th Bombardment Group in World War Two* by Ian MacTaggart of Braintree Road, Gosfield. The 410th were stationed at the base in 1944.

It is difficult to believe that things were ever any different.

"...sometimes," came the memory, "you'd see a plane coming in with smoke pouring out of an engine – only forty to fifty feet above your head – and you'd hope it would land all right. Perhaps they'd clear the whole airfield for it. Other times, they weren't successful, and it would crash and there would be a big explosion.

When things like the bomb loading disaster happened we weren't immediately told. Later the American servicemen would just say quietly 'they caught a packet today'."

From these – gravest – of recollections we move to others. Of the aeroplanes testing their machine guns and weapons – by firing them into a big bank of soil; of the perimeter guards with their pistols and sub-machine guns; of the endless convoys of lorries on the narrow lanes as they brought in the petrol, the bombs, the food and supplies, but maybe, most of all, of the noise.

"Just try to imagine all those aeroplanes – hundreds of them – going over when they went out on a mission. And then, when they came back, you'd see some breaking off from the great mass to land at Gosfield, or Stradishall, or elsewhere."

But no summary of sound would be quite complete without a recollection of:

"the quieter more peaceful days – when they'd play Glen Miller music over all the tannoys. When the wind was right we could hear it quite clearly at Mashey Corner – that always cheered us up!"

There must be similar stories, memories and impressions from every other airfield in East Anglia. They deserve to be recorded.

We complete our picture with statistics from another excellent book, *Action Stations – Wartime Military Airfields of East Anglia 1939-1945* by Michael J. Bowyer.

"By 1943 the U.S.A.A.F. was mounting fighter-escorted bomber operations with up to a thousand aircraft and more. It often took well over two hours before the entire force was in formation.

By 1944 there were as many as 4000 and even 5000 flights being made daily over East Anglia."*

Little wonder that so many contributors spoke in awe of the, "sky almost dark with aeroplanes as wave after wave came thundering overhead."

And yet this is a local book; of local people and places.

Let us make one final tribute then. To all those involved in the services. To the Americans and the men and women of the villages of which we have written. Those who were born and schooled in our lovely Colne-Stour countryside, and who served on land, on sea or in the air.

And especially to acknowledge, and pay our last respects to those who came not home.

This is the book's shortest chapter. It is deliberately brief. That its brevity speaks louder than our words.†

---

* From Earls Colne for example 1000 paratroopers departed on March 24th, 1945, for Operation Varsity – the airborne crossing of the Rhine. (Source: *Halstead and Colne Valley at War*).

† A special thought is always due to those from the Sudbury/Halstead area whose memories of 'The Burma Campaign', are included in *The Khyber Connection*. In 1944 they were known as the 'Forgotten Army'. Half a century later many feel their endeavours are still unrecognized.
    They especially deserve to be remembered.

THE HOME FRONT

"A lot of my relatives in Bulmer were involved with threshing machines or the traction engines which pulled them. In fact when my uncle (Jim Rowe), joined up for the First World War, the first thing the army did was to send him down to Wiltshire, – to take charge of a traction engine – which was baling hay for the horses at 'the front'! They even made him a sergeant for it!"

"Were there any others?"

"Yes! My brother Fred. They sent him baling hay for a while as well – but eventually they posted him to France, where he drove a steam-waggon carting supplies to the Front Line. He actually lost a thumb and two fingers there, but when the war was over he still carried on threshing and later became landlord of The Cock and Blackbirds."

TOM ROWE of Bulmer on World War One

"The winter of 1939-40? Oh yes. That was very, very sharp. Exceptionally severe. Not a lot of snow – but continuously cold, icy and frosty. Trouble was, there were hundreds of acres of sugar beet that never got lifted. But when the ground finally thawed out in the spring, we just found rows of black holes – just like soot where the beet had sort of dissolved."

"But what about all this land?" I wondered. "How did you plough it up?"

"It didn't need ploughing! It was so fine and tilthy – from the frosts – that we could just work it straight on top."

BERT SURRIDGE, Gestingthorpe

"In the War there used to be gas-fuelled buses and cars. You'd see these big bags on top of them – and as the gas got used up the bags would slowly collapse. But I'll never forget the ol' gas bus which went to Ipswich. I mean we always had to get out and walk when we went up Martlesham Hill!"

MARY ALLESTON, Sudbury

"Before I joined the Royal Engineers in 1942, I worked 'on the land' for Mr. Ruffel at Parkgate Farm.But the first year I was in the army they actually gave me six weeks 'special leave' so that I could go back and help get the harvest done. That's how desperate they were for farmworkers!"

LES 'LUKE' SMITH, Gestingthorpe

"The G.I.'s would come and meet us schoolboys. I was given five comics and a packet of chewing gum by one of them for introducing him to my sister...unfortunately she wasn't interested. Worse, I had to give the comics back!"

BARRY WALL, Sudbury historian

"Sudbury was suddenly exposed to all manner of people, creeds and colours... It was the first time for centuries that the world had come to Sudbury rather than vice versa... The influx – not just of G.I.'s – but also of East European refugees, Commonwealth and British troops, evacuees, German and Italian POW's was enormous... In general however, I think that Sudbury coped very well."

ANDREW PHILLIPS, Sudbury

✤   ✤   ✤   ✤   ✤

Chapter Twenty One
CIVILIANS

"When I was a child there were a lot of outdoor turkeys on the farm where my father worked at Poslingford.But when these big aircraft came screaming in low they'd all take fright. So during the Summer holidays they'd get me to bang the side of the water butt when the planes came over – so that it was a steady, continuous noise – rather than too much of a sudden roar."

AMY SAUNDERS, Cavendish

Every single civilian in our area was involved in the war effort. So too was every parish. As early as March, 1938, many were circulated with a letter inviting residents to serve as Air Raid Wardens; First Aid Volunteers; or Auxiliary Fire Fighters, etc. Another requirement was to appoint a billeting officer: "But THAT WAS A THANKLESS TASK!" exclaimed several contributors.

"The problem," explains Elmsett's Janet Cooper, "was that nobody really wanted the children in their houses. People had the idea that they were infected with all sorts of London diseases and so forth."

The billeting officers' first duty was to complete an 'Evacuees Survey'. That for Great and Little Henny was conducted by the Rev. Alexander.
Beside the address of each – often already overcrowded house – the rector's observations range from:
"Old and infirm...quite impossible."
"Would take two girls – but only in daughter's room – boys impossible."

242

to:

"Would not I think refuse, if really necessary."

or:

"Might do in an emergency."

Yet despite everything a surprising number of families did actually volunteer.

On 3rd September 1939, hostilities were declared. Thousands of children were rushed out of London. School Logs reveal a colossal influx to our area. It lasted throughout September...and some of October. But by Christmas, the great majority of youngsters – unsuited to rural life – had returned to London.

But not all families could have actually accepted evacuees: their houses were simply too small. "So I did land work instead," explains Bulmer's Phyllis Billimore:

"Oh yes! I've done thistling, hoeing and rogueing and set potatoes! We used to go from nine in the morning to four in the afternoon."

Within the 'great campaign of producing food' there was also the regular Land Army.

"And it was wonderful," says farmer Dennis Holland of Lavenham, "to see the spirit of some of those girls – pulling beet, pitching muck, weeding corn, pea-picking – or whatever needed doing."

Some were detailed to threshing duties...where Jack Cornell's first instructions were: "HACK THOSE BLESSED FINGER NAILS OFF!" However – as quoted in *The Long Furrow* – "between August 1944 and May 1945 (a threshing year), he achieved a record 17,419 sacks with their assistance."

So pressing was the need to increase food production that Rene Cross of Halstead – who by day was a 'silk twister' at Courtaulds – continued 'on the land' in the evenings as a member of the less well-recorded *'Women's Emergency Land Corps'*. One evening – half a century later – she enthusiastically recalled those times:

"How did you come to be involved?"

"Being as Courtaulds were making parachutes, I was in a

243

'reserved occupation', so I couldn't join the N.A.A.F.I. – which is what I'd really wanted to do – but then I saw this advert to help on the land. Anyway at Halstead about a dozen of us volunteered to do farm work during our holidays and on summer evenings."

"How often did you go?"

"Every night of the week if it was fine – and they had something for us to do. I've weeded corn for Mr. Gosling at Maplestead, done pea-picking for Wilfred Williams, cut rape for Frank Read, and all sorts of jobs like that. We were paid 'piece rate' wages for it – and we did have some fun together. Beet singling was hard work though!"*

But even as night fell and the girls were brought back to Halstead – in a lorry with canvas sides – the commitment did not end.

"About four nights a week," continues Rene, "I slept at Nether Priors (the Civil Defence H.Q. where the Red Cross, Home Guard and A.R.P. were). I shared a room with about a dozen other women and we all slept in bunks. Then at 6 o'clock we'd get up and I'd go home for a wash and breakfast before going to work at Courtaulds for 7.30am."

Rene was not alone in 'doing everything she could'. At Sudbury, May Cresswell was on 'fire watching' with four other girls who were responsible for the Market Hill and North Street area, although, "if there was no siren we could remain in the H.Q. and play cards". (H.Q. was a warehouse at the rear of Heads furniture shop).

As the war continued a new challenge emerged. It was the raising of funds. By October 1940 a collection had been started in Gestingthorpe (by Mrs. Gardiner) towards the cost of buying a Spitfire, whilst in June 1941, "a sub-committee was formed," minuted the Parish Council, "to co-operate in the national 'War Weapons Week'."

---

* As a 'silk twister' Rene had to take particular care of her hands and consequently soaked the handle of her beet-hoe in water each night. However she also remained busy with the Womens Emergency Land Corps. during her summer holidays and went fruit picking in Hereford. "After Halstead," she says, "Hereford was wonderful – we felt safe there as it was out of the War Zone. But back here at Halstead we had those wretched doodlebugs!"

Every village was similarly involved. In 1942 Sudbury and Melford District designated February 21st-28th as WARSHIPS WEEK. A target of SEVENTY FIVE THOUSAND POUNDS was set – being the amount required for the warship *Scarab*.

Yet, incredibly, "by Wednesday February 25th," reports *The Suffolk Free Press*, "the indicator outside the Town Hall had moved up to...

...£142,537 14s. 0d."

Of this:

Sudbury Borough had raised	£49,788	4s	0d
Acton	£3,151	6s	0d
Alpheton	£3,817	18s	0d
Assington	£3,225	7s	0d
Bures	£2,380	4s	6d
Chilton	£2,219	5s	0d
Gt. Cornard	£19,528	7s	6d
Long Melford	£10,579	11s	6d
Nayland with Wissington	£2,313	1s	6d
Newton	£3,284	5s	0d
Shimpling	£3,906	13s	0d
Stansted	£3,678	16s	0d
Stoke by Nayland	£2,515	9s	6d
Gt. Waldingfield	£6,954	13s	0d
Glemsford	£10,141	7s	0d*

But how on earth were such staggering amounts raised? Glemsford we learn had a football match between the Army and Civilians: the Army won 7 – 1. At Great Cornard there was a film display by the Ministry of Information; Acton had a Children's Concert; in Long Melford a parade was followed by a Church Service. All had a rich variety of 'whist drives', concerts, 'darts evenings', dances, rummage sales and 'penny a week' funds throughout the year whilst at Bures the 'Warships Week' actually lasted a fortnight – "since the village was deemed to be in both Suffolk and Essex!"

However the real war could never be forgotten – even during the fund raising.

---

* During 'Warship Week' Halstead Urban and District Council adopted the *H.M.S. Harrow*. Later both Castle Hedingham and Clare adopted ships named after their respective villages.

"You tried to select nights around the full moon for your dances and evening events – on account of people travelling in the 'black out'," explained one source. "What's more, on moonlit nights, there was far, far less chance of a bombing raid!"

Yet often the air-raid siren was sounded, "…and it made a BLOOD-CURDLING wail," laments Alphamstone's Ena Twinn – for whom worse was to follow:

"It was the hideous sound of the doodlebugs aimed at the local airfields. They seemed to come straight up the valley towards us. They were terrifying."

But despite the doodlebugs, Luftwaffe, Hitler or Goering, there was one elderly Alphamstone lady who quite adamantly REFUSED to be rushed.

"My grandmother!" laughs Popsy Parker, "She was living with us at the time – but she was over eighty. And – oh dear– every time the siren went, she would very, very slowly fumble into her vest, camisole, corset, three petticoats, skirt and blouse. By the time she finally got downstairs, the 'ALL CLEAR' had usually sounded!"

With the enemy aircraft overhead the local searchlight crews would have swung into action. Some we know of include the units based at :
Upper Houses, Bulmer;
Hyde Farm, Little Yeldham;
near *Netherhouse Farm*, Wickham St. Pauls;
Rushey Green, Castle Hedingham.
Moreover in the open countryside between Gestingthorpe and Little Yeldham, there was, relate both Dick Finch and Bill Yeldham, 'a dummy airfield'. The latter explains:

"There were paper and canvas aeroplanes spread out, and at night the area would be slightly lit up, but at harvest the 'planes' would be folded up so that the fields could be cleared. The Germans dropped flares but I don't recollect it ever being bombed."*

* It was from the top of the Fruit Farm to Leys Wood. Frank Billimore similarly records a 'dummy airfield' at Cavenham to protect West Row, Mildenhall.
During the Second World War some 845 people were killed in Essex during bombing raids.

Just as the real war was never far away, so too the real army were also in the area – often being billeted at local 'Big Houses' (e.g. in Nissen huts at Dynes Hall, Great Maplestead; in Kentwell Hall and Long Melford Hall; in the grounds of the *Auberies* at Bulmer and also the *Cedars*). Also utilised was Gosfield Hall which not only housed thirty evacuees, but, recalls Edith Hurry:

"Some Hussars who had come straight from Dunkirk. They were in a dreadful state; their uniforms were torn and tatty and until they got re-equipped they really did look like beaten men."

Someone else to be temporarily billeted at Gosfield – in one of the attic rooms – was Albert Cross (our contributor to 'rural postmen', page 77), who was also based around Halstead "on and off, for a couple of years whilst the 'Second Front' was being prepared."

Asked about the influx of soldiers into the town, one female contributor exclaimed, "Oh, Halstead loved the soldiers! They said it was the friendliest place they had ever been".

The contributor's name is Rene Evans and, in time, she and Albert became engaged... However I couldn't help wondering if the blackout helped to induce the romance?

"What!" exclaimed Albert. "Be romantic with your gas mask, tin hat and rifle! You must be joking!"

Yet Albert did provide one endearing story... and he is adamant we should print it! It is to do with a dog. A dog called Scruffy.

"He was a mongrel whom we'd adopted after Norway and become our mascot. He was a lovely old dog and before we paraded down Halstead High Street, he used to tear about, barking away, and clearing the road for us. Then when we marched down the hill he would quietly walk beside us. When we were transferred to Europe we left him in good hands – and when I came back two years later he could still remember me! Today, he is buried beside the Sudbury Road."*

* Being attached to the 'Signals', much of Albert's time in Halstead was spent in repairing telephone wires and installations besides undertaking routine guard duties etc. Of his spare time he particularly recalls the dances at the Queens and Co-op Halls together with the inevitable queues to get into the Savoy or Empire Cinemas.

Dedicated work was displayed in all walks of life. Harry Gilbert spoke of the thousands of bombs that were brought in on the Colne Valley Railway – and then hidden in the surrounding woods for use at the newly built airfields.

For the little railway that had never really been a commercial success, the delivery of these dangerous consignments was undoubtedly its finest hour.

From John Frost, of Halstead, I learned more of the vital contribution of local industry.

"At Hunts Foundry, in Earls Colne we worked for 12 hours a day, 6 days a week and sometimes on Sundays as well. We made a lot of 'one-offs' to Ministry specifications. On the munition side, we were told to make propeller shafts and bearings, and thousands of pulleys for the landing craft which were used for D-Day and elsewhere. We also made 'paying out gear' for PLUTO (the Pipe Line Under The Ocean), which pumped petrol under the Channel to France, whilst we also produced sleeve bearings for mine sweepers."

Similarly, the famous 'Tortoise' stoves – made by Portways of Halstead – heated many an army hut, Courtaulds produced silk for parachutes, whilst at Sible Hedingham, Rippers manufactured landing craft, pontoon bridges and tail-fins for Mosquito aircraft. So important was their work, that they were subjected to a daylight bombing raid.

At Great Yeldham, Whitlocks built, "hundreds of Nissen huts in addition to agricultural implements", Bulmer Brickyard was directed to make drain pipes for airfields,* Gestingthorpe' blacksmith Dick Nice, was ordered to make a THOUSAND mule shoes for the army, whilst the Sudbury silk mills not only produced parachutes for the forces, "…but," declares one source, "parachute underwear for all the girls who worked there!"

---

* Many brickyards had to close during the hostilities since their fires could be seen by enemy aircraft. "Fortunately, Bulmer's," explains Peter Minter, "was a 'down-draught kiln' and as such the glow was not visible from the sky."

Further afield, Ransomes of Ipswich made gun trolleys and bomb racks, whilst I.C.I. produced explosives at Stowmarket. Curiously the mule shoes which Dick Nice made were all designated to be the same size. To the end of his life he wondered whether they were ever used.

Then there was agriculture. Whose great achievement was to turn TWENTY THOUSAND ACRES of derelict land between Colchester and Haverhill into productive farmland. The first directive to Essex 'War-Ag' was quite simple. It read:

"INCREASE THE ACREAGE OF WHEAT
AT THE EXPENSE OF GRASSLAND"

Other directives were to follow. Many holdings were required to grow acreages of potatoes, sugar beet and sometimes flax.* Farming standards were closely monitored. Anyone unable – or unwilling – to maximise production could be relieved of their farms. (At least two holdings between Sudbury and Halstead were actually requisitioned). They were desperate measures. For desperate times. But how did the system actually work?

"Nearly every market town like Sudbury or Halstead," explains the author's father, "had a branch of the 'War-Ag' with a couple of officers, whilst in every single parish a leading farmer would be appointed to the War Agricultural Committee. It was his job to report on whether instructions were carried out and objectives met.

"Most problems however revolved around 'hobby farmers' – who had a meadow to keep a hunter or pony on, and that they didn't want 'ploughed up' and put into wheat. In those situations the 'War-Ag' would 'serve an order on the field' and the occupier would be told to get the work done. If they didn't do it – or, weather permitting, made no attempt, the 'War-Ag' would send a contractor in to do it.

"Sometimes a farmer might complain that the land was too wet for cropping – possibly because it had 'gone behind' in the depression – and the 'War-Ag' might get it 'mole drained'.†

---

* It was utilised for canvas tents, fire hoses and army kit bags etc. "When it was ready to harvest, a special 'WAR AG' machine came and pulled it out of the ground – as the best fibres are low down on the stalk. The machine then tied it into bundles which we 'shocked up' like wheat. Then we'd build a stack to keep it dry and wait until the flax factory at Glemsford called for it."

† In the county of Essex some 50,000 acres were out of cultivation. (From *Sunshine and Showers* by Ralph Newman Sadler published by Ingoldesthorpe Publishing Ltd.) At Gestingthorpe the WAR AG ordered the ploughing up of the twelve acre Rents Field (see page 71). In Germany some 700,000 people are believed to have died from malnutrition.

249

As noted earlier the Women's Land Army played an invaluable role in the colossal task. And Prisoners of War were also co-opted.

"They were 'tidy herberts' some of these 'I-ti's," [Italians; pronounced, 'eye-ties'] recalls Jack Cornell of those allocated to his threshing gang, "but by and large I could work them all right. They'd even give you food – well a little anyway. In fact, later on the 'I-ti's' could bike down to Sudbury and pretty much come and go as they pleased. They were clever as well. They'd make miniature boats in Lemonade bottles and all such things as that... Course the German prisoners were a different kettle of fish altogether – oh no! You couldn't be so relaxed with them!"*

Despite the manual input, local agriculture was already dependent on machinery. But there was a chronic shortage of equipment. New tractors were strictly 'on allocation only' – via the county 'War-Ags' – and second hand models and other implements could only be obtained at auctions, "if your name got pulled out of the hat!"

One insight into this little known aspect of the war was provided by Johnny Hart (b.1923), who rose from workshop apprentice to general manager of 'Mann Egertons', Ford tractor agents for Ipswich. In his latter role – he visited numerous farmers in the area, offering 'competitive quotations' against a rival Ford tractor supplier situated in Sudbury's Cornard Road! It was on one such foray – shortly before retiement – that he recalled war-time agriculture:

"Tractors didn't start very well in those days and if they were idle for a while it was *vital* to keep the engines turned over – especially if they were new. At one point – before a big military operation – the army put THIRTY THREE into our store at Ipswich. Being as I was young, I was given the job of starting them up – every week. It was a job as well! I remember one week, I just got the last one running by late Friday afternoon and on Monday morning I had to start all over again!"

There were also other difficulties.

"One of our biggest problems, was the complete scarcity of good

* There were P.O.W. Camps at Ashford Lodge, Halstead, (which held about 500 inmates), at The Auberies, Bulmer (where they lived in huts down the drive) and at Borley and Liston Hall (which held about 100 each).

fitters – because so many had been 'called up'. Piston rings and 'big ends' used to give a lot of trouble in those days and in the worst months there was a FOUR MONTH backlog of major repairs. In fact, if we were on 'fire duty' and it was a quiet night, we would use the time by putting new sleeves in an engine."

Surprisingly the firm were not allocated any extra petrol when travelling to vital 'on farm' repairs. On one occasion John bicycled:

"Right up to Debden – about twenty miles from Ipswich – with my tool kit and a new set of piston rings. It was summer time and being as I didn't quite finish the job I stayed overnight and slept in the barn on some hay. But next morning, when I started the 'old girl' up, she back-fired – and almost broke my arm. So I had to bike back to Ipswich swerving all over the road with just one hand to steer by!"

Yet as the days slipped by into seasons, and the seasons into years, the war began to go the Allies' way. By May 1944 the entire region had become a giant holding area for the impending invasion of Europe. On May 26th the *Halstead Gazette* announced:

"Following the assault, our churches will be open all day for prayer and special services. Holy Trinity 11am, St. Andrews 7pm, High Street Congregational 3pm."

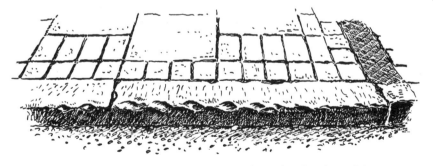

Sudbury historian, Michael Hills, kindly points out that the edges of the pavements along North Street (and until they were recently replaced – in Friars and Gainsborough Street), were scalloped out by the tracks of the Sherman tanks – "dozens of them – on their way to the Normandy Invasion." The above however can still be seen in Gainsborough Street – just a few yards from 'Bazaar Gift Shop'.

251

Then it was June 6th. 'D-Day'. Everyone who lived through those historic times has vivid memories.

"It was unforgettable," says Peter Minter (b.1933). "I was woken up by this terrific rumbling. Not very fast but continuous. The road past Bulmer Brickyard was full; so full that I couldn't get to Salters Hall School in Sudbury. In fact I had to walk. But I still didn't get there till lunchtime. On the road from Sudbury, the traffic was 'nose to tail' with jeeps, army personnel carriers, tanks, motorbikes, armoured cars, masses of bren gun carriers, big guns, big howitzers – the lot. It actually carried on most of the day... Even when I'd finally got to school I just gazed out of the window watching it all go by."*

Three months later, occurred the Arnheim air lift.

"It was a Sunday. I sat on top of the kiln and looked up. The sky was full with wave after wave of aircraft and gliders – as far as the eye could see... They looked mammoth things. I remember a tremendous feeling of elation because although I was only a child, I somehow knew then – at that moment – that we were going to win the war."

This then has been our brief account of the Colne-Stour countryside during those years of war. It was a period when the roar of aircraft was daily overhead and when the bombing raids and doodlebugs ensured that the conflict was never far from those who dwelt here.

Today, there are still the lingering reminders of those times; the 'Pill boxes' which stand grey and squat beside the River Stour at Bures, Henny, Sudbury, and Long Melford. In the giant hangars of Chilton airfield. In the names of U.S. airmen whose signatures still hang within the Lavenham *Swan*; and in the silent memorials that quietly record the names of those who died in every town and parish church.

* One contributor, who was actually in a tank 'en route' for Normandy, remembers coming down North Street and over Ballingdon Bridge before camping at Ashford Lodge on the outskirts of Halstead. "But," recalls Gordon Pritchett with a laugh, "my wife was living at Twinstead, so naturally I wondered 'dare I go and see her?' The Sergeant Major said 'No!' but my Officer said 'I'll look the other way'!

Finally there is the Home Guard. Often parodied , it is still the core of this section. Summing up his own feelings, John Frost declares:

"The Home Guard undoubtedly had its 'Dad's Army' side but it also did a great deal of very useful work. Basically it took military defence and personal surveillance right down to the smallest hamlet in the land. In the event of an invasion that infrastructure would have been crucial.* As it was, this detailed knowledge was invaluable in locating crashed aircraft and making it difficult for German spies – the fifth column – to operate successfully. Moreover, by undertaking so many observation and checkpoint duties we released the full time army for other duties."

On December 3rd 1944, the 15th Essex Battalion of the Home Guard formally 'stood down' with a parade through Halstead.

And yet…can we really leave the local Home Guard on this serious note? Indeed, for our most quoted Bulmer contributor of all, it was not this parade that was remembered, but another one, when…

"Right in the middle of the crisis, we had to parade through Halstead High Street – down that bloomin' hill. Talk about a laugh! Off we went, arms swinging like proper soldiers and trying to keep in order. In order! Huh! There's an iron manhole cover half way down Halstead hill and we all had these new hobnail boots on – I bet nearly half the platoon slipped over on it!"

Fifty years later there are literally hundreds of books and countless films on the war at large, yet only one, Dave Osborne's 'Halstead and Colne Valley at War' monitors its repercussions on the North-East Essex area. Thank you Dave for your contribution to this section.

---

* In *The Last Ditch*, David Lampe investigates the 'underground resistance' which was in readiness if East Anglia had been invaded. (A network of well hidden subterranean bunkers were constructed in remote woodland situations, from where a six-man unit could have opreated 'behind enemy lines' to cut off supplies etc. One such bunker is reliably reported to have been sited in a wood some two miles from Gestingthorpe).

Similarly, at Elmsett in mid-Suffolk the author's grandfather was given a sealed package: it was stamped "TOP SECRET; ONLY TO BE OPENED IN THE EVENT OF AN INVASION". At the end of hostilities it was returned –unopened – to the Ministry of Defence... How we now wish we had known the contents!

PART SIX

THE CONTINUING LINK

"I've had dozens of rabbits down Belchamp Meadows – and just with a big stick. You see if a rabbit is sitting under a tuft of grass first thing in the morning and there's been a dew – well the heat from the rabbit's body dries the grass and you can spot where they're sitting... We almost used to live on rabbits years ago."

Charlie 'Bommy' Martin, Belchamp Walter

"If you find where a red squirrel has buried hazel nuts, and then dig them up, you'll never find a bad one... But years ago old people round here would pick hazel nuts when they were green and put them in a tin which they'd seal and bury. That way they'd get them before the squirrels did! Course there's no real need to bury them, but people usually did – just to make certain that the air couldn't get to them. And then in time these nuts would ripen on their own."

Oliver Prentice and Claude Alleston, Sudbury

"I've heard that years ago an old poacher near Monks Eleigh used to get all the sloes from sloe gin – and then he'd scatter them about near the 'feeders' that the gamekeepers put out – and the pheasants would pick over them and they'd go a bit silly – and then he could catch them right easily after that!"

Ken Partridge, Sudbury

Chapter Twenty Two

THE VILLAGE AND THE HEDGEROW, WOODLAND AND MEADOW
Countryside Lore – The Wildlife Survey Continued

"If a robin shrieks in a barn – then it is sure to rain!" exclaims Bulmer's Gertie Coe . There is a pause – I give her a long, hard, sceptical look. "Oh yes its right you know! I remember one time Dad was getting ready to go threshing – at Cornard I think – but he heard this robin shrieking in the barn. So he 'phoned the farmer and told him not to take the thatch off the stack – but would he listen? Course not! He told Dad that he'd GOT to come. But it was his own fault, wasn't it. Because it rained torrents after that!"

Thomas Gainsborough's painting 'Cornard Wood' is dated 1748. Fallen branches are being gathered for kindling; faggots are being 'withied up'; a young man is digging clay – possibly for the bricks of a local building; donkeys are being used as pack animals, whilst a Suffolk Dun cow* and many Silver Birch trees stand mute beneath metallic black clouds.

Thus we continue our enquiry into the uses of our hedgerows, woodlands and wildflowers begun in *The Long Furrow.*

Let us start with the faggots which Gainsborough depicts being 'withied up' and which were later burnt in brick ovens for baking,

---

* The identification is somewhat speculative. However, it does appear to be 'polled' (i.e. have no horns) and is pale in colour – as was the Suffolk Dun – although the breed eventually developed into the well-known Red Poll.

255

beneath 'coppers' for washing, and on the fires of every home for warmth and cooking.

"People used to bring the wood in during the evening so that it could dry out," relates Jack Cornell. "That way you could get a nice fire going in the morning – to make a cup of tea and cook your breakfast on. But at Belchamp Otten I had an old neighbour who would put the kettle on the faggots, go off to the privy – about half a bloomin' mile down the garden – and then time he'd got back the twigs would have burnt through, the kettle would have tipped over and the water would have put the blasted fire out! Huh! He weren't very wonderfully polite then!"

Others provide more rewarding memories of woodland produce. John Dixey described the door hinges which Sid Rowe made from the stubs of nut hazel, Daisy Nice remembered an old lady picking sloes at 'a shilling a bushel', whilst,

"at Belchamp Walter," says Gertie Coe, "Mr. Cobbold who lived at the Rookery Farm just cut down a great big heap of Blackthorns, brought them back to the farm on a horse and cart and picked the sloes off them there."

At Bulmer the late Philip Rowe described his father collecting the bark from oak trees for the tanning factory at Bures, whilst Harry Gilbert recalls gathering sweet chestnuts in Chalkney Wood, Earls Colne, and picking hazel nuts:

"by giving the branches a good shake so that the nuts would 'slip the hods' and be easy to pick. Course to get good nutting," he continues, "the hedge needs to be regularly cut down and 'kept young'. Years ago hazel was regularly coppiced – for thatching, hurdle-making, pea stocks, faggot withies and so forth. It was just the normal thing."

"Did you ever go acorn picking for farmers?"

"Did we! Scores of times! It was an annual thing. I mean Herbert Whybrew the foreman at Hungary Hall used to let his pigs run out in the woods for acorns and sweet chestnuts – but if they heard you shaking the trees they would soon come and pick them up! They would pick 'em up quicker than you could!"

But possibly our most pertinent comments on the produce of garden and hedgerow come from horticulturalist Tom Gilbert (b. 1922), who today lives in Little Maplestead, not far from the big water tower. With his sunburnt features and ready smile he radiates enthusiasm for all aspects of gardening, and vividly recalls his Father's 'fruit and vegetable' business – which was based at Little Yeldham:

"Dad used to go round the local villages in a pony and cart and sell greengroceries. But there were some things like walnuts, greengages and bullace that he would actually buy from some of his customers. It's difficult to believe, but before the war this was one of the best areas in the whole of England for greengages and now – well you hardly see any. But I've seen greengage trees round here with branches almost breaking down with fruit."

"What about the bullace?"

"Well, that's another thing. We used to buy bushels of them! People picked them in their gardens or nearby woods and then we'd put them in bushel skips and send them from Little Yeldham railway station to Hammond Brothers in Spitalfield Market. We'd often send 200-300 bushels of bullace and even more greengage to London in a season. That time of day almost everyone had a bullace bush in their garden."

"And the walnuts – how did you get them?"

"From GOOD STRONG LADS – who would climb the trees with long hazel poles and then sit up there and thrash them off!"

"Was there anywhere in particular that comes to mind?"

"Oh yes. There were an awful lot at Spencer Grange in Great Yeldham; at Shearing Place and The Hall in Belchamp St Pauls (at

---

* Tom who now lives in Little Maplestead describes an additional quandary which his Father faced:
    "When summer came, all the people Dad had been supplying in the winter, wanted to sell him their surplus fruit and vegetables! But he just couldn't take it all. It was heartbreaking really. Sometimes he'd even buy things and then throw them away – just to keep people's custom!"

the latter they were on the grass between the farm and the Church); at Stambourne Hall; and at Blacklands Farm, Cavendish. In our record year we once sent over THREE HUNDRED bushels of walnuts off on the train!"

"Did you just send them off or did you have to skin them?"

"No! That was the bugbear. We had to 'hod' or 'leem' them all first. My poor mother used to sit at home hodding these walnuts day and night – and she hated it. Her hands got so bad that she even wore gloves in bed, but the stain still came through onto her face. Luckily I was out during the day so I only had to do it at night. Oh no! There was only one good moment in that job. And that was taking them to the station because you knew it was finished!"*

But the old countryside produced more than food-stuffs and building materials. On one visit to our 'countryside oracle', Harry Gilbert, he quietly picked up his walking stick and explained:

"It's made from sallow and was quicker to grow than my ash stick which I used for 'beating' at shoots and so forth. In fact the ash stick is probably twice as heavy."

"How did you make them?" I asked.

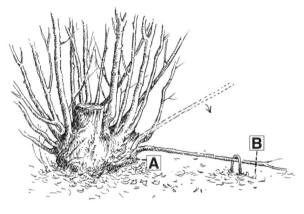

"Well, it might take you two or three years, but what you did was this:

...first, find a good coppiced ash stem, keep pegging it down (at A) to make a natural bend. Obviously you couldn't do it all at once because it might split. Finally, however, you can peg the stem down with a notched stick, then leave it until it is big enough (2-3 years) when you cut through (A and B) leaving a good walking stick."

"If holly is cut down to the stub and then allowed to grow up again, it also makes lovely sticks. They used them as handles for the driving whips on coaches. You would see them standing upright in a socket beside the driver. But it was very rare ever to peg holly down. I only ever did them as 'straight-up' sticks; but they are a good deal heavier than ash."

Another retired countryman, Frank Billimore of Bulmer Street, – whose traditional cottage garden is always such a delightful profusion of colour, described his method of keeping earwigs away from Dahlias.

"You simply get a handful of hay – about the size of a cricket ball – wedge it on top of a three foot stick, and then put an old mug on top – just to keep the rain off, and they'll settle there much more happily than among the flowers."

From garden flowers to wild ones. Tom Rowe (b.1903) tells of his grandmother "picking all the leaves of Horehound – to make an infusion of tea". Bert Surridge of Gestingthorpe was told that 'every yellow flower [e.g. Ragwort] contains either a medicine or poison'.

"Years ago, one of my neighbours lived to be well over eighty, without a single day's illness. His explanation was Agrimony tea and he let me try it once. But it was too rank for me. It was like old fashioned medicine... I couldn't abide it."

On another occasion in the nineteen forties:

"We went 'darting' and I met a chap who was well over eighty and he was as active as hell! Danced all night and kept larking about all the time. 'Whatever keeps you going?' I asked. 'The root of Yellow Rod (Aarons Rod) boiled up and kept in a little bottle' he replied 'and if I am ever feeling under the weather I have just a little'."

Another root which is reckoned to have both medicinal and poisonous – properties, is White Bryony.

"They used to say," continued Bert, "that if you boil the root for a couple of hours, it will become rock hard. But the juice is a good

259

cure for rheumatism if you've got any around you. I remember one old man who worked on a steam engine for Baldocks – one of them that never got ill – and he kept a Bryony root in his pocket and every now and then he would just cut a bit off with his penknife and nibble it."

Other gifts of our natural world have also emerged. Paul Mann enthused about moorhen eggs as being "really lovely", whilst Eric Warburton confirmed that peewits' eggs (now protected by law) had had a similar reputation. On the subject of herbs and medicines, Harry Gilbert pointed out:

"If you set some new pasture for cattle, they would always wander back to the old meadow for the herbs and wild flowers to 'doctor' themselves up with."

Among the wild flowers would be bees gathering pollen...of which Jack Cornell provides his own story:

"One night when we boys were all in the *Blackbirds*, this old man came stumping in with a bucket which had an old sack on top of it.
"Just caught a swarm of bees," he said, pointing to the bucket. Anyway, he drew up a chair and put the bucket beneath it.
"Well, all us lads kept looking at this bucket. Then the old man rose up and leant towards the fire to light a piece of paper for his fag. In a flash, someone had half-pulled his chair away. He almost sat in the bucket! Course, no harm was done, but just think of that – taking a bucket full of bees into a pub!"

From bees to hedgehogs and the traditional belief that they 'can milk a cow'. However Wickham St. Pauls farmer Jim Ruffle reveals that:

"when a cow's udder is completely full, a little milk may seep out and hedgehogs have been seen licking up those drops."

Hedgehogs were in fact, much prized by gypsies who ate them, although as Jim explains, "They were first baked in clay – to remove the prickles!" By comparison Reg Rippingale describes a traditional means of catching the eels which once swam in the Belchamp Brook:

"Unravel a sock and put the wool in the edge of the water. The eels will suck on the wool – and then you can haul them out."

Another memory comes from Jimmy Theobald (b.1919) who worked for many years at Borley watermill:

"Years ago we used to catch eels in traps or nets near the 'flood gates'. If we caught a lot we'd even send them to London – on the train from Melford station. In fact the biggest amount I caught came to nearly a hundredweight."

"But how did you get them to London alive?"

"Eels will live for twenty four hours without water, so we put them in boxes with a few air-holes in. But the holes mustn't be any bigger than a pencil! Don't they'd find their way out! They'd go out tail first!"

From eels to bats.

"And at night," exclaims Dick Halls, "the sky was FULL of them. They even came into one of the bedrooms at Rectory Farm, Gestingthorpe."

Then there were lapwings:

"And on cold winter afternoons," says horseman Bert Surridge, "all the lapwings would get in the last furrow you'd ploughed – where it was warm. And then next morning there would be a long line of white from their droppings."

By comparison it was late spring when Stanley Sharp of Hall Farm, Stanningfield, came to a Lapwing's nest whilst ploughing a fallow with two horses:

"Well it seemed a shame to go and plough them in. So I made a little hollow in the soil that I'd just ploughed and then moved the eggs across – and when the mother bird returned she did actually go and sit on them!"

Something to return to Gestingthorpe during the writing of this book – and which we are most happy to report – are badgers. Years ago when walking to work however, Bert Surridge had often seen,

261

"the bumble bees' and wasps' nests they'd dug out for the little honey comb which they liked".

From bumble bees to wasps – and the latent danger of traditional farmwork.

"On Belchamp Meadows," recalls Jack Cornell "an ol' farm-worker was pitching up hay when he picked up a wasps nest on his fork…and the damned things were so angry that his mates had to cover him up with sheaves to protect him. As it was, his hands were so badly attacked that the skin blew up as thick as gloves."

Another pest is rabbits – which both graze crops and bite young trees. However Bulmer's Ken Day provides a panacea to prevent the latter. It is quite simple. "Just surround them with string which has been dipped in creosote." The deterrent he says, lasts for about three months.

Then there are the local nicknames – which we were so keen to record in *The Long Furrow*. Recent additions include:

Yaffles for	.....Green Woodpeckers
Bread and jam	.....Sheeps Sorrel
Piddle-pan	.....Dandelion
Scratchcock	
Crotchweed	} .....Cleavers
Sweetheart weed	

("the latter name for cleavers," says Claude Alleston, "originates because it clings to you so").

Interestingly Olive Bettinson of Glemsford referred to Sparrows as 'chookeys', whilst Harold Cooper of Elmsett described them as 'spadgers'. Indeed Oliver Prentice instantly exclaimed of having "spudgeon pie in my youth". (Spudgers or Spudgeon seems to have been a particularly common name for sparrows in the Sudbury area – although the word also appears in the *Oxford Pocket Dictionary*).

Within a lifetimes love of the countryside there are also those utterly special moments when we witness the unforgettable.

For the author it occurred on the frost-white morning of Sunday, 25th October 1987. The location was Old Barn Field, Bulmer. Spiders had covered the entire 35 acres of cultivated soil with a mass of gossamer cobwebs.

Then the sun began to rise over Jenkins Farm to my east. And suddenly, the sunlight was diffused by the frost-covered gossamer into brilliant, rainbow-like shafts of spectacular light stretching across the field. It is something I shall never forget.*

And finally for Bert Surridge – who has given so much to this book, the most memorable moment occurred outside the Gestingthorpe *Red Lion* (now *Pheasant*):

"We saw this bird swoop down and pick something up. Then it rose. It went higher and higher into the sky and seemed to be fighting its prey. Then, suddenly they stopped, and crashed down onto the road. They were both dead. The bird was a sparrowhawk."

"And what was its prey?"

"A stoat!"

* The experience lasted for maybe half an hour. And no. It wasn't photographed. Four reels of film had just been used up. Recording hurricane damage.

Chapter Twenty Three

SOUL OF THE PARISH
Church and Chapel

In twenty two Chapters we have progressed from the manor to the parish and from thence to more recent village memories. Yet throughout it all – across all these centuries, there has been one enduring focus within our communities. It is the parish Church.

The history of Christianity in our locality is an absorbing subject. It takes one back, to churches with thatched rooves; medieval monasteries; the arrival of Saxon missionaries, (like St. Cedd who built a church at Bradwell-on-Sea about 655 A.D.) and ultimately to the fourth-century Roman Church at Butt Road, Colchester.

Our churches have been constantly evolving. We can imagine their humble, timber-hewn Saxon origins: the later gathering of flints for permanent walls, and subsequently the medieval bequests that built the towers, the porches and belfries. But the transformation has been more than structural. In medieval times vivid murals, gilded walls and elaborate statues decorated the interior. But as yet there were no pews. So the infirm were allowed to rest by the wall, (giving us the expression 'weakest to the wall'). Meanwhile rushes were scattered over the floor,

"Whilst the nave itself," says Richard Slaughter, "was also used for the secular feasts and festivals which today we hold in village halls."*

Further – and more bewilderingly for our manorial predecessors – services were conducted in Latin whilst English translations of the Bible were suppressed. Then came the Reformation and a century later Cromwell's puritanical Protectorate. The walls were white-

* From, *A Guide to the Church of St. Andrew, Bulmer, Essex* by Richard Slaughter, published by Bulmer W.E.A., 1987.

washed, the statues defaced or destroyed and the stained glass windows smashed. In the oft quoted extract from Dowsings Diary of 1643 he records:

"Gregory Parish, Sudbury: We brake down 10 mighty great angels in glass: in all 80."

The changes were to continue. In the eighteenth century it became fashionable to install towering, three decker pulpits and high enclosed 'box pews' – often with a fire place for the squire. Then came the Victorian improvers: they restored the fabric of the building, incorporated underfloor heating: discarded the high pews and lowered the pulpits...

Yet each parish has witnessed stirring issues of conscience. In 1527 there were furtive 'underground' readings of Tyndale's English translation of the Bible – which led to arrests at Steeple Bumpstead, Ridgewell and Birdbrook. Later in the century came the turbulence of the Reformation whilst in August 1662 occurred the final rupture between the official Church of England and other Protestant 'nonconformists'.

From that date were 'formally born' numerous Congregational (and some Baptist) Chapels along the Suffolk-Essex border. Initially they suffered persecution, harassment and denial of privilege. To worship collectively they had to meet secretly in barns, in fields and in woods. Sometimes their ministers – who had often resigned from the official parish Church – were imprisoned for their beliefs.

Eventually – from about 1710 – the non-conformists were allowed to, 'officially licence places for Divine Worship'. Many were in private houses. Every parish in our area had examples. In time some developed into the rural chapels – of which so many villages have lingering reminders.*

It is perhaps their later 'lay preachers' who best deserve to be remembered. Redoubtable rural men with outspoken convictions and rigorous principles: self-taught artisans who sermonised on Sundays but who toiled with pitchfork or horse team, 'blacksmith's

---

* Literally scores of local premises – such as barns and cottages were 'officially licensed for worship'.

At the West Suffolk Record Office the applicant's details are particularly easy to obtain. The following is a typical example:

"10th July, 1801: ...hereby certified that the lower part of the dwelling house and premises of WIDOW VINCE situate in KERSEY STREET are set aside for Religious worship of Protestant Dissenters."

hammer', or 'mill-bill' for the intervening six days. As Albert Cross explains:

"In the early days, many lay preachers could neither read nor write…they learnt their sermons by heart."

Harry Gilbert recalls the Pebmarsh chapel of his youth:

"Signalman Gosling would preach there sometimes. And my goodness he was wonderful. Mind you, chapel people were more serious about religion. But it was more down to earth; the sermons were a lot simpler. And in those days when working people weren't so well educated as now, the Bishops and parsons did rather talk over our heads. That's why I enjoyed listening to Signalman Gosling so much; he had a wonderful grasp of the Bible and for his time was a well learned man."

John Dixey tells a typical story of a 'Chapelite' meeting at Bulmer Tye.

"Henry Paine who farmed at *Clapps Farm* often preached at the Chapel. But at the end of the sermon he'd often say to one of his men in the congregation: 'Well John bor, we'll just have one more hymn 'fore we go and feed they bullocks!'"

The Suffolk-Essex border has been a veritable stronghold of independent religious worship.

"Not far from the Maplestead *Cock* beside the Halstead – Sudbury road," records Albert Cross, "a Congregational Chapel was built in 1841. Now that's quite a remote place. But in 1867 an additional £370 was spent to increase its seating capacity to FOUR HUNDRED people! But where did all the people come from? They must have come from surrounding villages. And the great majority must have come on foot – in all weathers – many walking several miles to worship."

Yet we should not forget the Church of England. For, despite its eighteenth century decadence, it was – by Victorian times – re-emerging as a spiritual force. Yet it still came as a surprise to discover that in 1896 Gestingthorpe not only had a Men's Bible Class – but that its "average attendance was nearly FIFTY".*

In the following March a mission by two evangelists was arranged. Extraordinarily in a parish of just 536 inhabitants no less than sixty one services were arranged over nine and a half days.

"Every night the church was almost full…and at the women's services there were from fifty to seventy every afternoon."

Doubtless some (especially those 'in service') were 'persuaded' to attend by their employers. Others would have been invited from neighbouring villages. Yet the mission's success still testifies to the Rector's enthusiasm. As the late Douglas Hasler recorded:

"Reverend Bromwich was totally committed to the village. His funeral in 1917 was the only time the Church was completely full."

With the twentieth century came the Age of Technology. Eddie Tuffin recalls one major development at St. Barnabas' Church in secluded Alphamstone:

"We finally decided to get some electric in there," he explains, "but unfortunately the 'Board' were a bit slow about getting it done. However Mr. Stuck – my boss – had electric, but his house was on the other side of the road. But there's an old four inch land-drain what cross the road near there. So what I did was this. I put a line and collar on a buck ferret and put it in this pipe – and when it come out we tied an electric cable onto the line – and that's how we pulled it through and got switched on!"

In earlier centuries many rural churches had another innovation – the organ. And before organs? The music was led by the parish orchestra.

How appealing this concept is! Of men in buskins and hob-nailed

---

* Parish Newsletter.

Establishing the voluntary nature of late Victorian Church attendance is difficult. Lesley 'Luke' Smith commented:

"In my Father's time if your boss went to church then you went to Church"; Beryl Spillings adds, "there was a time when Reverend Bromwich would actually come and ask people why they hadn't been to Church". Yet even here the picture is not completely clear, for the large congregations which attended the non-conformist chapels went completely of their own free will.

Getting electricity to Alphamstone Church

boots with rough and calloused fingers guiding the congregation with their simple instruments.

In 1893 the *Halstead Times* reported:

"The death in Great Maplestead of an elderly resident and blacksmith named Hawkins... Mr. Hawkins was one of a quartet of players on stringed instruments who led the music in the church at Maplestead some forty or fifty years ago."*

How long then did the church orchestras survive? One presumes until the mid-nineteenth century. At Kedington, however, there *still is* a muscians' gallery. At Alphamstone the gallery wasn't removed until the early twentieth century while Belchamp Otten has the probable remains of a West gallery – which were once common in almost all villages.

* From *The Maplesteads; Then and Now, 1881 – 1986* published by Maplestead W.E.A.
For a good description of the parish orchestra see Thomas Hardy's *Under the Greenwood Tree.*

These then are our parish Churches. They have been – through many centuries – a catalyst of village life. Here, within their walls were the earnest 'Vestry' meetings of the parish government; here too was 'Relief for Poor Persons' often disbursed, or the early school children first taught. They have been built – almost without exception – from local flints and bricks, in a mortar of sand and chalk, that was often dug and slaked by parishioners themselves.

They are the churches also, to which so many of our contributors; "went to Sunday School and Church, followed by Church again in the afternoon". They were the churches to whose choirs almost every contributor belonged in their youth, (particularly enjoying the Choir Treat to Clacton!), and where some like Gertie Coe, were married by the same incumbents who had previously Confirmed and Christened them – AND also married – AND Confirmed *their parents!* They have been truly, at the very 'Heart of our History'.*

Throughout our research there have been endless stories of 'organ pumpers who fell asleep between hymns', of parsons who 'droned on and on', of 'absentees' who seldom visited their 'livings', and others, who dressed in fur-trimmed coats – and kept a coachman and horses whilst the working men went hungry around. Conversely there are other memories. Of kindly, concerned clergymen, who discreetly helped the infirm and the ill; who built almshouses and schools; and who encouraged emigration and the fulfilment of potential.

It is through their endeavours that for centuries past Christians have attended our parish churches. Week by week to worship and pray, celebrate and praise and seek communion with Jesus Christ.

Inside our churches and chapels have occured services to inspire and guide, uplift and console, motivate and rejuvenate spiritual energy.

And the work goes on. Quietly and with dedication. Despite change and transformation. That the message of Christ's hope and forgiveness, good-will and salvation can be radiated out into a new millenium.

Let us leave it then, to retired shepherd Eddie Tuffin to provide a final recollection. It is of a contemporary clergyman whose ministry in the area has epitomised the warmth and caring, kindliness and

---

* For readers with a greater interest in the history of Christianity along the Suffolk/Essex border, Ashley is producing a short booklet entitled, *Soul of the Furrow.*

compassion of true Christian love:

> "We had Reverend Howard from Belchamp Walter here once – and I liked him. Anyway, he came to take the Harvest Festival. But when he walked into the Church – he'd got one of those big, black, plastic bags – what you have for dustbins! 'Well that's a rum thing' I thought. But when he went up to the pulpit – he actually took it with him! Next thing was, he pulled a great ol' sugar beet out of it! 'What the darvil-are-you-going to do with that?' I thought.
>
> "But do you know, he stood there, and he preached as good a sermon as ever you'd heard – about that 'ere sugar beet. And nothing to read by; no notes or anything. He just came out with it, and everybody said, 'What a wonderful sermon he preached – and what an inspiring person he was'."

Like Eddie Tuffin and Trevor Howard, the contributors to this book – every single one of them – have been at the crux, the very essence, and the ultimate, 'Heart of our History'.

Thank you for allowing me to visit you, and for giving me your wonderful memories.

Ashley Cooper
Hill Farm, Gestingthorpe. October 1994.

✤ ✤ ✤ ✤ ✤

St. Barnabas Church, Alphamstone

Bibliography

PART ONE

Bulmer Then and Now: Compiled and edited by Basil Slaughter; first published by Bulmer W.E.A. 1990 edition by Simon Harris.

The Domesday Book: edited by Alexander Rumble, from a draft translation by Judy Plaister and Veronica Sankaram. Published by Phillimore, 1983.

White's Directory for Essex 1863.

White's Directory for Suffolk 1844.

Victoria County Histories of Essex and Suffolk.

The Diary of Ralph Josselin, 1616–1683: edited by Alan Macfarlane. Published by Oxford University Press 1976.

Essex Quarter Sessions Order Book, 1652–1661: D. H. Allen. Published by Essex County Council; Essex Record Office Publication No. 65.

Colne Engaine: Village, Church and Parish: Vernon Clarke.

Colne Engaine: The Story of an Essex Village: edited by Peter Watson. Published by Colne Engaine History Society, 1992.

Beyond Living Memory. The History of Little Waldingfield: Harry Clive, 1979.

Great Waldingfield – The Babergh Village: Louise Kenyon, 1986.

Cavendish Contrasts: Richard Deeks,1990.

St. Barnabas Church, Alphamstone: P. R. Tuffin, 1981.

History of Long Melford: Sir William Hyde-Parker. Published late nineteenth century.

Wills of the Archdeaconary of Sudbury, 1630-35: editied by Nesta Evans. Published by Suffolk Records Society.

Notes on the Parish of Gestingthorpe: Compiled by the late Alfred Patchett, 1905.

Mount Bures: Ida MacMaster, 1980.

A History of Little Yeldham: Adrian Corder-Birch F. Inst.L.Ex., M.I.C.M. Published by Halstead and District History Society, 1981.

The Legacy of the Rural Guardians: George Cuttle. Published by W. Heffer & Sons Ltd., Cambridge, 1934.

Chartism in Essex and Suffolk: Dr. Arthur Brown. Essex Record Office Publication No. 87, 1982.

Halstead, in old Picture Postcards: Percy A. L. Bamberger, European Library, 1987.

The Discovery of Britain: Jack Lindsay. Published by the Merlin Press, 1958.

Elizabethan Life: Essex Gentry's Wills: F. G. Emmison. Essex Record Office Publication No. 71, 1978.

John Constable's Correspondence, Vol.IV: edited by R. B. Beckett. Published by Suffolk Records Society, 1962.

An Essex Pie: T. M. Hope. Published by Benham & Company, Colchester, 1951.

Crime and Criminals in Victorian Essex: Adrian Gray. Published by Countryside Books, 1988.

The History of Law and Order in North Hinckford (North Essex): Frederick W. Pawsey DFC, JP. Published by Halstead and District Local History Society, 1991 (price £9.95).

History of the Borough of Sudbury: C. K. Grimwood and S. A. Kay MA. Printed Sudbury 1952.

Castle Hedingham in the Olden Times: Edward Bingham (from a lecture he delivered in 1894). This copy reprinted by Maurice and Anne Stockhill, Magnolia House, Castle Hedingham, Essex.

PARTS TWO, THREE & FOUR

The Pattern under the Plough: George Ewart Evans. Published by Faber & Faber, 1966.

Schools and Scholars in Halstead and District: Mary Downey and Doreen Potts. Published by Halstead and District Local History Society, 1986 (price £2.50).

Captain Oates; Soldier and Explorer: Sue Limb and Patrick Cordingley. Published by Batsford, 1982.

A History and Description of Gosfield Hall: Published by the Wayfarers Trust Ltd.

Wickham St. Pauls; Some Items Towards Its Story 1662–1980: Published by Bulmer W.E.A., 1980.

A Pictorial History of Sible Hedingham: Adrian Corder-Birch F.Inst.L.Ex., M.I.C.M. Published by Halstead and District Local History Society (price £3.50), 1988.

Melford Memories: Ernest Ambrose. Published by Long Melford Historical and Archaeological Society, c.1970.

Essex Windmills, Millers and Millwrights: Kenneth G. Farries. Published by Charles Skilton, 1981.

The English Alehouse – A Social History 1200–1830: Peter Clark. Published by Longman, 1983.

The Land of England: Dorothy Hartley. Published by Macdonald and Jane, 1979.

A Directory of Nineteenth and Twentieth Century Suffolk Breweries: C. R. Bristow. Published by Salient Press, County Hall, Ipswich, 1985.

Cricketers of Sudbury, 1787–1987: Alan Cocksedge. Published by Sudbury Cricket Club, 1987.

PART FIVE

Combat Crew: John Comer. Published by Leo Cooper, 1988.

The Mighty Men of the 381st: Chaplain James Good Brown.

Action Stations: Wartime Military Airfields of East Anglia 1939–1945: Michael J. Bowyer. Published by Patrick Stephens, Cambridge.

Halstead and Colne Valley at War (1939–1945): Dave Osborne. Published by Halstead and District Local History Society, 1983. (£4.50).

East Anglia 1940: R. Douglas Brown. Published by Terence Dalton, Lavenham, Suffolk, 1981.

We'll Eat Again: edited by Margueritte Patten. Published by Hamlyn (and Imperial War Museum), 1985.

Sunshine and Showers: Ralph Newman Sadler. Published by Ingoldesthorpe Publishing Ltd.

PART SIX

The Maplesteads; Then and Now: Published by Maplestead W.E.A., 1986.

A Guide to the Church of St. Andrew, Bulmer, Essex: Richard Slaughter. Bulmer W.E.A., 1987.

Bibles in Barrells – A History of Essex Baptists: Doris Witard. Published by Essex Baptist Association.

A History of the Church in England: J. R. H. Moorman. Published by A & C Black.

Sudbury through the Ages: Barry L. Wall. Published by East Anglian Magazine Publishing, 1984.

A Thousand Years in the History of a Small English Town (Sudbury): Edith Freeman BA.

Gainsborough's Sudbury: Edith Freeman BA, 1987

Publications by **Halstead and District Local History Society** may be obtained from local bookshops at the prices indicated, or from:

    Adrian Corder-Birch,
    The Maltings,
    North End Road,
    Little Yeldham,
    Halstead,
    Essex CO9 4LE

plus 50p for postage and packing (except for *Law and Order*, enclose £1.00 for postage and packing).

BULMER HISTORY GROUP

The new edition of *Bulmer: Then and Now* is available from local bookshops price £3.50

Let's Get Up Agin the Table: by the late Basil Slaughter, which investigates East Anglian cooking and diet in past centuries is also now available, price £5.00

Either of the above may also be obtained from:

Mrs. Hilary Slaughter,
6 Park Lane, Bulmer, Sudbury, Suffolk.

plus 75p for postage and packing.

Heart of Our History

Further copies of all Ashley Cooper's books are available via book-sellers using Whittakers 'Tele-ordering' system. Please add £1.20 for postage and packing.

N.B. Despatch of books may sometimes be delayed due to farm work. Books are not usually available in August or September: otherwise every 3-4 weeks. For direct orders write to Hill Farm, Gestingthorpe, Halstead, Essex, CO9 3BL.

Of the Furrow Born

...is the second volume of *Heart of Our History*. Initially explored is the self provident countryside of earlier times. Brickyards and potteries, rural industries and implement manufacturers, wind and water mills are all recalled.

Farm diaries follow. Of particular interest are those from Foxearth (from the 1890's) – which vividly illustrate Horse Era farming. Yet agriculture was in decline. Parishes were experiencing a drastic decline in population - which is discussed – as is the influx of hundreds of farmers (often Scotsmen) to East Anglia. In turn the Tithe War, agrarian conditions of the 1930's and early mechanisation are all reviewed.

Available December 1997.

Countryside Journey

Part Three of Ashley Cooper's *Heart of our History* trilogy brings all the diverse threads of his previous volumes into a historical travelogue around the Suffolk-Essex border. The book will be a combination of historical research and rich rural anecdotes giving a new perspective to every village and by-road in our area.

Publication in due course.

The Long Furrow

Three thousand years of rural history from the Suffolk-Essex border telling the story of the land and those who worked it from the last ice age to contemporary times. Complete with the memories of over seventy local people including the horsemen, shepherds, drovers, blacksmiths and threshing contractors of the bygone era, the book also includes chapters on Roman Gestingthorpe; Arthur Young; the farmworkers' strike of 1893; Harvest time and horkeys; the Tithe War; the Great Depression and a special section devoted to wildlife, and a local ecological survey.

The Long Furrow is Ashley Cooper's first book and was largely quoted in *The Reaper's Year,* a play written and performed by the Eastern Angles Touring Theatre Company.

Fifth print now available. ISBN 0 900227-82-6

"I've enjoyed *The Long Furrow* immensely, in fact it's just the sort of book I wish I had written myself."
David Richardson
Presenter of Anglia Television's 'Farming Diary'

". . . Ashley Cooper in his excellent book *The Long Furrow*."
Quentin Seddon
Author of 'The Silent Revolution', BBC Books

The Khyber Connection
The Furrow and the Raj

Returning home from a rucksack expedition around India at the age of 23, Ashley Cooper was intrigued to discover that a neighbouring farmworker had also visited the sub-continent – with the Suffolk Regiment in 1921.

Eventually the author interviewed over 70 local people from the Suffolk-Essex border who had also served in India. Privates from the local regiments, Gurkha officers, retired tea planters and their wives, all describe their lives.

But the book is not all nostalgia. A complete section is devoted to local men who served in the **BURMA CAMPAIGN** of World War Two and who depict again the heroism of Imphal and Kohima and the jungle camps in which they lived.

Many other surprising connections between India and the Suffolk-Essex area are also unearthed, and by examining local newspapers, the reaction of East Anglians to the Indian Mutiny is investigated.

Finally the reader is taken on a 7000 mile journey from the plains of North India to the coasts of Kerela and from the snow packed Himalayas to the rugged boulders of The Khyber Pass as India is explored again.

ISBN 0-900227-81-8

"Fantastic. I'm thrilled that at last someone has recorded what the average soldier went through during the Burma Campaign. I've also had some good laughs as well. It's definitely written in a style of its own. Superb!"
Douglas Legg
Retired Sudbury Printer
Stationed in India 1942-45

"...an original and highly successful attempt to examine the impact of India on one small area of England. ...Cooper's book is one that merits the admiration of anyone remotely interested in India and is a work to be noted by historians amateur and academic..."
Chowkidar (Vol. 4 No. 6)
The magazine of the British Association for Cemeteries in South Asia

Tales of Woodland & Harvest

In *Tales of Woodland & Harvest*, Ashley Cooper writes with humour and great feeling of the contemporary East Anglian countryside.

They are fictitious stories of love – love of the land and the seasons, of the seedtimes and harvests; of the woodland and fields and of the people with whom the experience is sheared. They range from his immortal portrayal of Curley – a retired farm mechanic – and also include wily gamekeepers and poachers, the hero of a rural 'who-done-it' and an ageing horseman whom we enchantingly meet in a moment of true village cricket.

Each story is delightfully illustrated with the countryside drawings of Elizabeth Martland.

Reprint now available. ISBN 0-900227-84-2

Born at Gestingthorpe in 1952, Ashley Cooper describes himself as, "a fully committed working farmer with a passionate interest in local and human history." His first book, *The Long Furrow*, (published 1982)) has been reprinted four times and was followed by both *The Khyber Connection* and the fictitious, *Tales of Woodland & Harvest*.

For ten years he hosted an 'experimental trials centre' on his farm and in 1991 was awarded the *Farming News* prize for combining cereal husbandry with good conservation practice." He is a past President of Gestingthorpe Cricket Club and also wrote the hymn 'A Celebration of Sudbury's Countryside'.

Benjamin Perkins who illustrated this book devoted his life to painting and writing in 1978. His definitive book *Trees* was graced with a foreword by the Duke of Edinburgh, although his best known work is undoubtedly *A Secret Landscape* – which in prose, colour paintings and illustrations recounts the 'wildlife year' of a group of isolated meadows along the Suffolk-Essex border.